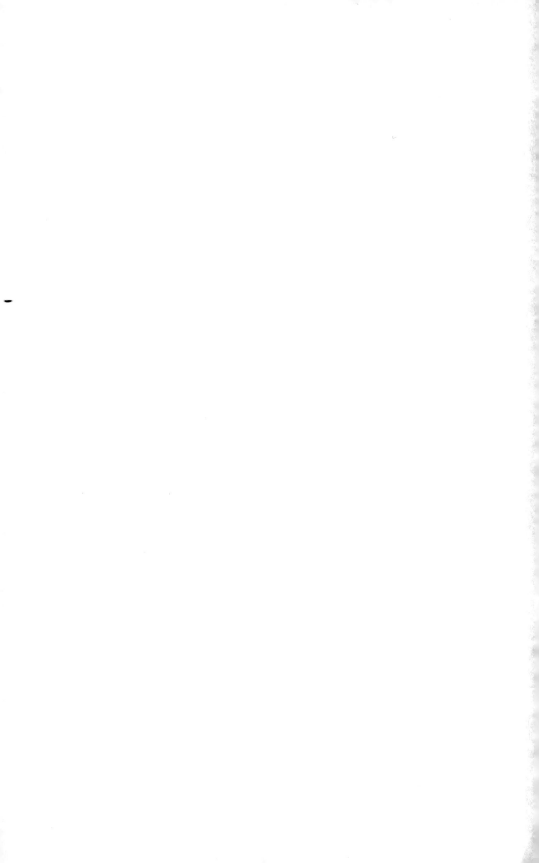

Connecting Kids to History
with Museum Exhibitions

Connecting Kids to History with Museum Exhibitions

D. Lynn McRainey
and John Russick

EDITORS

Left Coast
Press Inc.

Walnut Creek, CA

Left Coast Press, Inc.
1630 North Main Street, #400
Walnut Creek, California 94596
http://www.LCoastPress.com

Hardback ISBN 978-1-59874-382-1
Paperback ISBN 978-1-59874-383-8

Library of Congress Cataloging-in-Publication Data
Connecting kids to history with museum exhibitions / D. Lynn McRainey and John Russick, editors.
    p. cm.
  Includes bibliographical references and index.
  ISBN 978-1-59874-382-1 (hardcover : alk. paper) — ISBN 978-1-59874-383-8 (pbk. : alk. paper)
  1. Museums—Educational aspects—United States. 2. Museums—Social aspects—United States. 3. Museum exhibits—United States. 4. History—Study and teaching—United States. I. McRainey, D. Lynn. II. Russick, John.
  AM7.C596 2009
  069'.15—dc22

                                    2009029019

Printed in the United States of America

The paper used in this publication meets the minimum requirements of American National Standard for Information Sciences—Permanence of Paper for Printed Library Materials, ANSI/NISO Z39.48—1992.

Cover illustration and design by Michael Kress-Russick.

Part introductions' photography credits are as follows: Part I (page 27) *A Sailor's Life for Me?* photograph by Greg Cooper, courtesy USS Constitution Museum. Part II (page 93) *Imagining Chicago*, Chicago History Museum, photograph courtesy John Russick. Part III (page 197) Children's Discovery Museum, Normal, Illinois, photograph courtesy Ken Kashian.

The United States Holocaust Memorial Museum gave permission for the use of Figures 4.1–4, photos of *Remember the Children: Daniel's Story.* Please note that the views or opinions expressed in this book, and the context in which the images are used, do not necessarily reflect the views or policy of, nor imply approval or endorsement by, the United States Holocaust Memorial Museum.

DEDICATION

To Alan, who never forgot what it was like to be a kid

To Miss Ann and Archie

CONTENTS

Among the variety of museums in the United States today, those inter-preting history are the most numerous and, by virtue of their content rooted in the uniqueness of specific localities, also arguably the most diverse. Many museums devoted to preserving the past, or to capturing the ephemeral present as it quickly "becomes history," take familiar form as historic sites, house museums, or free-standing state and local historical societies. Others are devoted to the histories of particular cul-tural groups or to exploring historical narratives associated with the de-velopment of industries, art forms, and businesses (motorcycles, music genres, transportation, flour milling, and computers are only a few re-cent examples). Still other history organizations preserve sites imprinted with meaning by virtue of their association with significant events or with memorable personalities. And as diverse communities have blos-somed across the country's social landscape, new museums have also taken root, nurturing historical memory with collections that document these communities' origins, exhibitions that celebrate their achieve-ments, and heritage programming that connects the generations.

Because they are so numerous and diverse,[1] these history organiza-tions collectively offer the public a broad variety of museum experi-ences and, because they represent the places, people, and events of our shared daily experience, they also have the potential to make significant connections with American museum audiences. Research indicates that, even more than the first-hand accounts of family members and others, museums are Americans' most trusted source of information about the past.[2] However, compared to other types of museums, attendance at indi-vidual history museums is quite low,[3] indicating a substantial gap between their potential to engage the public and the fulfillment of that promise. Today, many history museum professionals are seeking to understand the factors behind this disconnect, looking for ways in which their orga-nizations can become more resonant with the audiences who are not yet coming through their doors. Among the constituencies increasingly recognized as underrepresented in their audience profiles, children and families can be one of the most important opportunities for history museums to broaden public engagement with the stories latent in their collections. But until quite recently, many—indeed, perhaps most—history museums have extended only minimal gestures to reach these audiences.

For example, for quite some time (at least as long as we have collected systematic data, and likely much longer), the Chicago History Museum's most numerous visitor segment has been older adults, primarily empty nesters who visit alone, in pairs, or in organized groups. Until quite recently, this visitor profile was presumed satisfactory: efforts to engage families with children focused primarily on once-a-month weekend programming and on an aged "Hands-on History Gallery" whose isolated and outdated demonstration units lacked any kind of unified storyline or purpose. Children were seldom if ever seen as the primary audience for new exhibitions and the museum staff had little experience with the interpretive and design tools needed to engage them. Our narrow audience focus shaped our exhibition processes and products in ways that are evident only in retrospect. We knew our collection and how to explain any one of its objects with no more than seventy-five words on an attractively designed label panel. We had honed our editing skills to encapsulate whole chunks of history into three-minute videos and posing Q&A issues on flip-up labels. Once in a while our budgets allowed us to develop an interactive computer program. We figured we knew which stories mattered, and since the way we told them was so interesting to us, we didn't pay much attention to who else was listening. Almost (but not quite) unconsciously, we had chosen to make exhibitions for ourselves, relying on teachers, chaperons, parents, and docents to do the heavy lifting for kids. This practice ignored the fact that about a third of our museum's total attendance was comprised of student groups, the majority from elementary school classrooms.

Although, like the Chicago History Museum, most history museums' attention to children may still be in its infancy, over the past twenty or more years some of these museums have instead been very engaged in audience development focused on issues of diversity, representation, and interpretive voice. While many museums (including most state and local historical societies as well as house museums) continue to enjoy enduring relationships with the traditional constituencies that have built their collections over generations, they also recognize that the demographics of their surrounding communities have changed. Many of their new neighbors feel an uncertain connection—or no connection at all—with the past that traditionally has been represented in history museum exhibitions and programs. Recently arrived in a new location, families are focused on making that place a foundation for their future, and a history that does not include them seems peripheral to their concerns. In common with previous generations of Americans, these audiences look to the future and seek pathways to it. We envision a future lying before us. History lies behind, and we often struggle to see any value in looking back.

As history museums become experienced in audience research and more nuanced in its interpretation and application, data demonstrates that these museums cannot build effective and long-lasting bridges with diverse communities until they are attractive to these communities' families and their children. Research shows that visitors' most enduring connections with museums are based on their experiences as children during family visits. Reflecting on findings from a survey of museum attendance studies, John Falk posits, "Proactive efforts to involve more families in museum experiences will lead to increased attendance and support in the future."[4] Recent market studies by the Chicago History Museum also remind us that ethnically diverse audiences, like other free-choice visitors, are most likely to seek museums as members of intergenerational family groups.[5] These families must have reasons to visit us, they must feel welcomed, and their experiences must be rewarding. To gain their attention, we must compete with myriad other scheduled commitments and attractive entertainment options. History museums need to recognize and embrace their opportunity to attract these families by offering unique leisure experiences that are not only entertaining but also meaningful for children.

A generation ago, natural history museums began to transform themselves, inspired by progressive work in British[6] and American[7] science museums. Borrowing scientists' techniques for engaging visitors in a discovery process, natural history museums began to allocate space and budgets for interactive exhibitry that would encourage audiences to explore the context and meaning of anthropological artifacts and natural specimens. In a similar vein, exhibitions practitioners in history museums now look outside their institutions for models and practices to engage our audiences, particularly children and families. Today's methodologies draw from a broader base of technology, utilizing not only museum precedent but also other applications from our media-rich environment. We benefit from the body of data that has accrued over several decades of visitor research, and a new generation of museum professionals embraces audience-centered thinking and recognizes the value of creative collaborations among museum staff from varied disciplines.

Several years ago, my colleagues Lynn McRainey and John Russick were asked to conceive an exhibition for children to be a centerpiece of the newly renovated Chicago History Museum, replacing the obsolete "hands-on" center with a more vibrant environment that would be engaging for young visitors and would offer coherent and meaningful history content. Lynn and John's thoughtful development process was a model partnership between gifted professionals with different but complementary experience and interests, and as they examined the opportunities inherent in their project, they looked for lessons and inspiration from colleagues throughout the country. Their research and wisdom gave life to a fun, new history exhibition for kids called *Sensing Chicago.* This exhibition became the cornerstone of a successful campaign to transform the institution's visitor demographics, and brought reality to our vision of the museum as a destination for families and children. It also inspired the current volume of essays, which coheres the knowledge and creativity of experts across museum disciplines and offers insights to inspire a new generation of history exhibitions for young visitors.

Phyllis Rabineau
Chicago History Museum

NOTES

1. While there is no definitive or "official" count of these organizations, the American Association of Museums estimates there are approximately 6,692 history museums and historical societies in the United States, and an additional 1,942 historic houses and sites. Collectively, they comprise more than 48% of the total number (17,744) of the country's museums. Elizabeth E. Merritt and Philip M. Katz, eds., *2009 Museum Financial Information* (Washington, DC : American Association of Museums, 2009), 22-23.
2. Roy Rosenzweig and David Thelen, *The Presence of the Past: Popular Uses of History in American Life* (New York: Columbia University Press, 1998), 21.
3. Data from participants in the American Association of Museums' 2008 survey shows that median attendance for historic houses or sites is just 11,700 visitors annually; history museums fare even worse, with 10,000 visitors a year. Elizabeth E. Merritt and Philip M. Katz, eds., *2009 Museum Financial Information* (Washington, DC: American Association of Museums, 2009), 43.
4. John H. Falk, "Visitors: Who Does, Who Doesn't, and Why," *Museum News* (March–April 1998): 42.
5. For example, see Lipman Hearne, "Summary of Research: American History, Abraham Lincoln, Benito Juarez" (compiled for the Chicago History Museum, Chicago, IL, 2008).
6. Roger S. Miles et al., *The Design of Educational Exhibits* (London: Unwin Hyman Ltd., 1982).
7. Hilda Heine, *The Exploratorium: Museum as Laboratory* (Washington, DC: Smithsonian Institution, 1990).

Is this for me?

Have you ever picked up a book, read the title, looked at the cover, scanned the table of contents, and wondered, Is this for me? Will I enjoy this? One can imagine that kids ask themselves similar questions when they go into our museums and exhibitions. Is this for me? Will there be anything for me to do? Will I have fun?

So how do you know if this book is for you?

If you are ready to see kids as a valued museum audience, requiring the same level of commitment from us that we give the adults who bring them, then this book is for you. If you recognize that kids are a unique and complex audience and that reaching them with history content demands that we approach our work differently, this book is for you. And, if you are looking for new ideas and new methods for engaging kids in experiences with the past, this book is for you.

It would have been for us too had it existed in 2003 when we began work on the premiere exhibition for a new children's gallery at the Chicago History Museum. Opening in 2006, *Sensing Chicago* was produced by a team led by an educator and a curator. Throughout the exhibition development process we often lamented the fact that this book did not already exist and wondered why. We also discovered that our partnership was uncommon and we wondered about that too.

The complex and sometimes contentious history of educators and curators working together in American museums is firmly grounded in preconceived notions, often fueled by turf wars, and sustained by an array of stereotypes. So when a veteran educator and curator were paired to create an exhibition for children at a venerable history museum, there were far more questions than answers about our professional practice, desired process, and expectations for the final product. After all, what could an educator know about making exhibitions? What could a curator know about working with children? Dialog and debate became our means for understanding each other's perspectives, for defining our approach, and for discovering the competencies and capabilities of kids.

In late 2003, the conversation began. Not having worked together on previous projects, we started with shared experiences to initiate the dialog and to draw from as we advanced the project. To that end, we made site visits to museums across the country that had a tradition of reaching out to kids and family audiences. Although we found few successful history exhibitions specifically developed and designed for kids, we did experience a range of interactive spaces that targeted children. We were able to expand our conversations to include colleagues who had already grappled with questions similar to those we were facing. These individuals were all generous with their time and expertise, from helping us become versed in how to identify and accommodate kids' unique characteristics, to educating us on ways to engage kids and their families so they could influence our work. Eventually these conversations extended beyond the museum profession to include others whose work was focused on kids: youth psychologists, education specialists, youth marketers, toy developers, designers, and classroom teachers. And of course, throughout this process we heard the same steady chorus from all these experts: go talk to kids.

Through a rigorous regimen of classroom visits, focus groups, testing, and prototyping, children became our experienced guides, leading us back to childhood and what it was like to be a kid. They were the wise sages who reminded us that they too can have meaningful experiences with history. And they became our willing partners, there to advise us when something was not working and propel us onward with their smiles of delight when they (and we) got it right.

The project also benefited from a continuous dialog between and among members of a highly dedicated and experienced team comprised of Chicago History Museum staff and external designers and media consultants. Team members were willing to deviate from the tradition of prioritizing content and collections in order to focus on audience. Instead of defining what "it" would be too early, our process allowed children to take the lead. The exhibition would be defined by watching, listening to, and interacting with more than one thousand children over the course of its development.

This book is a continuation of the conversation that began between an educator and a curator. The chapter authors were selected by the editors and invited to join in this discussion, and they brought with them their diverse perspectives and expertise on kids, history, and exhibitions. Read individually, chapters identify the range of opportuni-

FIGURE P.1. Dedication to the ideals of a project by both internal and external team members is central to its success. Members of the *Sensing Chicago* project team pose for a reunion photo in 2007. *From left:* Tamara Biggs, John Russick, Andy Anway, Dorrie Brooks, Sara Smith, Caleb Donat, Steve Bressler, Lynn McRainey, and Scott Rabiet. Courtesy D. Lynn McRainey and John Russick.

ties available for reaching out to kids and recognizing their abilities to connect with history; read as a whole, the book presents an argument for assuming our responsibilities to create the spaces in which these exchanges can occur.

Since the focus on kids as a core audience for history museums is an emerging practice, the breadth of exhibitions for kids is limited. While a range of successful experiences are cited as examples, in some instances the same exhibitions are featured in multiple chapters. Authors examine these experiences from different perspectives to mine them for the insight and direction they can provide us as we consider how to connect kids to history. Practitioners in small and large museums can use these examples to spark conversations with their colleagues and to shift institutional thinking about kids.

We have chosen to focus primarily on kids and not the families or school groups they are a part of to emphasize kids as individuals and as an important museum constituency in their own right. While docents, gallery facilitators, teachers, parents, and caregivers play important roles in navigating children's visits to museums, we have focused on unfacilitated exhibitions to show that museums can create experiences in which kids have meaningful encounters with history that invite them to take the lead, make choices, and be engaged. The chapters are organized into three parts:

I.   *Valuing Kids*—understanding who they are, what they can do, and how to collaborate with them;

II. *Connecting Kids to History*—expanding our and their interpretive toolkit to include story, imagination, play, the senses, and place; and

III *Creating History Exhibitions for Kids*—rethinking familiar exhibition elements of design, interactives, collections, labels, and media with kids in mind.

We are grateful to many individuals who have been part of this unfolding dialog. We benefited tremendously from the support and generosity of our colleagues in children's museums, science centers, and art and history museums. In addition to helping make *Sensing Chicago* a success and an honorable mention in the American Association of Museums' 2007 Excellence in Exhibition competition, these individuals challenged us to think differently about our audience and to see that the issues we were grappling with were bigger than those of a single exhibition project and needed to be shared with the larger museum community.

We are indebted to the contributing authors to this volume for their willingness to join our conversation and to ponder and reflect on the challenge of developing history exhibitions for kids along with us. Their collective experience is a testament to our profession; their diverse perspectives and valuable insights offer a range of possibilities for our future work with kids. We are grateful for the support of Phyllis Rabineau, vice president for interpretation and education at the Chicago History Museum, whose foreword offers a context for these and other conversations surrounding kids, history, and museums. We extend a special thanks to Michael Kress-Russick of www.kindredpixel.com whose artistic talent allowed us to put kids first even on the cover of this book. He captures them perfectly as ready, willing, and waiting for us to take action. We acknowledge the ongoing support and encouragement of Gary T. Johnson, president, and Russell Lewis, executive vice president and chief historian of the Chicago History Museum. Interns Elizabeth Leiserson, Lindsey Parker, and Angela Argentati assisted on a range of research and administrative details, and we thank them for their work. And finally, our thanks go to Jennifer Collier for her skills in the production of this book and Left Coast Press for ensuring that this conversation can reach others.

By committing to this audience, undertaking the research to know and understand them, and doing the hard work to create meaningful and memorable experiences with history for them, we do more than influence the lives of children. We engage our colleagues and ourselves in a conversation that is destined to reveal new ways of thinking about history. We push our museums to more fully embrace accessibility as a goal for all we do. And we challenge our profession to define and express the value of history for everyone, everyday. In the end, our museums and our audiences reap the benefits. And room is made for a younger voice to become part of the conversation.

Still reading? This book is definitely for you.

Who Needs History?

Our lives are history. In fact, every moment we have ever lived is now a memory. At the same time it is our history that makes us real and gives our lives meaning. For both adults and children, our ability to reach back and connect to the past is the central mechanism in knowing and understanding who we are.

In *The Presence of the Past*, Roy Rosenzweig and David Thelen chronicle their experiences collecting the perspectives of people from across the nation about the value and meaning of history in their lives. In a personal afterthought, Rosenzweig writes about the challenge to history professionals from ordinary people both engaged in the ideas of history and passionate about their personal stake in it. In a passage about how these people viewed official history, Rosenzweig writes,

> our respondents were more interested in talking about the experience and process of engaging the past. They preferred to make their own histories. When they confronted historical accounts constructed by others, they sought to examine them critically and connect them to their own experiences or those of people close to them. At the same time, they pointed out, historical presentations that did not give them credit for their critical abilities—commercialized histories on television or textbook-driven high school classes—failed to engage or influence them.[1]

The audiences for history are numerous and diverse, complex and thoughtful. They are interested in what we have to offer, but at the same time they bring a critical eye to our work. They are already invested in history and they know whether they have been invited into or excluded from the experience. And they are bored, even turned off, when it's not done right. If history museums are to be successful they must understand their audiences in nuanced ways and be ready to provide meaningful points of access for them.

But what does the audience for history look like? Is it everyone for whom history could or should have meaning? If not, to whom should we direct our efforts? Who needs history more? Is it older adults who have the longest relationship with the past, recent immigrants trying to ground themselves in the culture and tradition of their new home, individuals with limited education looking to expand their horizons, or kids who are just becoming aware of their relationship to the past and who will be the leaders of tomorrow? Is there a group we can ignore? Are there people for whom history does not matter?

If history is important for all these groups then logic dictates that history museums have an obligation to provide meaningful experiences with the past for anyone who walks through our doors. We have to become accessible to all, and accessibility means more than conforming to the legal requirements of the Americans with Disabilities Act. From bilingual labels to free admission days, museums are mining the dimensions of accessibility. In recent years, several high-profile American historical societies have tried to appeal to wider audiences, some even shedding their founding title and incorporating words such as "center" or "museum," including the Chicago Historical Society (now the Chicago History Museum). But if our goal is to expand audiences for history and champion accessibility and inclusivity we need to do more than simply change our names. We have to change the way we do business.

In "Interactivity and Social Inclusion" Jocelyn Dodd asserts that museums are not always as inclusive as we may hope. Dodd advocates for a more equitable approach to audience through "pathways to inclusion" that move our interpretive practice away from the authoritative voice of the specialist or scholar, to an interpretive approach that offers visitors of all ages points of connection, relevance, and cultural ownership. Dodd advocates dismantling "the barriers—physical, intellectual, sensory, emotional, attitudinal, financial, cultural and technological. The removal of these barriers is complex, involving a holistic approach by the museum."[2] Museum barriers limit more than just physical access. They are evident in the topics we select, the spaces we design, and experiences we create. They communicate who is welcomed and able to participate in the exploration of history. Whether young or old, if any visitor is unable to access the information or engage in the experience because of the vocabulary used, height of cases, or simply overall comfort in the space, the museum is to an extent communicating, You are not welcome, or at least, We didn't make this with you in mind.

Do History Museums *Get* Kids?

When it comes to kids and history museums, our barriers are many and points of connection few. Our spaces are typically formal, our voice is usually authoritative, and our content loaded with ideas unfamiliar to most kids. Not only are our physical spaces ill considered in anticipation of kids, but also we create barriers through our expectations of their behavior.

For many history museums, kids represent a discrete and particularly challenging audience. We watch their behavior in our museums and they confirm our preconceived notions that kids do not have the patience or focus to grasp the depth of the content. Nor do they posses the reflective nature to spend concentrated time considering their place in our collective past. We are repeatedly told (and we echo the message) that kids think history is boring. Through this casual analysis, kids seem an unlikely target for our efforts.

Too often we see only the obstacles rather than the opportunities that kids represent. Although we were all once young, we forget what it was like to be a kid. Their interactions with and reactions to the world around them are quite different from our own—it is full of movement, noise, emotions, and energy; behaviors we have not considered or even imagined, let alone accommodated or encouraged in creating our exhibitions. We often seek ways to control and limit these traits through behavior management and the creation of tools to keep kids occupied rather than harnessing these attributes as means for engagement and points of connection.[3] In terms of exhibitions, we often simply retrofit our adult-centered spaces with quick fixes such as scavenger hunts or a flip label to target younger visitors. While a dedicated gallery for children is a first step, it also segregates the experience to a confined area of the museum as if there were two histories, one for kids and another for adults.

If our goal is to connect kids to history with exhibitions, we are faced with the questions, What does a meaningful and memorable history exhibition experience for kids look like? How can we explore the "then and now" with an audience centered on the "here and now?" In opening our minds and spaces to children, we find ourselves struggling with the nuances of our practice—the tensions between scholarship and memory; education and entertainment; authoritative messages and personal meaning making.

Do Kids *Get* History?

In his autobiography, comedian and civil rights activist Dick Gregory shares many tender, funny, and heartbreaking stories from his impoverished youth in St. Louis, Missouri, including a wonderful anecdote about the interpretation of history by kids. "We used to root for the Indians against the cavalry, because we didn't think it was fair in the history books that when the cavalry won it was a great victory, and when the Indians won it was a massacre."[4] Writing as an adult, Gregory reflects on how his personal circumstances shaped his critical eye on historical events. As a poor African American child living in segregated America his identification with the people of color in the story upends the accepted lessons of history and anticipates the movement away from the portrayal of American Indian communities as a menace expertly and forcibly removed for a noble cause. In part because of his race, but also because of his youth and the fact that he had no investment in the traditional interpretation of manifest destiny, Gregory was free to imagine an alternative meaning for this widely accepted history.

Four decades after its initial publication Gregory's story suggests how a child's perspective can be more than simply unique. It can be instructive. The way kids think about the past can highlight opportunities for museums to make connections with them, to use their natural instincts and interests as the basis for creating experiences with history designed for them.

An adults' consumption of history tends to be a reflective, contemplative act that draws on their personal inventory of life's experiences, knowledge, and personal meaning. By contrast, children are still figuring out life and themselves through experiences that allow them to explore, participate, and play a part. While their consumption of history may seem quite different, they too are drawing on experiences, understanding of self, and personal meaning. Children are all too eager to make comparisons between how they do something and how others did it. Their imaginations can transport them to places in history and into the lives and circumstances of people of the past. While they are finely tuned into their own perspective of me, myself, and I, children can step into the shoes of another person through role-play that allows them to be an American Indian or a newly arrived immigrant, even the president. While their boundaries of time do not always fit neatly into the prescriptive framework of timelines, children are comfortable moving back in time, as their favorite stories of princesses or dinosaurs demonstrate. And kids can appreciate the firsts, the lasts, the bests, the worsts, and the mosts of history.[5] Is this so different from the way adults experience or appreciate history?

Experiencing History

If kids are already equipped with the tools to make sense of the past then how do we invite them in? How do we make exhibitions that connect them to the past? What do those exhibitions look like?

As adults, we come to view history as something that is researched and composed by others and prepared for us. Adults expect to read or listen to or watch history; we tend to step back and leave the work to the experts. These passive experiences often fail to engage kids who learn in motion and through interaction. Moreover, historians are quick to explain, our interpretation of history is not and should not be fixed. In fact, history needs our ongoing participation. In "Why Study History? Three Historians Respond," William H. McNeill explains,

> Historians are always at work reinterpreting the past, asking new questions, searching new sources and finding new meanings in old documents in order to bring the perspective of new knowledge and experience to bear on the task of understanding the past. This means, of course, that what we know and believe about history is always changing. In other words, our collective, codified memory alters with time just as personal memories do, and for the same reasons.[6]

If history is open to new ideas and new perspectives, if it grows and remains vital because of new input and the participation of many, the opportunities to present history as an interactive work in progress has the potential to redefine the history museum exhibition experience. History is waiting for people—old and young—to bring their own perspective to bear on it and make it meaningful.

In our effort to illustrate history as a process, as an exchange between the present and the past, museums frequently claim our products "bring history to life." This dubious phrase sends a very clear message; history is dead and needs someone to revive it. While we use it to imply interactivity and infuse the historical process with relevance, it brands the past as dormant, stagnant, as if it needs constant resuscitation to make it powerful, relevant, and accessible. But what if instead of approaching the past as a dead thing we occasionally bring to life, we bring history to our lives, and our lives to history? In this twist on the old phrase, the life of history is found equally in the scholarly research of an historian, the reflective contemplation of an adult visitor, or the active engagement of a child.

What if our exhibition development process began with the identification of desired experiences and behaviors we wanted visitors to have and demonstrate? Like life, the space would demand participation and invite queries, debate, and discoveries; and most of all, like life itself, every visitor—old and young, experienced and novice—would leave their mark and change the space just because they were there at that moment in time. Perhaps we need to start thinking about history as something we do in the present rather than something someone else did in the past.

This book is an elaborate argument for targeting kids with history exhibitions. In these pages, multiple authors consider kids from diverse perspectives and note countless opportunities, rather than endless obstacles, for connecting them to history. The chapters in this book explore why, how, and when to connect kids with history content, and the exhibition examples featured provide evidence that some museums have begun to tackle the challenges of this underappreciated and undervalued audience in meaningful and memorable ways.

D. Lynn McRainey and John Russick

NOTES

1. Roy Rosenzweig, "Roy Rosenzweig: Everyone a Historian," in *The Presence of the Past: Popular Uses of History in American Life*, Roy Rosenzweig and David Thelen (New York: Columbia University Press, 1998), 179.
2. Jocelyn Dodd, "Interactivity and Social Inclusion" (Conference Proceedings: Interactive Learning in Museums of Art, Victoria and Albert Museum, May 17–18, 2002), http://www.vam.ac.uk/res_cons/research/conferences/learning/index.html (accessed January 31, 2009), 3.
3. In "A Short Review of School Field Trips: Key Findings from the Past and Implications for the Future," Jennifer DeWitt and Martin Storksdieck review the discrepancies in research literature on the effects that "attention focusing devices" have on the student group experience. The debate surrounds the tension between structure and choice when devices, such as worksheets, are created as a means to manage behavior rather than stimulate discovery and inquiry (*Visitor Studies* 11, no. 2 [2008]: 185–186).
4. Dick Gregory with Robert Lipsyte, *Nigger* (New York: E. P. Dutton & Co., Inc, 1964).
5. Kieran Egan of the Imaginative Education Research Group (IERG) explores the active engagement of a child's imagination in learning through cognitive tools found in different levels of understanding. The different "understandings" that children develop over the course of their lives, as described by Egan, suggest opportunities for connecting kids to history content. For example, Mythic understanding (comes with oral language) draws on story and the affective organization of content, and Romantic understanding (comes with literacy) draws on the limits of reality, the extremes of experience in a child's growing fascination with the real world ("Cognitive Tools," last modified November 5, 2006, http://www.ierg.net/about/cogtools.html [accessed August 12, 2009]).
6. William H. McNeill, Michael Kammen, and Gordon A Craig, "Why Study History? Three Historians Respond," in *Historical Literacy: The Case for History in American Education*, ed. Paul Gagnon and The Bradley Commission on History in Schools (New York: Macmillan Publishing Company, 1989), 105.

PART I

Valuing Kids

W hy kids? In 2001, the American Association of Museums publication *Excellence in Practice* challenged museum professionals to explore the dimensions of accessibility to "provide multiple levels and points of entry into content, including intellectual, physical, cultural, individual, group, and intergenerational."[1] History museums have made considerable strides over the past two decades to break down barriers—mental, physical, psychological, and emotional—for ever-increasing subsets of the museum's potential audience. However, when it comes to kids, many history museums have failed to grapple with a host of formidable barriers that limit accessibility. We tend to justify why kids are not a fit for history exhibitions rather than exploring ways to make them feel welcome; we blame schools for giving history its bad reputation of being boring rather than taking a hard look at how our approach to interpreting history in exhibitions might engage younger audiences.

In "Interactivity and Social Inclusion," Jocelyn Dodd writes about museums shifting to a more equitable approach to serving diverse audiences: "As museum professionals we are not well placed to understand the feeling of being excluded from museums, because of our professional interest, knowledge, and experience. Yet understanding this is an important step in meeting the needs of those who are socially excluded."[2] Although we all would like to think our museums are "socially inclusive" of children, our practices, as Phyllis Rabineau noted in her foreword to this book, depend on the adult companion to do the "heavy lifting" in providing access for children in their groups through identifying points of engagement and connection. The height of cases, length of labels, and even content selection weigh heavily in favor of adult visitors. Even our rhetoric when referring to children contributes to this dismissive attitude toward a younger audience. Perceptions that developmentally appropriate content is "dumbed down" and that interactive, whole-body experiences are not suitable formats for addressing serious subject matter and will lead to inappropriate museum behavior foster a culture in which children are not valued or taken seriously as a core audience. When staff members, confronted with the challenge of developing meaningful exhibitions about history for kids, claim "it will never work here," they allow the museum to take a pass on kids, to rationalize why accessibility for younger audiences is not a priority. In short, by not challenging ourselves to create inviting environments and engaging experiences for children, we are telling kids and families, "there's nothing for you here."

Appropriately enough, the chapters in this part of the book put kids first. Making history accessible to kids is no different than providing access to other audiences. To be successful with any audience we have to know them, understand them, engage them, and most importantly respect them. We were all kids once, have memories of being kids, and in some cases live with kids, but these personal associations should not lead us to make uninformed decisions or craft quick solutions to serving younger audiences. Instead, our approach to understanding kids must be driven by research, literature reviews, developmental frameworks, and audience studies. Although children's visits to museums are always defined in terms of a group experience (family, school, and youth), younger visitors are complex individuals who come with their own set of needs, expectations, interests, and desires that warrant experiences beyond the printed handout or the occasional flip label.

In turning to children, we can discover how they learn, explore, and understand the world around them, and the role history plays in their lives. The chapters in this part offer exhibition team members new approaches and models for making kids an institutional priority. Research into educational theories, designing developmental frameworks, and collaborating with kids are critical steps toward a more equitable approach for connecting kids to history. Children are part of the continuum of the past, present, and future and should be seen as active participants in the unfolding dialog and story that are at the heart of history. As the subsequent chapters will reveal, children have an active and logical sense of the past.

Recognizing the unique characteristics of children, in Chapter 1, "Never Too Young to Connect to History: Cognitive Development and Learning," Sharon Shaffer challenges us to consider two important questions: Are children required to understand history in the same manner as adults? Do children have critical cognitive abilities relevant to understanding history that remain unrecognized? This chapter encourages us "to know them" by examining the educational theories on how children learn that apply to our field. All exhibition team members will benefit from this review, because it exposes learning as a dynamic process of personal meaning making through experiences, social interaction, and multiple intelligences. This chapter provides a context for familiar terms within the museum field—constructivism, learning by doing, and multiple learning styles—allowing practitioners to revisit these terms and their applications for connecting kids to history. Kids emerge demystified as an eager, viable, and desired constituency for history.

In Chapter 2, "It's about Them: Using Developmental Frameworks to Create Exhibitions for Children (and Their Grown-ups)," Elizabeth Reich Rawson challenges readers to know their younger audiences as well as they know their content. Her charge, "to understand them," puts theories into practice as projects shift from being *about* something to being *for* someone. With a commitment to audience, a developmental framework provides an exhibition team with the knowledge and insight to make choices that will empower kids during their museum visit. Rawson advocates for the rigor and discipline to research, design, and apply a developmental framework for every project. Through benchmarking kids' social, cognitive, and physical milestones, exhibition teams can more effectively match experiences and content to desired messages and affective outcomes.

All team members become audience advocates as museums reach even farther from exhibitions developed for someone to exhibitions developed with someone. In Chapter 3, "Experts, Evaluators, and Explorers: Collaborating with Kids," Anne Grimes Rand and Robert Kiihne advocate for museum professionals to reach out to children and involve them in every stage of the planning and development of exhibitions, "to engage them." From focus groups to prototypes, kids are given a voice to inform and define exhibition concepts, object selection, and design. This new model welcomes children as active agents as they inform and influence the creation of more meaningful and engaging exhibitions. Team members realize that planning does not occur behind closed doors but rather out in the galleries and in classrooms as they seek opportunities to observe, converse, and interact with kids, and to learn from and be inspired by them.

We must value kids. By knowing, understanding, and engaging kids, staff members become more skilled at creating experiences for them. In turn, the process gives kids a voice and a stake in our work, and our products become environments that provide them with physical, cognitive, and emotional access to history.

Why kids? The answer lies in a museum's commitment to accessibility for diverse audiences and requires individual and institutional commitment to a process that puts children at the forefront of exhibition research and development. By focusing on children, museums are extending an invitation to children; an invitation to be engaged, to make discoveries, to contribute, and to feel welcome. By knowing, understanding, and engaging children, museums can fully embrace a practice that welcomes and expects kids, values diverse learning styles, seeks collaborations with kids, and makes content accessible through interactive experiences.

NOTES

1. American Association of Museums Standing Professional Committee on Education, *Excellence in Practice: Museum Education Principles and Standards* (Washington, DC: American Association of Museums, 2002, revised 2005), 7.

2. Jocelyn Dodd, "Interactivity and Social Inclusion" (Conference Proceedings: Interactive Learning in Museums of Art, Victoria and Albert Museum, May 17–18, 2002), www.vam.ac.uk/res_cons/research/conferences/learning/index.html (accessed January 31, 2009), 1.

CHAPTER 1

Never Too Young to Connect to History: Cognitive Development and Learning

Sharon Shaffer

American museums are recognized around the world as places of learning that have contributed to the educational landscape of our society. Most American museums were established on a commitment to subject or collections, and some even considered audience at their inception, but few recognized children as a discrete segment of that audience. In recent years, museum professionals have sought to develop exhibits and programs to address the interests and needs of children. With this increased commitment on the part of museums to reach a young audience, exhibition project teams are looking for best practices that will serve as models.

To engage a younger audience in a meaningful way, more museums need to embrace approaches to exhibition development that are grounded in what we know about how children perceive and construct meaning about their world, or what is often thought of as cognitive developmental theory. A strong theoretical foundation in child development and cognitive theory, which have been important tools in the development of models for learning in museums, increases the likelihood of developing effective educational experiences for this audience. This chapter reviews key theorists and concepts, setting the stage for subsequent chapters, which bring these ideas into museum practice.

A child's ability to connect to the past and construct meaning about history requires an understanding of the development of concepts of time, sequence, categorization, and classification as well as exploration of the role of experience, language, and culture in the learning process. Educators grounded in learning theory acknowledge that a child's understanding is qualitatively different from that of an adult. In making connections to the past there is a need to categorize and integrate information in a meaningful way, as well as think abstractly, skills not always identified as strengths of children. We ponder important questions: Are children required to understand history in the same manner as adults to be viewed as learning history? Do children have critical cognitive abilities relevant to understanding history that are currently underutilized? To consider these questions, we must both revisit how we define and understand history and become familiar with how children think about and construct meaning of the past.

The Power of History

History is not simply an abstract concept. It is important to most individuals in daily life. Researchers Roy Rosenzweig and David Thelen conducted a survey about Americans' interest in history.[1] Their findings suggest that ordinary people are deeply engaged with the past and that the connection to the past develops through personal experience, interests, and family culture. What is this connection to the past and the role of history in the lives of ordinary people? Are the connections similar for children?

Historians recognize that history is socially constructed and that there is seldom consensus in interpretation. An individual's interests, experiences, and culture play a pivotal role in constructing meaning about the past. History is never a simple record of the past, recounting details of ideas or events in time, but rather an interpretation from different points of view, often with varying degrees of clarity. "The fabric and design of history, like the threads of experience in our own lives, are woven in intricate and complex patterns."[2]

From a child's perspective, history is envisioned as everything that has already happened. It is seen initially in the broad context of the past and the relationships to people, places, and events that have occurred, rather than through a detailed sequence of events across a continuum of time. This ability to recognize and categorize events as present, past, or future is an early framework for a child's capacity to think about history and typically is grounded in personal history. As children gain the ability to organize ideas about the past cognitively, a relationship to history is born. More nuanced appreciations develop as children see connections or common links among everyday experiences, thus creating an infrastructure for organizing ideas. It is through social interactions and everyday encounters with stories, customs, holidays, places, and even mainstream media that ideas about the past are introduced, later to be sorted and classified.

Educational Theory

For centuries, humans have pondered the wonders of the mind and posited theories of learning that continue to influence practice today. As we entered the twentieth century, the examination of learning theory expanded from the arena of philosophy to include psychology and education, bringing together perspectives of philosophers, psychologists, and educators to shape our current understanding of learning and advance our knowledge of cognition and effective teaching practice.

Within the museum field and history museums in particular, we seek a common language to discuss ideas relevant to informal learning and refer to the writings of respected theorists in an effort to shape practices for creating meaningful and memorable connections to the past for children.

Cognitive Theory: Biology or Environment

Theorists have long pondered the origins of learning and wondered whether an individual's capacity to learn is most influenced by genetics or by experience. This discussion of nature and nurture continues to evolve. There is a strong indication by cognitive theorists that a blend of biological (nature) and environmental (nurture) circumstances predict cognitive growth and that, indeed, experiences are crucial to cognition. Nature is reflected in developmental stages, innate abilities, instinctual differences, and learning styles.

Although the biological factors are viewed as important to this discussion, there appears to be even greater consensus in recognizing the import of experience through interaction with the environment as crucial to the construction of knowledge. Experience becomes prior knowledge and serves as a building block for future learning.

Cognitive Theory and Children's Learning of History:
A Constructivist Framework

In an analysis of cognitive theory and its implications for teaching history to children through exhibitions, a broad theoretical framework can serve as the foundation for our understanding. A brief definition of cognitive theory, or educational theory, establishes common ground for further thought. According to George Hein and Mary Alexander, who discuss constructivist theory as it applies to museum work in *Museums: Places of Learning,* "an educational theory requires a theory of *knowledge* (an epistemology), a theory of *learning,* and a theory of *teaching* (a pedagogy)."[3] Theories can be classified across a continuum representing diverse perspectives. On one end of the continuum, knowledge is seen as residing in the real world, outside the individual; at the other extreme, knowledge is viewed as an internal mental construct, existing within and interpreted by the individual. Theories require a view of knowledge as well as perspectives on how individuals learn and how we should teach.

Widely accepted views based on ideas of theorists and coupled with beliefs of educators as practitioners can be gathered within what is known as the *constructivist framework*. This framework rests on the belief that knowledge is internally constructed and influenced by external factors. Each theorist identifies specific elements that are perceived to be most critical to learning and then describes the role of each factor in the process of learning or constructing knowledge. For some, experience is the most salient factor, whereas for others it might be social interaction. In either case, many museums have embraced constructivist thinking and have sought to develop and design experiences and environments in which visitors construct meaning. Their efforts have been largely based on the work of the educational, developmental, and psychological theorists featured in the following pages.

A review of selected theorists regarded as constructivists provides insight about cognitive development and influences on learning. Although there are common threads in their thinking, there are also nuances that offer opportunities for interpretation that shape today's beliefs about learning in relationship to museums. The underlying tenets of cognition as portrayed by constructivists rely on a belief that learning is an internal process influenced by interactions with the environment and experiences of the individual. It is that process of constructing knowledge, and how and when that occurs, that is the beginning of this conversation of learning.

John Dewey (1859–1952)

John Dewey, recognized by many as the most influential thinker in American education in the twentieth century, is best known for his belief in experience as a way of learning and knowing. He emphasized that experience becomes knowledge once it is acted on and that abstract ideas take on meaning only in their application.[4] Dewey framed learning as an active encounter with the environment, with the learner making connections to prior knowledge to create meaning. Reliance on prior knowledge and the need to see meaningful ties or relationships to ideas that are already known is integral to Dewey's thoughts and beliefs about the process of constructing knowledge. The phrase *learning by doing* is often associated with Dewey and suggests that knowledge is gained through active engagement rather than passivity. He is recognized for a child-centered approach that builds on a child's natural interests and instincts.

In his writings, Dewey suggests that reflection and questioning lead to further thought and reflection. Learning is not about acquiring information but rather creating meaning from experience, action, and thought. A belief in experience as the most critical element of learning is the hallmark of Dewey's philosophy of education. Dewey lays the foundation for all constructivist theorists to come, and his influence on museums is immeasurable.

Lev Vygotsky (1896–1934)

Russian psychologist Lev Vygotsky contributed to the discourse on cognition by suggesting that all learning is contextually and socially mediated. His writings indicate a belief that intellectual development is the result of interaction with the environment and that social interaction with adults or peers influences the level of performance exhibited by an individual.

He recognizes the benefits of learning in social settings and suggests that learning is fostered by the support (or what Vygotsky terms *scaffolding*) that comes from individuals who possess more sophisticated abilities. It is the guidance of adults or collaboration with more capable peers within *a zone of proximal development* that increases learning. Vygotsky's *zone of proximal development* is described as the distance between the actual developmental level determined by the individual's ability to perform independently and the potential developmental level as defined by performance with guidance from more knowledgeable individuals. This guidance or *scaffolding* is not to be mistaken for adult-directed learning but rather as facilitation that enables more sophisticated learning. The focus remains on the individual child's action to construct meaning. By clearly situating learning in the context of social interaction, Vygotsky suggests that language is integrally linked to thinking and knowing.

In *Thought and Language* Vygotsky describes the stages of concept development, indicating that the process begins with the naming of objects within the environment.[5] Named objects are then grouped into random categories that ultimately take on more meaning as the individual recognizes common traits or attributes. It is this more sophisticated view of world experiences and relationships among them that is critical

LANGUAGE DEVELOPMENT

During the 1990s researchers documented the process of language development, recognizing its complexity and suggesting that exposure to language produced neurological changes in the brain.[6] The number of words heard by two years of age was seen as the precursor to future vocabulary development, leading to later competency in language. In this stage, young children associate tone and gesture with meaning, connect words to concrete experiences, and begin to gain understanding that is attached to language. Language acquisition is a process that requires many different experiences. It is the product of actions and reactions in social settings beginning with an infant's first days, strengthened by each new experience and exchange. Language development evolves incrementally over time and requires nurturing of both expressive and receptive capabilities.

Long before infants and toddlers can speak, they comprehend. We see evidence of this in their actions, and we know that it is social interaction and modeling of speech that is the groundwork for that knowledge. The building blocks of language are not always visible in the process of learning yet are absolutely essential to help young learners strengthen their command of language.

An examination of similarities between the learning process of language and that of history provides a framework for understanding the relationship between history and children. Just as language acquisition begins long before there is ever an expectation of acquiring language, gaining an understanding of history begins long before we ever think of the possibility of learning history.

to understanding. In this stage of concept development, "traits of objects are analyzed and concrete factual bonds or relationships among diverse objects are established through direct experience."[7] With new experiences, children garner new perspectives and ultimately revise and reshape the connections between objects and ideas. As children approach adolescence, concepts gained by concrete interaction with the environment are translated into more abstract thought and a more mature understanding of ideas and relationships, marked by a capacity to think with a clear sense of logic and abstraction.[8]

In his writings, Vygotsky also explores play and suggests that fantasy play may be the "leading factor in cognitive development."[9] Not only does Vygotsky draw a clear connection between fantasy play and similar symbolic representation with words, he also recognizes imaginary play for its strength in building understanding of the world. Play is no longer viewed in its simplest state of representing symbolic schemes but rather as a child's interpretation of the world through rule-governed behaviors.

Vygotsky linked cognitive and social development in his understanding of cognition: he situated learning within the context of social experience and interaction, rather than as occurring solely within the individual. This view of jointly constructed knowledge advances our way of thinking about learning and has increasingly been accepted by educators and employed by museums.

Jean Piaget (1896–1980)

The cognitive theories of Swiss psychologist Jean Piaget have influenced educational practice for nearly half a century and have provided insight into the development of intelligence in children. Although his ideas have been carefully studied and at times debated, particularly his theory of developmental stages, it is clear within the educational field that many of Piaget's theories continue to be valued and play a vital role in defining learning as a constructivist activity. It is this process of learning and the notion that children perceive their world in a way that is qualitatively different from adults that are integral to Piaget's beliefs.

Piaget is well known for describing developmental stages, rooted in biological development, that explain how a child thinks and understands the world. This stage sequence of development offers a continuum that moves from learning that is concrete and dependent on the senses to a more formal abstract way of understanding. Characteristics of the child define each stage and provide insight into learning at that specific chronological age and occur, according to Piaget, in a specific sequence. For example, Piaget suggests that in the early stages of development a child's initial world is centered on the self—an unconscious egocentrism is central to all actions and thoughts.[10] As a child matures, he gains the capacity to recognize multiple points of view, which changes his thought process. Piaget suggests that external forces or experiences have little effect on moving a child from one stage to the next and that nature supersedes environment. Although it is generally accepted that young children are typically egocentric beings, there is some suggestion that a child's capacity to see another point of view emerges earlier than Piaget thought and that this egocentrism is not inflexible.

Current thought is that stages of development typically occur in the relative sequence suggested by Piaget but are less rigid than he presumed, particularly as reflected in the chronological age spans suggested. Piaget does, however, acknowledge that the stages cannot be given a constant chronological date and that they differ across society.[11] Most important, there appears to be general consensus that children view the world in a way that differs from that of adults and that children acquire new cognitive insights during ages 3 to 12 that alter their view of the world. Ultimately they adopt the more logical adult perspective.

According to Piaget, children make sense of their world by interacting with concrete objects. This interaction leads to recognition of similarities and differences, which allows for sorting, classifying, and organizing and thereby, results in more sophisticated knowledge. Children organize their world through a process of classification, dividing objects into categories based on specific criteria. This skill emerges as early as 2 or 3 years of age but becomes more sophisticated by 10 or 12. A child might arrange a collection of family photographs into categories of new and old (*today* and *long ago*) based solely on visual cues such as style of dress, hairstyles, cultural artifacts or objects within the image, and the photograph itself. This process begins with intuition for younger children. Older children are better able to articulate the reasons for assigning specific photographs to categories and may even be able to create more discrete groupings based on multiple factors.

Constructivism is at the heart of Piaget's research and theories and is exemplified by his discussion of how a child develops knowledge of concepts through a process of *assimilation* and *accommodation*. *Assimilation* is the process of integrating reality, or the perception of reality, with the internal structure of knowledge. The modification of internal schemes or structures to reflect the experience or reality is called *accommodation*.[12]

Schema, or basic constructs that capture the essence of an idea, become the basis for cognitive development. An initial encounter or experience begins the formation of schema; over time, schemes are modified by further experience that relates to the concept. For example, a child develops an understanding of the concept of *wheel* with exposure to toy cars, trucks, and trains as well as with experience riding a bicycle. The construct of *wheel* originates with personal experience. When new information is introduced (assimilation)—through such experiences as looking at illustrations in a book or a visit to a museum—that conflicts with what is already known, the individual redefines or modifies (accommodation) the original concept to meet with the newly acquired knowledge. Today's familiar version of *wheel* is expanded to accommodate a more diverse understanding that could include size of wheels (gleaned from an encounter with an antique bicycle), materials (rubber, wood, plastic, metal wheels) from versions of bikes across time, design, and even purpose (for example, a steering wheel in a maritime exhibit). This newly refined construct of *wheel* will be tested multiple times and see many iterations to maintain current understanding. This process implies an emphasis on experience as critical to learning since each encounter contributes to redefining and rethinking internal constructs, which in essence shapes all knowledge.

Although aspects of Piaget's theories may be debated, the essence of his thought is generally accepted. His belief that children learn by doing reflects that of his predecessor, John Dewey. He extends the notion with the thought that children formulate ideas through play and experience, thereby arriving at knowledge, albeit in different ways.

Howard Gardner (1943–)

A new voice joined the conversation about learning with the publication of Howard Gardner's *Frames of Mind: The Theory of Multiple Intelligences.*[13] Gardner was influenced by his work with Jerome Bruner, a theorist who believed that learning was a social process that required active engagement of the individual, and by Erik Erikson and his beliefs about the evolution of the individual and the influence of culture on behavior. Gardner espoused a new way of thinking about human intelligence that differed from the accepted linguistic/logical-mathematical model of the past that privileged verbal and reasoning skills, equating these with intelligence. Gardner's model placed value on different ways of knowing and attached the label of intelligences to each.

His study resulted in seven distinct categories, and, while retaining the categories defined as linguistic and logical-mathematical, he added musical, bodily/kinesthetic, spatial, interpersonal, and intrapersonal intelligences to his model. In recent years the idea of multiple intelligences has been expanded to include naturalist and existential as ways of knowing.

Gardner suggests that there are myriad ways of knowing and processing information and that education should celebrate and embrace diverse learners by respecting the different ways of learning. He encourages educators to adopt a way of thinking and teaching that supports students with different strengths and interests, thereby building on the innate capacities of the individual rather than thwarting growth. With the introduction of Gardner's theories, museum learning gained validity as a means of constructing knowledge through nontraditional experiences. Museum environments broadened the context for informal learning with the high degree of visual experience in exhibitions, the expansion of interactive elements within exhibitions, and the broad sensory immersion that takes place in a museum setting.

Gardner's research offers new insight for museum professionals. He suggests that museum collections are a means to an end—they provide the opportunity for research and public education—and that by understanding the visitor, museum professionals can support the institution's educational goals through the display of collections. This understanding of diverse audiences and valuing of individual learning capacities is at the heart of Gardner's thinking.

Characteristics of the Young Learner

A few minutes in the company of children clearly shows that they are unique and distinct beings. Their world is in motion, and each child is actively engaged, utilizing multiple senses to explore something new or purposefully examining objects to create meaning. Adults often wonder how children have the energy to maintain their level of activity throughout the day.

In considering the learning styles of children, one must recognize that they are actively engaged in sensory-based experiences (sound, sight, taste, touch, smell) as ways to explore the world; they engage in imaginative play; they assume roles of others; they observe and interact socially to gain new knowledge; they imitate what they have seen or heard and attempt to practice those newly acquired words and skills; they recreate scenarios through dramatic play or in games in an effort to make meaning; they express ideas and knowledge of their world through narrative; they compare and analyze; and they build on prior knowledge by redefining what they already know based on new experiences.

Understanding that children see the world in a way that is qualitatively different from that of adults is critical in shaping learning experiences, whether in the design of a museum exhibit or an educational program. Yet at the same time, we must recognize their potential for learning and acknowledge their capacity to grasp concepts that are sophisticated and complex. Over the years, as children develop a sense of time, accumulate a personal history, and develop sequencing skills and sorting and classification skills, they are also building their capacity to engage with and understand history.

Sense of Time

In listening to the words of constructivists, we begin to see the value of experience in forming the building blocks that create a foundation for understanding history and building connections to our past. A parent rarely thinks about teaching history when cuddling an infant. Yet early experiences and relationships between a young child and a parent are rich with vocabulary and expressions that introduce the concept of time. Think of all of the words that are connected to the concept of time—soon, not yet, in a few minutes, yesterday, today, tomorrow, before, next, once upon a time.

Time vocabulary begins to appear in a child's early verbal expressions. "We went to the beach last week" might indicate an event that clearly took place in the past but may not have actually occurred last week. As a child experiments with language and meaning, everything in the past was *last week*! While a child is referencing the past with the words "last week," he likely does not have an understanding of time in a temporal sense. Intellectual understanding of time comes through experience and maturation.

In conversation, a sense of time is frequently invoked to provide contextual meaning, which is essential to understanding the notion of history. As children grasp the meaning of new words, they not only learn to label objects and actions but also attain further information through words that describe or offer contextual insight. The significance of these early experiences in communication must not be underestimated. It is this immersion in language rich in time-related vocabulary that is a building block for future understanding of history and that contributes to a child's ability to recognize the difference between *now* and *then*.

A Personal History

A child's personal history gives meaning to time and is also paramount as a step toward understanding history in that it allows a child to distinguish the difference between what is currently happening and something that has already taken place. Personal events such as birthdays create meaningful reference points for a child, much like other traditions and holidays. Children collect personal experiences that will one day serve as prior knowledge. It is this knowledge, organized into specific categories, that helps to shape a child's first thoughts of history. A sense of time evolves and meaning emerges as ideas and experiences are linked.

Children gain a sense of the past through conversations with family members and celebration of family traditions. Baking pumpkin pie for Thanksgiving using a recipe written by Great Grandma, telling stories of gatherings from past holidays, or examining an aunt's collection of dolls from long ago—these are traditions that connect children to their heritage and to the past. Children's interests develop as well as a sense of identity through this personal connection to history.

Ten to 12-year-olds are entering a formative stage where shaping personal identity takes precedence in life. Family culture, traditions, interests, first-hand experiences, and social interactions play an important role in forming personal identity and ultimately connect children at this age to the past.

Sequencing

Everyday conversation and experiences help a child to comprehend the meaning and significance of sequence. A simple activity such as baking a birthday cake reinforces sequence and gives temporal context to the experience. This specific activity is particularly salient for a young child and takes advantage of a child's interests. New information is gleaned as a child carefully observes and notices precise steps that proceed in a given order: mix the ingredients, pour the batter into the pan, bake in the oven, cool, then eat and celebrate! A child quickly learns the order of each step and recognizes the importance of the sequence of events.

Through maturation a sense of number and sequence develops in children. The role of sequence becomes important in understanding relationships and in comparisons much like cause and effect, skills that are used by older children in critically examining events in history. For example, an important connection exists between the Boston Tea Party and the Revolutionary War, but without knowledge of sequence or order, interpretation is skewed. Knowing the sequence of events informs understanding, but at an early age it might be important to know only that the Boston Tea Party occurred before the war. As children develop an increasing capacity to analyze and understand events in the past, it may become important for them to know that it was only two years between the "party" in Boston Harbor and the outbreak of war. Ultimately, content goals must be measured against the cognitive abilities of the target audience.

Sorting and Classifying

Piaget and other theorists believe that children innately sort, order, and classify as they begin to perceive similarities and differences in their world. Sorting and classifying are also closely connected to Piaget's concept of assimilation and accommodation, a process that begins with a child's recognition of similarities and differences, leading to reformulating of mental concepts or schema.

Embedded in this act of sorting and classifying is the concept of comparison. To successfully sort or classify, comparison is required with a focus on similarities and differences. For young children this ability to observe differences leads to classification. For children ages 8 through 12 it is the basis for critical thinking and comparative analysis. This skill of observing differences becomes important if children are to grasp change over time by noticing differences between *now* and *then*.

Children strengthen their understanding of concepts from the past by grouping experiences that have common elements. Family gatherings, media, school experience, and visits to libraries and museums expose children to new ideas that are the beginning of internal schemes or concepts. It is common practice for children to learn about George Washington in school when Presidents' Day is celebrated. Stories are told and books are read that share the tale of Washington as a boy and a man. A family trip to Mount Vernon offers a personal look at George Washington's life on the farm and background about his role as a war hero and political leader. Each new experience builds on the previous knowledge and allows for redefining of concepts. It is unlikely that a young child can accurately place Washington on a historical timeline, but the collective experiences become a building block for future learning and can be categorized as long ago. Associations between ideas and experiences play an important role in understanding history and serve as prior knowledge.

History Museums and Children: Building for the Future

Today's history museums are welcoming children in a new way and are designing exhibits and programs to create meaningful experiences in the galleries. By acquiring knowledge of cognitive theories, museum professionals gain insight and understanding about the unique characteristics of children and appropriate strategies, which can help them to create exciting new environments for learning and connecting to the past. This book explores many concrete ways in which the theories of learning and cognitive development reviewed here can inform and improve history exhibitions.

Knowing that children naturally seek opportunities to explore and learn through their senses offers a starting point for developing and designing experience-based learning environments in museums. Sight, sound, taste, touch, and smell . . . the senses contribute to understanding and can thoughtfully be considered for inclusion in the exhibit. Mount Vernon's Donald W. Reynolds Museum and Education Center appeals to the senses and seems to take the visitor into the past, standing beside a soldier asleep on a bunk during the war. The soldier moves sleepily, trying to stay warm under a rough blanket in the worst of winters. In another part of the exhibition, the firing of guns signals the onset of war. Stacks of shipping crates offer a tactile connection to one of the stories behind the war, a story of taxation and lack of independence under British rule. Throughout the exhibition, the senses are aroused, and visitors form a personal connection with the past in a holistic way through multiple sensory experiences.

In the museum, sensory experience must be relevant, engaging, and, as John Dewey would say, educative. Simply creating an exhibit that allows the visitor to open and close panels to read text and find answers misses the point, particularly for children who most likely are opening and closing the panels to listen to the noise or for the physical, tactile experience. This design element does not further the story. When carefully conceived, experiences that engage multiple senses can enhance the design. An exhibition on baskets that encourages visitors to feel the textures of different reeds and grasses used in basket making or allows for exploration of the weaving process through a hands-on activity adjacent to the exhibition is likely to provide a relevant and meaningful sensory experience for young visitors.

Storytelling or narrative is a critical strategy that supports a child's way of thinking and constructing knowledge. As the exhibition's story is crafted, it is best to begin by creating a simple, compelling narrative that can be communicated through objects, experiences, media, or graphics. Not only can the story be told, and sensory elements added when they will enhance the experience, but through imagination, young visitors will be drawn into the time and place recreated by the exhibition. The imagination is a powerful avenue of learning and exploration and, as education theorist Kieran Egan and other researchers suggest, the way that most children understand their world.

The combined strategies of narrative, imagination, and sensory experience become apparent as a child enters the National Museum of American History exhibition entitled *Within These Walls . . .* , a display that portrays life in the home and community in the historical past. One part of the exhibition makes it easy to imagine the drudgery that comes with washing clothes long ago. A child steps back in time by picking up the old wooden bucket that replicates the act of carrying well water to the house for washing and is able to feel first-hand the amount of effort required to lift the bucket ten or twenty times. Imagination in this exhibition is not invoking fairies and goblins, rather it refers to applying imaginative powers to real world experiences to make meaning.

FIGURE 1.1. The laundry exhibit from *Within These Walls* . . . offers a first-hand experience for the visitor. Courtesy National Museum of American History, Smithsonian Institution.

Children are naturally curious and are drawn to objects that are unusual. Comparing unfamiliar objects with those that are commonplace or known is an exhibition strategy that builds on a natural inclination of children. By including opportunities for comparison, children apply those natural abilities to observe, recognize detail, identify similarities and differences, and then draw meaning. The story is the combination of two objects—an old-fashioned eggbeater next to an electric mixer—accompanied by text that asks questions about these objects. In what ways are they the same? How are they different? What was the benefit of the new way of mixing? Guiding text supports the informal learning experience for children and families by providing parents and teachers with suggestions for social interaction that explores pivotal ideas within the exhibition.

Conclusion

With an increased focus on audience, today's museum professionals are striving to meet the needs of diverse visitors and are incorporating programs and strategies that acknowledge children as an important segment of society. In this effort, many professionals in the field are committed to designing new exhibits and programs that target this audience.

Knowledge of cognitive theory is increasingly important for museum professionals as children are welcomed into the museum and programs and exhibitions are designed to serve this new audience. Theories of constructivism introduce the belief that learning is an internal process that is influenced by genetics and environment and that young children construct knowledge by integrating experiences through a process of assimilation and accommodation, building and refining concepts as new information is acquired. It is commonly accepted that concrete, sensory-based experiences offer a foundation for developing more abstract understandings and that beginning with simple ideas allows for the eventual exploration of more complex concepts. Theorists also acknowledge that children's curiosity and imaginative spirit provide powerful opportunities for learning and that through play, children reenact and reinterpret their world.

Children have a natural sense of history that begins at an early age. Museums can nurture and encourage that connection to the past by creating exhibitions that allow children to experience history in meaningful and age-appropriate ways. Constructivist theorists offer museum professionals insights about the unique learning style of children that can help shape gallery experiences that appeal to young children and use their ever-expanding cognitive toolkit to connect with history.

NOTES

1. Roy Rosenzweig and David Thelen, *The Presence of the Past: Popular Uses of History in American Life* (New York: Columbia University Press, 1998).
2. Wayne J. Urban and Jennings L. Wagoner, Jr., *American Education: A History.* 3rd ed. (New York: McGraw-Hill, 2004), xviii.
3. George E. Hein and Mary Alexander, *Museums: Places of Learning* (Washington, DC: American Association of Museums Education Committee, 1998), 30.
4. Hein and Alexander, *Museums*, 29.
5. Lev S. Vygotsky, *Thought and Language,* ed. Alex Kozulin, trans. Eugenia Hanfmann and Gertrude Vakar (Cambridge, MA: MIT Press, 1986 [1934, 1962]).
6. Paul J. Eslinger, "Brain Development and Learning," *Basic Education* 41 (1997): 9.
7. Lisabeth Dixon-Krauss, *Vygotsky in the Classroom: Mediated Literacy Instruction and Assessment* (White Plains, NY: Longman Publishers, 1996), 12.
8. Dixon-Krauss, *Vygotsky in the Classroom*, 12.
9. Laura E. Berk, "Vygotsky's Theory: The Importance of Make-believe Play," *Young Children* 50, no. 1 (November 1994): 30–9.

10. Jean Piaget and Bärbel Inhelder, *The Psychology of the Child,* trans. by Helen Weaver (New York: Basic Books, 1969), 13.

11. William Cooney, Charles Cross, and Barry Trunk, *From Plato to Piaget: The Greatest Educational Theorists from across the Centuries and around the World* (Lanham, MD: University Press of America, 1993), 257.

12. Piaget and Inhelder, *Psychology of the Child,* 6.

13. Howard E. Gardner, *Frames of Mind: The Theory of Multiple Intelligences* (New York: Basic Books, 1983).

CHAPTER 2

It's about Them:
Using Developmental Frameworks
to Create Exhibitions for Children
(and Their Grown-ups)

Elizabeth Reich Rawson

I was educated to understand that if the traditional curatorial perspective for exhibitions were translated into questions, those questions might be, What is this exhibition about? Or, What story am I telling? Exhibitions developed in response to these questions, grounded in literary conventions, can lead to the presentation format commonly referred to as "a book on the walls." In my experience, the best of these exhibitions are well organized by theme, chronology and/or argument, and utilize various design devices to assist the narrative and to create focus points, modulate the pace of information, and heighten visual drama. However, as long as the exhibition curator's operative question is, What is this exhibition about? the exhibition development process is likely to yield a product that will fully resonate with a very narrow audience, individuals who have life experiences, educational attainment, and interests similar to the curator's own. As a curator and exhibition developer at several historic houses and history centers I had opportunities to experiment with introducing some touchable displays and games for children into thematic exhibitions for family audiences, but it was after I accepted a role at Brooklyn Children's Museum that the foundation of my personal curatorial perspective was shaken.

Once I became a part of an organization whose mission and experiences were dedicated entirely to children and families, the key curatorial question for me to address had suddenly shifted from, What is this exhibition about? to Who is this exhibition for? Changing the dominant emphasis from content to audience challenged me to rethink my approach to all aspects of the exhibition development process—from concept through production. My primary obligation was no longer to present an argument, or tell a story from a singular perspective for people I assumed were much like me, but rather to understand a diverse audience and provide them with opportunities for multiple insights, experiences, and meaning making. This realization transformed the entire nature of exhibition development for me, as well as the definition of what an exhibition is and can be. What I was striving to create evolved for me from a (really good) "book on the walls" into a more accessible experience for most visitors (in Brooklyn's case, children and their caregivers), inviting and inspiring action, shared input, and creativity.

Starting with a goal of understanding audience and learning as much as possible about them—how they sort out information, what matters to them, what they already know about a topic—is in a sense inviting them to join and contribute to the process. This goal radically changes the terms of the conversations that an exhibition developer will engage in with expert advisors, with museum colleagues, with exhibition and graphic designers, fabricators, indeed with anyone who participates in creating an exhibition. Asking questions about audience every step of the way forces us to rethink how we approach content and design. Once chosen, the stuff that makes up most exhibitions is somewhat immutable—a group of objects, a set of images, a series of words, a work of art, or a moment in time. Children, in contrast, are variable, changeable, and in constant motion. They require a range of environments and mediums that allow active explorations of content. Creating effective exhibitions for them demands that our interpretation and presentation of content is based on a clear understanding of who they are and the best ways to engage their talents, skills, and interests in exploring an exhibition's themes and messages. If we, as exhibition developers, want to create exhibitions that are accessible and understandable by a broad range of children, it is a fair demand that we, in turn, understand them. A useful tool for advancing this understanding, and creating more powerful and engaging experiences, is a developmental framework.

In this chapter, I describe how we use developmental frameworks, also called audience profiles, at Brooklyn Children's Museum to research, create, and apply key insights about our audience to the exhibition process from the concept phase through fabrication and beyond.

What Is a Developmental Framework?

In their most common form, developmental frameworks provide benchmarks or milestones of a child's general growth: social, cognitive, and physical. These tools are familiar to many caregivers, educators, and pediatricians. Open just about any parenting guide on children's growth from birth through age 5, and you are likely to find a developmental framework.

In the exhibition process, however, developmental frameworks expand to include data from a variety of sources about our intended audience into an easily referenced tool. Developmental frameworks, as referred to in this chapter, distill research on children's capabilities at various ages as they relate to specific exhibition content and the social learning that can be supported through activities in an informal learning environment. An exhibition team's active participation in a focused investigation of audience (through the creation of a developmental framework) early in the exhibition's conception may be even more critical than the resulting document. The framework itself represents a set of dynamic notes—a valuable and ongoing summary of your team's growing insight into audience. Creating a unique developmental framework directly linked to the specific subjects, themes, and concepts of your singular exhibition demonstrates a team's commitment to its audience and discovering the best possible exhibition solutions for them. Adapting and updating existing data is necessary up to a point, but in order to own, absorb, and apply the findings effectively, the research for a developmental framework must be one of an exhibition team's first tasks.

A developmental framework ensures an exhibition is shaped—not only by content and a point of view but also by a focused understanding of kids: who they are, their needs and interests, and their readiness to engage with the proposed subject. Developmental frameworks don't dictate content—rather, they help identify developmentally appropriate themes and an approach that is most likely to increase children's access and receptivity to the ideas and information of the exhibition. Moreover, a framework enables an exhibition team to find ways to connect what they know to what children are ready to investigate, and a solid framework may inspire the confidence to tackle those themes more robustly. In other words, it ensures that the team members know audience with the same certainty that they know content. A developmental framework increases its value when used hand in hand with an evaluation process that tests the team's conclusions about audience throughout the exhibition's development.

Researching Developmental Frameworks

Researching developmental frameworks for exhibition projects at Brooklyn Children's Museum follows four lines of inquiry:

1. What are children's general developmental milestones or "ages and stages"? More specifically, what are children's capabilities at various ages and stages of development related to the particular exhibition

themes and social learning that can be supported through activities in an informal environment?

2. What does our audience know and understand about the proposed exhibition topic? Undertaking front-end audience interviews and observations with our own audience enables us to assess their knowledge of and interest in our projected concept and topic and suggests possible points of engagement.

3. What have other researchers learned about our audience's understanding or knowledge of our proposed exhibition topic? Conducting literature reviews helps us learn from what other researchers across a variety of disciplines have already established about children's understanding of our proposed subject matter.

4. What are the formal educational objectives or curriculums that are aligned with the proposed exhibition topic? Analyzing local and national curriculums and standards for themes relevant to the proposed exhibit informs how the exhibition might support formal learning goals and school programming.

This comprehensive approach may require more time and staff resources than some organizations are willing or able to spare. However, I would argue that even if an exhibition team can research only one or two of these questions, they will gain insights that will be invaluable as they design for children.

Developmental Milestones

The first task in creating a framework is determining the general physical, intellectual, and social developmental milestones across the target audience that are relevant to an informal exhibition environment: What are children's social contexts for learning? How do they process information and experiences at various points in their development? What are their abilities and readiness for attempting and completing physical tasks at various points? Are there gender and cultural differences among learners in our age group? Gathering this type of information helps an exhibition development team understand the limitations and capabilities of the children of various ages who will be sharing the exhibition space at the same time.

Our milestone research for the *World Brooklyn* developmental framework (Table 2.1) revealed the vastly different physical, social, linguistic, and cognitive abilities of our target audience of 4- to 11-year-olds. *World Brooklyn* is designed to encourage our target audience to gain a greater understanding and appreciation of Brooklyn as home to people of many different cultures and countries through settings, objects, and stories drawn from real people and places in the borough's diverse communities.

Table 2.1 Excerpt from Developmental Milestones from the *World Brooklyn* Developmental Framework

PHYSICAL CAPABILITIES

Age 4–5	Age 5–6	Age 6–7	Age 7–8	Age 8–9	Age 9–10	Age 10–11	Age 11–12
Sometimes clumsy, awkward; spills and accidents common; enjoy large muscle play and activity; fisted pencil grasp typical	Often stands up to do work; need a good deal of physical activity; relaxed games or free play	More aware of fingers as tools; noisy	Likes confined space; works with head down on desk	Speedy—works in a hurry; somewhat awkward	Increased coordination; pushes self to physical limits; race against each other or against the clock	Need a great deal of physical activity or energy will spill over as acting out behavior; particularly enjoys tracing and copying as fine motor skills strengthen—maps, cartooning	Vast appetite for food, physical activity and talking; good fine motor capability—can do delicate work, confident of skills

SOCIAL CAPABILITIES

Age 4–5	Age 5–6	Age 6–7	Age 7–8	Age 8–9	Age 9–10	Age 10–11	Age 11–12
Loves working with friends, but still much parallel play; moves quickly from one thing to the next; short attention span	Oppositional; not sure whether to be good or naughty; insecure with feelings	Highly competitive and can overdo need to win and be first; sometimes dishonest, invents rules	Doesn't like to make mistakes or risk making them; inward, withdrawn and sometimes moody, sulking or shy	Likes to work cooperatively in groups; prefers same gender activities; resilient, bounces back from mistakes	Highly competitive; self aware; individualistic	Fairness issues peak and can be solved; works very well in groups	Moody, sensitive, extremes of emotion; oppositional, tests limits

(continued)

Table 2.1 Excerpt from Developmental Milestones from the *World Brooklyn* Developmental Framework *(continued)*

LANGUAGE CAPABILITIES

Age 4–5	Age 5–6	Age 6–7	Age 7–8	Age 8–9	Age 9–10	Age 10–11	Age 11–12
Expansive, likes using big words; parallel reading with an adult—child "reads" one page of familiar story, you read the next	Verbal answers may not equal cognitive understanding—more words than ideas; elaborates and differentiates in answer to questions	Likes to "work," loves jokes and guessing games	Likes to send notes; interested in codes	Talkative; likes to explain ideas; listens, but so full of ideas cannot always recall what was said	Loves vocabulary and language play information; age of negatives: I hate it; I can't, it's boring, yeah right.	Good listeners, actively receptive; expressive, talkative, likes to explain	Argumentative, debater; impulsive—talks before thinking

COGNITIVE CAPABILITIES

Age 4–5	Age 5–6	Age 6–7	Age 7–8	Age 8–9	Age 9–10	Age 10–11	Age 11–12
Music and rhythm, repeating patterns—manipulatives important—puzzles, interlocking cubes; scoops, funnels, measuring cups in sand etc.; likes to imitate adult roles through imaginative play—dress-up, dramatic play	Begins to try new activities more easily; makes lots of mistakes, recognizes some	Games popular—poems, riddles and songs delight and illuminate, teaching through games produces stronger learning patterns; artistic explosion—needs to feel that attempts are valued—no right or wrong way	Likes to review learning; needs closure, must complete things	Engrossed in activity at hand, loves to socialize at the same time; likes groups and group activity	Industrious and self critical; dawn of "bigger world"	Able to concentrate and read for extended periods of time; loves geography, sports and TV facts, spelling, math, computer and electronic games, singing, poetry, plays, seriation, collections, height of concrete organizational skills	Prefers new tasks and experiences to reflection or revision of previous work; able to think abstractly

For example, at age 4 children are still physically clumsy and have difficulty with fine motor skills such as grasping a pencil. They find it hard to sit still and prefer activities that allow them to jump, run, and climb; by age 11, children—although still restless and full of physical energy—can enjoy and excel at delicate handwork that requires fine motor skills. Five-year-olds prefer to work standing up, whereas 6-year-olds have a tendency to fall backward out of chairs. Socially, 7-year-olds are generally moody and withdrawn and dislike making mistakes. By age 8 they have gained some resiliency and can bounce back from setbacks and enjoy working in peer groups, preferably of the same gender. Between the ages of 8 and 10, children's vocabulary and reading skills expand, and they delight in talking and explaining their ideas. Cognitively, children on the younger edge of the chart learn best through direct experience—what they can see and do—whereas older children are beginning to think abstractly (though they still learn by doing).

Although it might be tempting to undertake this research once and transfer it from one framework to the next, a cursory survey of child development resources revealed an explosion of research and information in the last ten years. The Additional Resources section at the end of the chapter lists some of the resources used by Brooklyn Children's Museum and other museums, but it is by no means exhaustive. There are innumerable online and print sources available targeting parents, educators, and healthcare professionals. The breadth of resources suggests that any research in child development might be productively updated for each project. Over time you will create a baseline of information, but best practice dictates that the data are revisited and updated, not just so new information is included but also to allow the team the opportunity to seek resources that may allow greater insights and deeper connections to your specific project—an inevitable result of doing the work yourselves rather than copying the work of previous teams.

What Do Children Already Know and Understand about Our Topic?

With a general understanding of children in hand, the next steps are determining children's understanding and knowledge of the proposed topic. This effort requires gathering information from self-generated research undertaken specifically for the exhibition such as a *literature review*, a *front-end evaluation*, and a *curriculum review*. Questions that might guide research include:

- What do children already know and understand about X?
- What do they want to know about X?

- When and how do these understandings develop?
- What are their frames of reference for understanding X? When do these references expand or change?
- When and how are these themes introduced and expanded in school?
- What is the adult role in supporting and extending children's engagement and understanding of X?

For the *World Brooklyn* project on global cultures, some of our questions included: What are the primary characteristics of children's understandings of culture? When and how do these understandings develop? What are their frames of reference for understanding the world—self, family, school, friends, and so on? When do these references expand or change? When and how do they process differences in people? When and how are world cultures introduced and expanded in school? What is the adult role in supporting and extending children's engagement and understanding of world cultures? The following sections illustrate how literature reviews, front-end evaluation, and curriculum reviews are means for finding answers on children's level of understanding.

Literature Reviews

Literature reviews of interest here are exploratory surveys of what researchers across a variety of disciplines have already learned about an audience's understanding of the proposed subject matter. Conducting a literature review may include consulting with subject experts (for example, for *World Brooklyn* we spoke with professors at Harvard and Columbia Universities who studied and taught about children's understanding of culture); searched online catalogs of public and academic libraries, ERIC Digest database, and visitor studies databases for relevant studies and curricula; and compared recent research bibliographies.[1]

Another avenue of research that falls within this review phase is investigating exhibitions with similar themes (even if it was intended for adults) to find out what approaches were or were not effective with audiences. Although the number of exhibitions fortunate enough to have a formal summative evaluation is growing, more often you will have to rely on your own observations (assuming the exhibition is still on view) and/or anecdotal information gathered from speaking with staff to learn about a project's effective audience strategies.

CHILDREN AND HISTORICAL THINKING

For an assignment in the Museum Leadership Program at Bank Street College of Education, Mari Shopsis created a developmental framework—detailing children's ages and stages, insights from her literature review of children's historical thinking, and how adult caregivers can expand a child's experience at each age (Table 2.2).

Her findings for 5- to 8-year-olds (excerpted here) is another example of how a literature review of children's understanding of specific subjects can provide a starting point based on data, rather than guess work, for initiating the development of an exhibition experience more likely to engage children in meaningful ways. For example, Shopsis found that although scholarship reveals that chronological history—dates and timelines—is too abstract for the youngest children, these children are able to talk about their own personal history with the help of a supportive adult.[2] Whereas, older children in the 6 to 8 age group can confidently categorize events as "long ago" and place them in time as past, present, or future.[3] Shopsis's findings suggest that children are interested in how life was different in the past, and therefore the stuff of museums—objects, images, and stories, if presented in a developmentally appropriate manner with opportunities for adult support, especially for the younger visitors—can help children make connections to the past and begin to help them build an awareness of history and their place in the world.

Brooklyn Children's Museum hired Selinda Research Associates in Chicago to conduct the literature review for *World Brooklyn* as well as several other projects. Their findings for *World Brooklyn* revealed that as children develop, their frame of reference for understanding the world expands from "me and my family" to include "my friends and my school." Children 5 and under notice physical differences among people, such as skin color, but these differences are not associated with stereotypes or evaluations. By around age 8, however, sexual, racial, and ethnic identities and group affiliations begin to emerge, and children are able to differentiate themselves from others and begin to place themselves within a geographic and cultural context.[4]

TABLE 2.2. Excerpt from a Developmental Framework
of Children's Historical Thinking by Mari Shopsis, April 2006

Age	Historical Thinking	Adult Role
5	Can rank family members in terms of age	Read stories together set in the past
	Know days of the week and uses time-vocabulary correctly (yesterday = just the day before today, and is not extended further into the past)	Provide access to images from both the recent past and the more distant past, allowing child to develop visual vocabulary of time
	Developing concepts of sequence, duration, and distance in time; can sequence basic visual materials relating to the past (e.g., "old-fashioned clothes" vs. modern clothes)	Look at family photos together, reminiscing and asking child to recount stories (building autobiographical memory and grasp of narrative form)
	Begin to use numbers and dates to represent the past; attempt to associate numbers/dates with people and events, with frequent inaccuracy	Provide exposure to a wide range of historical images and narratives, especially those built around a central character with whom children can identify
6–8	Use of general time spans—"long ago" outnumbers use of dates for time references	Create concrete visual references for concepts such as "number of days"—stack blocks and remove one each day
	Can categorize events as past, current, or future	Ask questions related to the sequencing and grouping of events

Source: Courtesy Mari Shopsis

Front-end Evaluations

Front-end audience evaluation assesses your audience's knowledge of and interest in the proposed subject. Brooklyn Children's Museum uses a naturalistic methodology (or a qualitative research approach) for our evaluations. Data are collected and analyzed in a real-life setting rather than in a laboratory-style experiment that tests a particular hypothesis. In other words, we go where the children are—in the museum galleries with their families, in the museum's after-school program, or in local classrooms. Our aim for all of our front-end studies is to gain a deeper understanding of what children know and understand and think about and the reasons why they do.

Data-collection techniques for a front-end study may include conducting audience surveys, convening focus groups of various audience segments, doing one-on-one interviews (or in the parlance of visitor studies "depth interviews") with children of various ages, and making unobtrusive observations of children and families in the museum. Purposive, rather than random, sampling is used. That is, respondents are deliberately selected to ensure all audience segments are represented. Focus groups include a small group of children of the same age and an interviewer. The conversations are recorded and later transcribed for analysis. The interviewer asks questions, and the children are invited to talk with one another about the topic. The advantage to this approach is that the group dynamic and interchange can provide additional and unanticipated data. For instance, one child in a focus group for *World Brooklyn* mentioned spending the summer in Barbados with extended family; others spoke up and related similar stories about spending summers in Barbados with extended family, which led to an interesting discussion about the differences between Brooklyn and Barbados.[5]

Interviews are done one on one in a quiet area of the museum. The interviewer poses a general question, such as, What can you tell me about your neighborhood? and then allows the child to answer in his own words in as much depth as possible. For audience surveys, visitors are invited to respond to a questionnaire by speaking with staff. Unobtrusive observations involve watching visitors interact in existing exhibition areas in the museum and later asking them questions about their experience. The observations help us understand the range of visitor behaviors, paying particular attention to family dynamics, quality of interaction, and in the case of the *World Brooklyn* front-end evaluation, interaction with cultural objects.[6]

As part of the exhibition development for the nine-hundred-square-foot traveling exhibition *Japan & Nature: Spirits of the Seasons,* Selinda Research Associates staff conducted front-end depth interviews with children visiting the museum to assess their perceptions about Japan, the seasons, and nature (three important keys to the concept plan). *Japan & Nature: Spirits of the Seasons* is a hands-on, object-based, interactive exhibition that invites children ages 5 to 12 to discover how nature is reflected and celebrated in Japanese children's everyday lives through special seasonal and everyday environments and activities.

One of the challenging, but not unexpected, findings of the study was that children assumed that all things Asian were Chinese. Often this Chinese/Japanese/Asian confusion came up when children viewed Japanese letters or writing. Other images that triggered this response were images of traditional homes and shrines and photographs of Japanese children. However, we were pleased to discover that children easily related to images of Japanese children engaged in day-today activities such as going to school or playing sports, and they could connect nature with the seasons. When children were shown drawings and photographs of Japanese landscapes, they picked up cues from nature to figure out what season it was; children pointed out that it was spring, because there were flowers on the trees, or that it was the end of spring or beginning of summer, because there were flower blossoms on the ground.[7]

These insights informed the exhibition's content and approach. To counter children's confusion of all things Asian, we developed an introductory computer component that allows children to "fly" from the United States to Japan; used maps and photos to "place" children in Japan; and repeated the words "Japan" and "Japanese" throughout the exhibition. Children experience *Japan & Nature* through four distinct environments reflecting Japan's seasons and unique geographic features. Welcome banners introduce each season and region and include a postcard from and photo of a Japanese child. The exhibition's activities are modeled on Japanese children's own experiences, and the exhibition is rich with real artifacts, photos, and videos gathered during our research of Japanese children.

Curriculum and Standard Reviews

Curriculum reviews are surveys of related formal and informal curriculum materials and standards and serve to inform how an exhibition might support school programming in the museum and naturally link to what children are learning in school. Formal learning objectives for social studies, the arts, literacy, and even math and science all have connections—some more concretely than others—to history concepts.

Federal, and many state and local, curriculum standards and benchmarks are available online. Most catalog what students are expected to know in a particular subject area by the end of each grade, provide a list of indicators for measuring their achievement, and give outlines for the sequence of topics. Local and state curriculums outline what topics are being taught by grade in area schools.

For example, the New York City Department of Education's *K-8 Social Studies Scope and Sequence* includes national standards, identifies ten thematic strands (such as culture; time, continuity, and change; people, places, and environments) and includes the New York State Core Curriculum. It also lists the essential inquiry-based "thinking skills" needed to process social studies concepts, such as "comparing and contrasting" and "using the vocabulary of time and place." Suggested time frames for the teaching of core content guided by essential questions are given by grade. Each unit of study includes the major content and concepts and their relation to specific standards, key ideas, and performance indicators.[8] A local historical society considering an exhibition for children on Native American culture should know that fourth-graders are challenged to explore "how did Native Americans influence the development of New York?" in unit one.[9]

The National Council for Social Studies publishes the periodical *Social Studies for the Young Learner* and the *National Curriculum Standards for Social Studies*.[10] The National Council for History Education is a resource for curriculum development, pedagogical methodology for history, and the report by the Bradley Commission, which outlines nine guidelines for developing a robust history curriculum in schools. Guideline number four states that "kindergarten through grade six social studies curriculum be history-centered."[11] The Commission argues that social studies at the elementary level should reach beyond the "expanding horizons" pedagogy of "myself, my family, my neighborhood, and my community" to include history, biography and mythology. Noting that although the use of dates is inappropriate for young learners, "children can begin to develop a sense of time and place ('long, long ago, far away') as they are introduced to historical literature." Children can be engaged by historical concepts when they are presented in formats that they can understand and enjoy—such as folk tales of different cultures; novels about important events and heroes and ordinary people in extraordinary times; immigrants' stories; poetry and songs.[12]

Resources such as these are enormously useful in helping exhibition developers find the intersection between what children are learning in school and the entry points and strategies developers might use in an exhibition. This approach is particularly true if one of the goals of the exhibition is to support and attract school groups to your institution. This research phase should also include a review of the textbooks being used in local classrooms and conversations with area teachers inviting them to share how an exhibit might support and enhance their work in the classroom. At Brooklyn Children's Museum, we have heard from teachers that making clear links between an exhibition and formal education objectives in school program descriptions helps them justify field trips outside the classroom.

In addition to formal school curriculum and standards, another rich resource for planning exhibitions for children is topical curriculums developed by nonprofit educational organizations—sometimes even museums—to promote their educational goals. These programs start with formal school standards and apply them using an interdisciplinary approach encompassing art, social studies, language arts, history, science, and math. Many offer developers ideas for connecting to content that can serve as starting points for unfacilitated hands-on activities in an exhibition environment.

One resource for our traveling exhibition on architectural design, *Building Brainstorm*, was a curriculum published by the Michigan Architecture Foundation for the elementary grades, *Architecture: It's Elementary!* The foundation's goal is for children to "gain appreciation of their built environment and the buildings, towns, and cities that make it up."[13] Each lesson uses an aspect of architecture as a starting point and shows clear links to federal and state standards for math, science, visual arts, language, and social studies. A lesson for kindergarteners, for instance, is about looking for basic shapes in photographs of buildings and labeling them with cut-out shapes. The activity supports national and state standards, which require kindergarteners to understand "shapes as the most basic element of form" and to "visualize shapes as simple forms of objects in the environment."[14] In the *Building Brainstorm* exhibition, this idea was realized as the "Shape Search Challenge," an activity in which children match two-dimensional geometric magnetic shapes to a mural fantasy skyline of famous buildings. Finally, this phase should include an investigation of the concrete ways adults might deepen children's exploration of history topics. This research might be achieved through interviewing parents and educators to determine what they need to facilitate their children's experience; conducting a review of family learning studies; speaking to institutions with successful family history programming; and consulting pediatricians, developmental psychologists, and youth-center and after-school coordinators.

Creating a Developmental Framework

Once the research is complete, the key findings are pulled out and summarized in a one- or two-page chart—a developmental framework. The finished product presents an intersection of key attributes through and across targeted age ranges: children's developmental readiness, understanding of relevant content, and formal education themes. In other words, it organizes what we've learned about children of various ages into two broad categories: (1) capabilities and (2) understanding and knowledge. Depending on what you want to accomplish, other columns can be added to detail goals or implications for exhibition development.

The aim is to take what you've learned and, rather than stick it on a shelf or in a file drawer, create something useful that every member of the team can refer to easily as you move through the exhibition process. This step requires that the team sift through the findings and determine what is the most critical to include in the chart. Written conclusions for the framework should be crafted so they identify opportunities for exhibition development and recommend actions for the project team.

Table 2.3 is an excerpt from the Research Conclusions section in the project team's developmental framework for the *World Brooklyn* project. Read vertically, the chart provides a depth of understanding for one audience segment. Read horizontally, it provides the potential breadth of engagement and understanding across our audience.

For example, the column for 4- and 5-year-olds, read top down, reveals that this age group has a fairly narrow worldview. Family and self are their frames of reference; and their understanding of place and community is limited to their homes, immediate surroundings, and the people in their neighborhood. They don't distinguish differences between them and others—to a 4-year-old, everyone is just like me! However, they're curious about the world—constantly "reading" and "labeling" their environment; and they enjoy figuring things out, such as puzzles (Learning through Activity). Social studies themes focus on helping them place themselves within their family and community. Add the developmental milestones discussed earlier in this chapter and you have a picture of an exuberant talkative child full of energy, enthusiasm, and imagination; a child eager to make sense of his or her world, who enjoys role-play and stories and learns best by engaging in active, hands-on activities.

Scanning across the category Self-Understanding we see that, although at all ages children have some knowledge of every aspect of themselves, young children's knowledge is very basic. In early childhood, their understanding of the self is dominated by bodily properties and material possessions. As children develop, their sense of self becomes more defined by their activities and abilities relative to others, and an emerging consciousness of sexual, ethnic, and racial identity.

The category Understanding Culture, Dealing with Difference reveals that, although younger children can understand that there are different perspectives, they may lack appreciation for the importance of someone else's perspective. However, at about age 8, children can begin to appreciate different perspectives in a reciprocal way. By the time they are on the edge of adolescence at age 11, they can imagine a neutral perspective or one completely different from their own.

Table 2.3 Excerpt from Research Conclusions
from the *World Brooklyn* Developmental Framework

LITERATURE REVIEW & FRONT-END FINDINGS

AGE 4–5	AGE 6–7	AGE 8–9	AGE 10–11
Frames of Reference			
Self, family	Family, school, neighborhood	Family, school, neighborhood, peers	Family, peer group, school
Self-Understanding			
Define themselves by physical attributes, activities and possessions	Realize that their humanity, gender, and individuality are permanent but base belief on physical and behavioral characteristics rather than something deeper	Begin to give psychological reasons for their permanence	Bodies begin to change; children begin to go through a "search for self "
Understanding Place			
Can draw pictorial view of their home and immediate surroundings (including people, sun and rainbows)	Include home and immediate neighboring homes with roads, trees viewed from slightly elevated position	Often include many buildings from local community using roads to provide structure; the view is high but roads are map-like and houses pictorial	Do aerial views of town/region with symbols for buildings
Understanding Community			
Fantasy stage, children concerned with needs and fantasy role-playing of occupations	Community interests now include details about stores of various kinds, the police station, the firehouse, and the hospital; interest in neighborhood roles continues	Ever-expanding interest in community life and holiday and seasonal activities	Interest in community service
Understanding Culture, Dealing with Difference			
Egocentric or undifferentiated perspective; others not different from self	Subjective, differentiated perspective; recognition of differences in other's perspective; see difference but tend not to understand the judgments that society attaches to those differences	Self-reflective or reciprocal perspective; awareness of how others might view one's thoughts and feelings	Third person or mutual perspective; ability to understand neutral perspective

(continued)

Table 2.3 Excerpt from Research Conclusions
from the *World Brooklyn* Developmental Framework *(continued)*

CURRICULUM & STANDARDS FINDINGS

AGE 4–5	AGE 6–7	AGE 8–9	AGE 10–11
Learning Through Activity			
Loves being read to and loves to do their own "reading" in picture books; constantly reading the environment—label objects frequently seen or used; needs validation; music and rhythm; repeating patterns	Loves to ask questions; likes new games and ideas; learns best through discovery; enjoys process, especially a group process, more than product; needs closure—must complete assignments	Loves group games—gravitates toward same gender activities but can easily get out of hand and needs boundaries; likes using "real/authentic" things when role playing; begin to see divergence in sexes i.e., girls dolls, boys tools; likes to manipulate objects	Can explore delicate work; art an important vehicle to greater focus in reading and math; interest in rules; challenging games, puzzles, even tests enjoyable, productive; has an increased ability for abstract intellectual pursuits
Developmentally Appropriate Thematic Studies: Social Studies			
Myself, my family, my neighborhood, my school; people helping each other; holidays and celebrations; transportation (cars, trucks, trains and planes); houses; pets	Social studies content must be connected to here and now; beginning understanding of past when tied closely to present; families; friends; school; jobs people do; differences; things we are good at; cultural and racial diversity	Our country and world; long ago and far away, *but not both*; history of culture; cultural, racial and ethnic diversity; neighborhood/community interdependence; community institutions; people, traditions, practices of communities around the world; meeting needs and wants	Current events, civics, history highly motivating when tied to issues of clear relevance to students; geography; immigration; industry; local history; social justice; also pop culture and materialism

Clearly, the challenge faced by an exhibition project team designing for children, is figuring out how to accommodate and engage a target audience with such a wide variance of developmental abilities and knowledge of themselves and the world.

Applying Developmental Frameworks to Exhibition Development

The value in creating a developmental framework is to focus the exhibition team's attention on audience early and help them to keep that focus over the course of the development process. Applying a framework consistently from the concept through the design phases helps ensure that the exhibition experience makes sense to children. During design development, using the framework to guide formative assessment helps your team test and clarify content and shape appropriate experiences.

Establishing a working definition of whom the exhibition is for ultimately saves time and money by eliminating ideas and approaches that won't resonate with your audience. What a framework won't do is determine what children don't know and what they need to learn. Frameworks won't help create an exhibition that speeds learning. And they won't help justify developmentally inappropriate content objectives.

Developmental Frameworks in the Concept Phase

Ideally, frameworks are completed and employed early in an exhibition's planning. In the concept phase, a framework helps refine and focus an exhibition's approach and preliminary activity development. At Brooklyn Children's Museum the framework is created by the core exhibition team (including staff from exhibitions, education, and collections). The framework is shared with expert advisors and senior staff and serves as a touchstone for crafting the exhibition's main message and experience and learning goals. Brooklyn Children's Museum has a strong commitment to, and history of, undertaking serious scholarly research in our exhibition planning. This approach includes assembling an advisory panel of content experts to help shape and guide every exhibition. Developing exhibitions for children, however, requires us to know our audience as well as we know our content. A clearly articulated framework guides the group to a place of understanding about audience that allows them to suggest attainable goals for content. The framework provides data that help shape reasonable objectives for our audience as opposed to carrying untested assumptions about children deep into the design process.

For *Building Brainstorm*, a traveling exhibition on building design, advisors thought children should "learn the work of architects." Our research indicated, however, that relatively few children could express what an architect did, although they could imagine being a builder or a designer. Knowing this shifted the conversation away from being an architect, or imagining themselves as someone else, to experiencing the act of designing. As a result the exhibition focuses on the concrete activities associated with designing buildings—thinking about how shapes fit together in space, considering what a building is for, playing with how light changes the feeling of a space, and researching and selecting building materials.

Using Developmental Frameworks During Design Development

Physical and graphic designers joining the team at the beginning of the preliminary design stage are given the developmental framework along with written guidelines for exhibition design based on our understanding of audience. Physical design guidelines detail the acceptable heights for tabletops and seating and the child-friendly treatment of component edges and surfaces. Graphic design guidelines address readability and layout standards appropriate for beginning readers.

At this point in the process the team has initiated content research, established the conceptual approach, and outlined potential activities. Our goal is to generate a wide array of experiences that will engage our audience at whatever point they fall on the framework. Each activity's operational description includes the target age range, main messages, and experience goals for one or more developmental milestones. These characteristics in turn set up the protocols for iterative formative evaluations of activity, text, and design moving forward. Most of the activities we start out with in the preliminary design stage will be dropped, modified, or replaced by new activities that emerge through evaluation.

When testing for an adinkra stamping activity as part of an exhibit featuring artifacts from West African and other world cultures, we referred to the framework to outline the range of experiences we might anticipate seeing. For the younger edge of our audience (ages 4 to 7) the expectation was they would enjoy the activity of stamping itself; this age group takes pleasure in repeating patterns and process. For the older edge of our audience (ages 8 to 11) we projected their interest in the meaning of the symbols and in making designs that illustrated a narrative; this age enjoys working with "authentic" materials, manipulating objects, expressing themselves through role play, poetry and drawing, and learning about cultures other than their own. They are also becoming more adept and confident in tackling delicate tasks and like challenges that require them to test their fine motor skills.

To check our assumptions, we supplied a simple blank template for the children to fill in along with a set of adinkra rubber stamps adjacent to a display of adinkra fabric, calabash stamps, photographs of people making and wearing adinkra, text describing how adinkra was made, and a key to the meaning of the adinkra symbols. Families approached the testing station on their own, as they would any other exhibition component, and were also invited to do the activity to ensure we had a broad sample of our audience.

After a period of observing the children and adults engaged in free play, we asked them questions about what they were doing, what the component was about, and what, if any, questions they had. Our evaluation was guided by a list of questions, including these: Do they read the labels? Are they curious about the meaning of the symbols, how or why they are used, and by whom? Do they make a connection between the objects and the activity? Do they connect the stamps to the meaning of the symbols on the key? What words do they use to describe what they are doing? What are their comments and questions about the stamps and labels? Do they use the stamps to create a story or to say how they feel?

We learned that visitors of every age were curious about how adinkra cloth is used. Many were surprised that the cloth is worn and were interested in trying it out themselves. This finding is something we really should have anticipated given that our research—the very same research we had consulted while developing the stamping activity—told us children enjoy learning about others, using "real" materials, and dramatic play. But we didn't even think of it until it came up in our conversations with children and adults. Long story short: there is a cloth-wrapping try-on activity in the exhibition, and the fabric is made in Ghana!

Most if not all of the respondents enjoyed looking at the stamps, learning the meaning of the symbols, choosing stamps based on their aesthetic and/or their meaning, and creating their own designs. That said, the fact that the symbols had meaning was not apparent to most visitors until they were engaged in the activity for a while—only then would they notice the label with the key to the stamps off to the side. Subsequently we tested having the symbol and its meaning on the back of the stamp itself, rather than on a separate key, and the problem was solved.

Another issue was that people were so engaged in the activity that few noticed the display of objects and images until we asked if they had referred to them at all while they were stamping their designs during our brief follow-up interviews. Once the objects were pointed out, there were lively conversations about the patterns matching the stamps and things made out of gourds—thus ending the interviews. In the exhibition, the component consists of a case holding fabric and stamps next to a large magnetic drawing board where children stamp their designs using magnetic blocks cut into adinkra symbols. The ledge that holds the magnet stamps is positioned next to genuine and touchable calabash stamps, which are just below real adinkra cloth printed with the very same stamps. This adjacency of activity to artifacts seems to work.

One thing we did get right was that older children were engaged in exploring the meaning behind the symbols and creating their own descriptive designs. Younger children enjoyed talking about what the symbols looked like and practicing the repetitive, wondrous process of placing a stamp down and leaving something behind again and again.

Employing a developmental framework late in an exhibition's design timeline can also facilitate a productive shift in a project team's perspective from content to audience. In the fall of 2007, the National Museum of American Jewish History (NMAJH) realized well into the design development phase for their upcoming permanent exhibition that they needed to consider children and families. While the story of coming to America and the immigrant struggle to make a new home was compelling to adults, the abstract concepts of a history exhibition—time, culture, identity, and change—was beyond the tangible experience of children up to 8 or 9 years old.

The team brought on museum planner Jeanne Vergeront to assemble the *Young Audiences Experience Framework and Activity Plan* to guide the development of exhibition elements and programming specifically targeting children and youth. Vergeront identified four critical factors for engaging children with history: (1) understand children's grasp of the exhibition's concepts of "time, place, identity, and change" at different ages and stages; (2) understand how adults can support and extend children's experience; (3) refine content messages to make them "more accessible to a broader age range;" and (4) provide a "range of environments and activities that support children's exploration, play, and learning in museums."[15]

Using Vergeront's plan as a guide, NMAJH translated the abstract concepts of their adult-focused exhibition on American Jewish immigration and migration—time, culture, identity, and change—into a set of six "take-away" messages that were more accessible to children: journey to America, making a new home, building a life, keeping tradition, becoming American, and acting on social responsibility. These messages were the basis for child-focused hands-on activities—meeting a friend, moving west, Purim play, Sabbath table, school desks, garment factory, and camp memories—integrated within the exhibition. In the "Moving West" area, children join a Jewish family traveling across the Great Plains by covered wagon and learn about life on the trail. Donning costumes, they do chores such as sweeping the trading post and setting the Sabbath table.[16]

A separate exhibition, designed specifically for children and youth, follows the real-life story of a girl, Fanny Brooks, on her trip west with her family. The exhibition features interactive experiences and environments that bring Fanny's story to life for the museum's younger visitors and likely resonates with older audiences as well.[17]

Developmental Frameworks in Final Design

In the final design phase, the framework is used primarily as a check against decisions about the final detailing of text, design, and activity. We generally opt for chairs with backs rather than stools, because they provide more stability for those members of our audience fond of balancing their seating furniture on one leg. Corners are rounded, manipulatives are "real" but safe, collection artifacts and case displays directly support and enhance experiences. Text is written at a third- and fourth-grade reading level and is short and conversational. Activity is designed to be intuitive, but where direction is needed, illustrations are used with a minimum of words and tested to ensure our intent is communicated. In one Brooklyn Children's Museum exhibition, a weighing-and-measuring activity was tested nearly half a dozen times before we hit on the right combination of text to illustration.

Conclusion

When an exhibition opens at Brooklyn Children's Museum, it has been tested and parsed and kneaded and massaged into something we are fairly confident will be engaging for most of the squirmy, raucous, curious, energetic, thoughtful, expressive, demanding, and discerning users we welcome through our doors every day. But even then, the framework is useful during remedial and summative evaluation as a guide for reminding us of the parameters and goals we established early in the project and for setting the protocols for measuring how well we met them throughout the design of the exhibition.

Is it worth creating a developmental framework? Absolutely. From a practical standpoint, exhibitions are expensive, time consuming, and long lasting. It is only sensible to take whatever measures are required to guarantee that your end product is as effective and meaningful to your audience as possible.

Developmental frameworks help project teams create exhibition experiences that take full advantage of their audience's skills and interests. Researching, creating, and returning to a developmental framework throughout an exhibition's development informs our processes, products, and most of all our perspective on what it means to be a kid. Making this research an essential part of a museum's exhibition development process transforms project teams into audience advocates and results in exhibitions that truly are learning environments tailor-made to engage all our visitors—even the short ones—in active explorations of content.

NOTES

1. Eric Gyllenhaal, Jill Gilmartin, and Cecilia Garibay, "Things in Common: Front-End Literature Review, Brooklyn Children's Museum" (report, Selinda Research Associates: Chicago, 2002), 4.
2. Mari Shopsis, personal communication, and "MyStory, OurStory! An Interactive History Experience for Young Children," a class assignment she developed for a child development course for the Museum Leadership Program, Bank Street College of Education, January 21, 2005, 2.
3. Shopsis, "MyStory, OurStory!."
4. Gyllenhaal, Gilmartin, and Garibay, "Things in Common," 6.
5. Lorrie Beaumont and Jill Gilmartin, "Things in Common: Front-end Evaluation, Brooklyn Children's Museum (report, Selinda Research Associates: Chicago, 2002), 7.
6. Beaumont and Gilmartin, "Things in Common," 6.
7. Lorrie Beaumont, "Japan & Nature: Spirits of the Seasons Front-end Evaluation, Brooklyn Children's Museum" (report, Selinda Research Associates, Chicago, 2002), 6.
8. New York City Department of Education, New York City *K–8 Social Studies Scope and Sequence, 2008-2009*, http://schools.nycenet.edu/offices/teachlearn/ss/SocStudScopeSeq.pdf (accessed August 22, 2008).
9. New York City Department of Education, *K-8 Social Studies*, 13.
10. National Council for the Social Studies, *Expectations of Excellence: Curriculum Standards for Social Studies* (Silver Spring, MD: National Council for the Social Studies, 1994 [published online 1996]), http://www.socialstudies.org/standards/curriculum (accessed January 29, 2009).
11. Bradley Commission on History in Schools, *Building a History Curriculum: Guidelines for Teaching History in Schools*, 2nd ed. (Westlake, OH: National Council for History Education, 2000) http://www.nche.net/docs/NCHE_BAHC.pdf (accessed January 29, 2009).
12. Bradley Commission, *Building a History Curriculum*, 18.
13. American Institute of Architects Michigan/Michigan Architecture Foundation, "Architecture: It's Elementary!" (curriculum guidelines, n.d.), http://www.k5architecture.org/ (accessed January 29, 2009).
14. American Institute of Architects Michigan, "Architecture."

15. Jeanne Vergeront, "Youth Experience Framework and Activity Plan, National Museum of American Jewish History, Philadelphia, PA" (report, Vergeront Museum Planning, Minneapolis, 2008), 1.

16. Vergeront, "Youth Experience Framework," 23–4.

17. Josh Perelman, PhD, deputy director for programming and museum historian, The National Museum of Jewish American History, personal communication, February 2008, and e-mail message to the author, January 2009.

ADDITIONAL RESOURCES

Alleman, Janet, and Jere Brophy. "History is Alive: Teaching Young Children about Changes Over Time." *Social Studies* 94, no. 3 (2003): 107–110.

American Association for the Advancement of Science. *Benchmarks for Science Literacy: Project 2061*. New York: Oxford University Press, 1993.

Barton, Keith C. "Oh, That's a Tricky Piece!: Children, Mediated Action, and the Tools of Historical Time." *Elementary School Journal* 103, no. 2 (2002): 161–185.

Beery, Robert, and Mark Schug. *Teaching Social Studies in the Elementary School: Issues and Practices*. Glenview, IL: Scott, Foresman and Co., 1987.

Berk, Laura E. *Awakening Children's Minds: How Parents and Teachers Can Make a Difference*. Oxford: Oxford University Press, 2001.

——. *Child Development*. 7th ed. Boston: Allyn and Bacon, 2000.

——. *Infants and Children: Prenatal Through Middle Childhood*. 6th ed. Boston: Allyn and Bacon, 2002.

Berk, Laura E., and Adam Winsler. *Scaffolding Children's Learning: Vygotsky and Early Childhood Education*. Washington, DC: National Association for the Education of Young Children, 1995.

Borun, Minda, Jennifer Dritsas, Julie I. Johnson, Nancy E. Peter, Kathleen F. Wagner, Kathleen Fadigan, Arlene Jangaard, Estelle Stroup, and Angela Wenger. *Family Learning in Museums: The PISEC Perspective*. Washington, DC: Association of Science-Technology Centers, 1998.

Cole, Michael, and Shelia R. Cole. *The Development of Children*, 4th ed. New York: Worth Publishers, 2001.

Durbin, Gail, ed. *Developing Museum Exhibitions for Lifelong Learning*. London: The Stationery Office, 1996.

Egan, Kieran. *The Educated Mind: How Cognitive Tools Shape Our Understanding*. Chicago: The University of Chicago Press, 1997.

Falk, John H., and Lynn D. Dierking, *The Museum Experience*. Washington, DC: Whalesback Books, 1998.

——. *Learning from Museums: Visitor Experiences and the Making of Meaning*. Walnut Creek, CA: AltaMira Press, 2000.

Fivush, Robyn, and Jean M. Mandler. "Developmental Changes in the Understanding of Temporal Sequence." *Child Development* 56 (1985): 1437–46.

Forman, George E., and David S. Kuschner. *The Child's Construction of Knowledge: Piaget for Teaching Children.* Washington, DC: National Association for the Education of Young Children, 1983.

Gessel Institute of Human Development Series. 10 vols. Dell Trade Paperbacks, various dates.

Gyllenhaal, Eric D. "A Generalized Developmental Framework for Planning Cultural Exhibitions and Programs" (report). Selinda Research Associates: Chicago, 2006, http://www.selindaresearch.com/goeast.htm (accessed March 4, 2008).

National Research Council. *National Science Education Standards for Scientific Inquiry.* Washington, DC: National Academies Press, 1996.

Nelson, Katherine, and Robyn Fivush. "The Emergence of Autobiographical Memory: A Social Cultural Developmental Theory." *Psychological Review* 111, no. 2 (2004): 486–511.

Paris, Scott G., ed. *Perspectives on Object-centered Learning in Museums.* Mahwah, NJ: Lawrence Erlbaum Associates, 2002.

Povinelli, Daniel J., Anita M. Landry, Laura A. Theall, Britten R. Clark, and Connie M. Castille. "Development of Young Children's Understanding that the Recent Past is Causally Bound to the Present." *Developmental Psychology* 35, no. 6 (1999): 1426–1439.

Reese, Elaine. "Social Factors in the Development of Autobiographical Memory: The State of the Art." *Social Development* 11, no. 1 (2002): 125–142.

Ringel, Gail. "Designing Exhibits for Kids: What Are We thinking?" Paper presented at the J. Paul Getty Museum, From Content to Play: Family-oriented Interactive Spaces in Art and History Museums Symposium, June 4–5, 2005, Los Angeles. www.getty.edu/education/symposium/Ringel.pdf (accessed August 8, 2008).

Schaefer, Jane, and Linda Pulik. *Teen Chicago Initiative Front-end Evaluation, Chicago History Museum.* Report. Selinda Research Associates: Chicago, 2002.

Stearns, Peter N., Peter Seixas and Sam Wineburg, eds. *Knowing, Teaching and Learning History: National and International Perspectives.* New York: New York University Press, 2000.

Vergeront, Jeanne. "Go East! Asian Exhibit Initiative Overview of Developmental Frameworks" (report). Association of Children's Museums, 2003, http://selindaresearch.com/goeast.htm (accessed March 4, 2008).

Vukelich, Ronald and Stephen J. Thornton. "Children's Understanding of Historical Time: Implications for Instruction." *Childhood Education* 67, no. 1 (1990): 22–5.

Wood, Chip. *Yardsticks: Children in the Classroom Ages 4–14: A Resource for Parents and Teachers.* Greenfield, MA: Northeast Foundation for Children, 1997.

CHAPTER 3

Experts, Evaluators, and Explorers: Collaborating with Kids

Anne Grimes Rand and Robert Kiihne

Shifting the Paradigm

THE CHALLENGE:
How can history museums create exhibitions that kids will use, learn from, and enjoy?

THE SOLUTION:
Involve kids in the exhibition development and design process.

This approach is easier said than done. Some history museums that seek to cultivate a family audience may not yet have kids and their parents strolling in the galleries, whereas others seek to enhance service to an audience that is already present. History museums can learn how to reach out to kids by talking to and learning from them. Kids are happy to share their opinions and ideas, if asked, and they are everywhere—in nearby schools, in after-school park programs, and some may already be inside your museum. And other museums, versed in working with kids, can provide insight, guidance, and proven strategies for initiating and sustaining collaborations with kids.

There are three main advantages of developing an ongoing working relationship with kids as a way to figure out how to attract and engage them. The first is that kids are experts at being kids. Like a content expert hired to provide background for an exhibition, kids can help guide decision making so projects appeal to them and anticipate their skills and needs. The second advantage is that kids become a regular, on-call evaluation cohort for the development not only of your current work but also of future projects. They can serve as test subjects for ideas that the museum is considering or a mock up of an evolving activity, always leading project teams to better decisions. Finally, having kids around the museum, working and sharing their humor and curiosity with museum staff, can ground project teams in the ways of being and thinking like a kid and help to prepare the entire museum for what it will mean to be family friendly.

History Exhibitions for Kids

To engage kids in the development of history exhibitions requires a change in approach to how we think about younger audiences and how we make exhibitions. Although they typically come to museums with a group—family or school—children are individuals who have distinctive interests, abilities, and needs. We must learn to see them as having the same level of complexity as our adult audiences and recognize that it has been a long time since we knew what interests a kid.

Children's museums lead the field in connecting with kids to create compelling exhibition experiences, and many of the lessons they have learned can and are being employed at history museums. This chapter follows the process of exhibition development and explores how kids can serve as audience experts, skilled evaluators, and inspiring collaborators throughout a project. The innovative work highlighted here offers new ways of approaching the development of history exhibitions and suggests ways to engage a young audience in both the process and the product. Although a number of history museums are already soliciting feedback from kids, the greater challenge is shifting the paradigm from exhibitions created for kids to exhibitions created with kids.

Kids First

It is never too early for an exhibition project team to seek the input of children. Often history museum professionals have developed the exhibition's theme, content, layout, and design elements before they speak with any children. When content is the priority, exhibition teams can easily create didactic exhibitions packed with artifacts that march visitors through time rather than engage them with ideas and experiences. Although there are always a few adult visitors who express a love of timelines and chronological treatments, historians have long recognized that chronological explorations of the past often misrepresent the dynamic processes that have shaped history. And although many kids are happy to memorize the name of every dinosaur that ever lived, most find that memorizing places, dates, and names in the order of their appearance on history's stage is not a satisfying or provocative experience. An alternative to chronological treatments is to develop experiences with historical content around the ideas, people, and events that interest kids. Then design exhibitions to play on their skills, interests, and abilities to draw them into an experience with history that in no way resembles a social studies lesson.

Through this approach to exhibition development, team members are forced to think about how to convey history themes through a variety of experiences to reach kids and adults with different learning styles. The interests, skills, and abilities of kids become a filter for content and design decisions. When each exhibition element is developed to engage visitors in the subject and communicate key messages, visitors become active users participating in the exhibition, rather than passive observers looking at objects and perhaps reading a few labels.

When developing exhibition elements that will appeal to children, the team must identify a specific target age range. Will the whole exhibition be targeted to one age group, or do you seek to engage an intergenerational family audience by developing experiences for different age ranges? Free play works well with the toddlers, whereas games target older kids. Team members need to conduct research on developmental stages and learning styles associated with their targeted audience to help create age-appropriate elements. In this scenario, all members of an exhibition team become audience advocates. Together, project team members seek to identify and meet audience interests, expectations, and needs.

Kids and Their Families

Children come to museums with adults. Exhibitions designed only for the kids or only for the adults often fail to serve either group. If both children and adults are engaged in exhibition experiences simultaneously, families have an opportunity to explore the exhibitions in depth and discuss what they see. Exhibitions can provoke questions, inspire wonder, and prompt conversation among family groups. Activities and games that require multiple hands encourage young and old to work together to achieve a common goal. Places to sit or put one's feet up and rest within the exhibition provide opportunities for conversation and reflection.

In *Learning from Museums* John Falk and Lynn Dierking assert that "families use museums as socially mediated meaning-making environments."[1] They point out that "museum exhibitions and programs, when done well, support opportunities for families to participate in and become more effective communities of learners, allowing group members to share, watch one another, have a new and novel experience, reinforce something they already knew, or see something in a new way. . . . All of this contributes to a highly personal experience, which is all important if meaningful learning is to occur."[2]

Turning to Kids

Often history museums reach out to children because they want more families and kids roaming the galleries. However, sometimes the audience is already there; the museum just has not quantified them. In 2003 the USS Constitution Museum, with the help of Dale Jones at the Institute for Learning Innovation, surveyed museum visitors in advance of an exhibition about the life of a sailor in 1812. One of the report's most significant findings was that 59% of the museum's summer audience came in family groups, and of the children in the survey group 54% were between the ages of 9 and 12. Knowing that the majority of visiting families included children between 9 and 12 years old provided a great point of departure for learning about them and creating experiences for, and eventually with, them.

Learning to see kids as experts at being and thinking like kids can lead to some interesting and unexpected decisions. At The Children's Museum of Indianapolis, staff asked one thousand kids an open-ended question, "If you could explore anything, what would it be?" The kids surveyed identified the top three topics: a coral reef, a dinosaur discovery, and an Egyptian tomb, which became the three content areas of the long-running exhibition titled, *What If . . .?* It is interesting that with such an open-ended question kids picked history subjects. Without the kids' input, would the staff have chosen these topics? Once a project team recognizes kids as insightful and knowledgeable experts, kids can begin to shift the discussion from what the team thinks kids want to what actually interests children.

For museums that do not always have easy access to significant numbers of kids or family groups, it can be a challenge to find kids that could become exhibition development collaborators. After-school programs, scout groups, and local schools are often looking for creative programming ideas. Package exhibit development as a fun activity, and these groups can become a great resource. Think about where kids gather in your community and consider going directly to them for input. Visit the after-school programs in your town or set up a table at a community event. Team up with the local library and visit the children's room on the weekend, or host a story hour on the subject of your next exhibit and get direct feedback from kids who have just learned a bit about the topic.

Rose Kelly took such an approach when she began developing the exhibition *Shipwrecked: Final Voyage of the Stella Maris* for the Bay Area Discovery Museum. Wanting to know which shipboard activities excited

FIGURE 3.1. When visitors climb into the "Hammocks" activity in *A Sailor's Life For Me?*, questions overhead ask, "Do you sleep more than four hours a night?" The response—"Not if you are a sailor on board USS Constitution"—invites kids and families to contrast their lives with the lives of sailors in 1812. Photograph by Greg Cooper. Courtesy USS Constitution Museum.

kids, she decided to go where the kids were, on the *Hawaiian Chieftain*, a tall ship that hosts school groups for day sails. The ship provided a great source of kids in the right frame of mind to answer her questions. As groups of fifth graders disembarked she asked them what they found most interesting about their trip. The kids expressed curiosity about how the ship's sails worked and how sailors steered the ship. They also told her about the bad food sailors had to eat, repeating a number of specific pieces of information they learned during their sail. The students' answers gave Rose an understanding of what kinds of activities could be successful in the exhibition and how kids perceived sailing ships. Specifically, she learned that the exhibition needed to include sail handling and some exhibit element related to how to steer a ship.

Determining whom the exhibition is intended to serve and what sort of experience you want them to have are important first steps toward collaborating with the audience. They will become valued partners with applicable knowledge throughout all phases of the exhibition process, helping to identify exhibition content and themes, to select featured objects, and to develop and design exhibition experiences.

Kids and Object Selection

As keepers of physical history, objects speak to museum professionals in a variety of ways. They can represent the stories of their past owners, a technology that changed the historical landscape or many other possible meanings. Although adult visitors may still need us to unlock an artifact's story, they know the language of time, and they are already clued in to the likely historical themes to be explored. For example, adults can anticipate the story behind a butter churn or a corset and can immediately identify the historical implications of a United States flag that has only forty-eight stars. Kids, however, have a different set of reference points. To find out which artifacts speak to them all you have to do is ask.

The Henry Ford Museum used fifth- and sixth-grade overnight dorm program participants as a focus group to identify which pieces of furniture interested the kids and why. Rather than hauling out each item of furniture, staff showed flash cards with photos of the collections that could be included in the exhibition. One of the objects that really caught the kids' imagination was a horn chair—the kids wondered if steers were killed specifically to make the chair. Such queries provide museum staff with entry points for engaging kids with objects that might otherwise fail to inspire a close look or even a passing glance.

Visual appeal is often just the tip of the iceberg for history museum artifacts. Younger visitors, just like the rest of us, can be drawn in by a curious object or a thrilling story. Cathy Donnelly at The Children's Museum of Indianapolis needed to know which fossils to include in *Dinosphere, Now You're in Their World*, a major exhibition about dinosaurs and how to introduce the fossils to kids. Lynn Dierking of the Institute for Learning Innovation suggested an approach previously employed at the Smithsonian Institution. In a classroom at the museum a curator laid out a number of artifacts. Cathy recruited families with kids from the museum floor. As the kids inspected the various artifacts and talked to the curator about them, Cathy observed and recorded the conversations both between kids and curator and within family groups. Listening to the curator's and kids' interactions she learned not only which objects had special attracting power for kids but also how to "hook" kids into the object's story. Cathy used the kids' own language within the exhibition interpretative labels.

She learned

how families (particularly kids) were really interested in dinosaur coprolites. We figured that would be a hook to get families interested in what dinosaurs ate. We display the coprolites . . . in our "Question Lab" within the context of "How do we know what dinosaurs ate?" [3]

The labels incorporate the kids' own words in the discussion of "dinosaur dung" but also introduce the term coprolites.

During the development phase of an exhibition on American history at the Chicago History Museum, co-curators Peter Alter and Joy Bivins led a team of interns in a research project to explore kids' reactions to four objects to discover if and how the kids related these objects to the idea of freedom. Researchers presented the kids with images of a rifle, slave manacles, a typewriter, and a television. In an unpublished internal report on the study, data showed that some of 11- and 12-year-olds found connections to freedom in these objects. However, most of the kids in this age group found a connection to freedom in the typewriter. Through follow-up inquiries the team discovered some details about the types of connections the kids made to the objects and the cultural and racial differences that emerged from the data and the interviews. Alter said, "The implications of the research are that we have a better idea of how to interpret these and other potential objects. And we have ideas for how to develop interactive experiences with these objects that will expose some of the history that kids expressed curiosity about." [4]

Kids and Content Development

Throughout the exhibition development process kids can be easily involved as sounding boards. They can respond to the work the museum has produced and give it a thumbs-up or thumbs-down. However, true collaboration begins when the kids' ideas shape the project, and the museum responds to their creativity, instead of the other way around. For these relatively complex and involved relationships, schools can help. Teachers that use your institution as a resource may be more than willing to have their students participate in collaboration with the museum. Such participation may be as simple as a written, in-class survey designed to solicit ideas and suggestions, or it may evolve into a long-term relationship over the life of a project that regularly brings exhibition teams and student groups together over the course of a semester or a school year. For the exhibition *Your Place in Time: 20th Century America*, the Henry Ford Museum asked students to pick favorite artifacts from their childhood as part of a class assignment. Students filled out a worksheet that asked what their favorite possession is and why. The museum included these objects and student quotes as part of the exhibition alongside items from the museum's collection. Kids were

SOLICITING FEEDBACK FROM KIDS

There are many ways to get feedback from kids:

- **Surveys:** ask specific questions about kids' interests, opinions, present knowledge, and preferences.

- **Focus groups:** talk to a group of kids to get a more in depth, qualitative view of how they perceive what you have to offer.

- **Artifact show and tell:** invite kids into a room with objects and a team member, and see what happens. Find out what in your collection really interests kids and how kids would interpret your artifacts.

- **Class assignments:** from essays to art projects, there are endless possibilities for collaboration with students, teachers, and schools. Their projects can offer insight into topics and collections.

- **Share sample labels and graphics:** grab a clipboard and mock-up of a label or proposed graphic, then discuss it with visitors and get a quick response to your work.

- **Cardboard prototype testing:** any interactive should be tested as a simple prototype with kids and adults. Building something out of cardboard gives you and your audience a physical representation of your exhibition idea to experience and to discuss.

- **Tracking and timing observations:** identify how much kids use your space—where do they go, what do they do there, and how long do they stay?

- **Behavioral coding observations:** identify what kinds of activities occur in your galleries. Do kids read, talk, touch, or completely ignore what you have to offer?

- **Talk back stations:** give visitors of all ages an opportunity to participate in your exhibitions while providing you with quantifiable feedback. This approach can be as simple as sticky notes and a piece of plywood with a question printed on it.

- **Exit interviews:** find out if you are succeeding in your exhibition's goals.

- **Your own creative form of feedback:** evaluation with the youngest visitors may involve asking them to respond by drawing a picture or rating your ideas with a smiley face, flat face, or frown. Use your imagination, but make sure your data-collecting method is rigorous and will provide you with solid information on which you can act with confidence.

able to see their world and their values compared and contrasted to a child's world from the past; and the museum gained important insights into the types and qualities of objects that attract kids and have meaning for them.

The team developing *Sensing Chicago* at the Chicago History Museum collaborated with students to develop age-appropriate label copy. Modeling an approach used by a local third-grade teacher, the team tested draft labels with the class. The exhibition curator described an activity to the students and then read aloud the label text that would accompany it. He then asked the kids to rewrite the label in their own words. Their versions changed the text, added flair, and even influenced historical interpretation, all of which helped the exhibition to capture and to inspire the imaginations of the target audience once the gallery opened. Language and tone for many of the final labels were drawn from the children's interpretations, and their writing and speaking styles. The students took the assignment very seriously, making sure they got all of the key information correct. Still, they had to have fun. For example, at the suggestion of the students the word, "Yum!" was added at the end of a label in the taste section. Throughout the label-testing process, kids continued to suggest adding descriptive words to punctuate the proposed text. In addition to label testing, this neighboring third-grade class opened its doors to the exhibition team throughout the process from early testing of activities to prototypes of gallery components. The class even came to the museum during installation of a media component to give it a dry run. The project team filmed the kids using the final interactive. The footage was eventually installed in the exhibition as an attract loop for the activity.

Children even weighed in on the final exhibition title through written surveys. Their responses to three possible titles revealed the messages that each communicated to kids and the expectations and possible misconceptions the titles might evoke in 8- and 9-year olds, the target audience. For example, one title under consideration was, *Awesome History Adventure.* Students' responses ranged from, "Does it have to be history?" to "I thought of dinosaurs and presidents and war." Another possible title was, *Chicago, Kid-Style.* One student thought it sounded boring, and another thought it would be about kids' fashion. In the end, *Sensing Chicago* was the title that most resonated with kids. They felt that an exhibition with this title would be "all about Chicago history," and "about discovering new things about Chicago." Children's honest assessment assured the team that the exhibition title would communicate clear messages to its key audience.

Kids Influencing Design

Successful history museum exhibitions require thorough research, creative content development, thoughtful object selection and inspired design. They are also fueled by the energy and skill of experienced curators, educators, and designers. However, when collaborating with kids the expertise of staff and their exhibition plans and proposals must be regularly and enthusiastically measured against the insights and inclinations of the audience. This influence is most noticeable on design, specifically because of prototype testing. During prototype evaluation, collaborating with kids has its biggest potential payoff. Kids serve as experts by behaving and responding like kids. They provide the exact level and type of evaluation needed for the project by being themselves. And this is the moment when staff proves that they are honest and responsive collaborators. Kids' suggestions may require changes to the exhibition's plans. The team needs to be open and ready to respond to both praise and criticism from children.

Beginning in 2003, the USS Constitution Museum embarked on an extensive and thorough collaboration with kids and families as expert evaluators, which has transformed the museum. Minda Borun of Museum Solutions worked with the staff of the USS Constitution Museum over a period of three years to conduct exhibit research and to evaluate the exhibition *A Sailor's Life for Me?*. The evaluation concepts and techniques described here are adapted from those developed by Borun and used to train staff at the USS Constitution Museum.

Since then the museum has adopted a belief that all successful interactive exhibitions require prototyping. The USS Constitution Museum has spent tremendous amounts of time inviting kids and families to try out prototype activities, listening to their feedback, changing the product, and repeating the process until families confirm that the exhibit elements achieve their goals.

Collaborating with Kids at the USS Constitution Museum

Prototypes can take many forms. The form depends on the types of exhibition experiences you hope to create for kids and the stage you are at in the exhibition development process. From showing a few versions of a label on a clipboard to testing an installed working version of a complex interactive element, you can, and will, get useful input from kids, and thus they become part of your team. The feedback will result in changes that make your offerings better. Even when prototyping an exhibit causes very few modifications, audience input is still validating and essential to the development process.

FIGURE 3.2. Conversations with families during prototyping improve exhibit elements and lead to a final product that kids actually use. Photograph by Greg Cooper. Courtesy USS Constitution Museum.

Kids and families will help you determine:

- Interest: Do kids find it attractive and compelling?
- Functionality: Will it work?
- Readability: Do kids understand what you are asking them to do?
- Comprehension: Do kids get the message of the activity?

Three prototypes from the USS Constitution Museum's exhibition *A Sailor's Life for Me?*[5] illustrated all the preceding outcomes. For example, the "Holystone the Decks" activity was immediately popular (interest). Kids liked rubbing a rock on a piece of wood (functionality), and they understood that it would be a lot of work to scour the *USS Constitution*'s deck (comprehension). But they also wanted more. What they and their parents asked for was sand and water—just like sailors used. Because this was a prototype, staff decided to try adding sand and observing how much dust the activity created. Adding a spritz of water each day kept dust to a minimum. Both the museum and audience benefited from the change. For the museum, the activity is effective at communicating some of the intangibles of life on board ship in 1812; for the audience, it provides a physical encounter with the past.

The "Pack Your Seabag" interactive prototype produced the opposite result. It consisted of a pair of magnet boards with a graphic seabag and movable magnetic images of everything a sailor needed and might want to bring with him. The goal of the activity was to illustrate the

---

SAMPLE PROTOTYPE PROCESS[6]

At the USS Constitution Museum, families were asked to try a number of interactives. Evaluations were conducted through a simple five-step process designed to provide quantitative and qualitative data. The combination provided the project team with both the input needed to fix problems and the confidence that the feedback was valid.

1. Record basic demographic information of each participant (for example, gender, age, and number in party).

2. Observe and note if families used the instructions and how they interacted with the exhibit element.

3. Ask the participants a few (no more than four) short questions about the content.

4. Ask the participants to rate the overall exhibit on a scale of one to five (like a five-star movie rating): "How many stars would you give this activity?"

5. Record their comments and ask for suggestions.

---

limited space a sailor had available to him and the few possessions he could keep. After three iterations, a few hundred families made it very clear: this activity was not effective. Kids simply were not interested in the experience. The exhibition team subsequently dropped the activity and sought alternate ways to communicate this content. Communicating what to do at an activity is not as simple as listing instructions.

The "Recruiting Interactive" at the USS Constitution Museum was a simple two-sided tabletop interactive with questions on one side and a related image on the other. The goal is for family members to have fun asking one another recruiting questions, such as "Are you willing to climb 100 feet in the air to furl a sail the size of a basketball court?" or "Have you ever swung in a hammock? Are you willing to do it next to 200 of your closest friends who haven't taken a bath in a while?" This interactive is intended to encourage conversation about joining *USS Constitution*'s crew in 1812. It was clear after fewer than ten families had tried the activity that the directions did not work for kids or parents. In terms of readability and comprehension, families didn't know what to do—even when staff tried to explain the interactive. The next day staff typed up new directions based on the concerns and suggestions from the first day's work After tap-

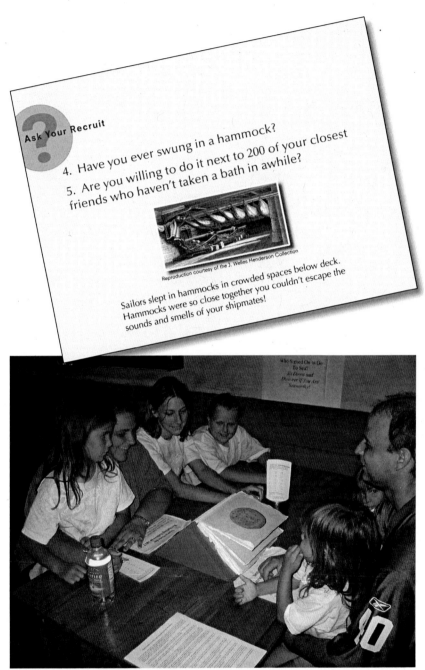

Ask Your Recruit

4. Have you ever swung in a hammock?

5. Are you willing to do it next to 200 of your closest friends who haven't taken a bath in awhile?

Reproduction courtesy of the J. Welles Henderson Collection

Sailors slept in hammocks in crowded spaces below deck. Hammocks were so close together you couldn't escape the sounds and smells of your shipmates!

FIGURE 3.3. Families test a tattered prototype and offer their suggestions to enhance the "Recruiting Interactive" in *A Sailor's Life For Me?*. Photograph by Greg Cooper. Courtesy USS Constitution Museum.

ing a piece of paper with new instructions on top of the nicely laminated original directions, staff tested the interactive with another ten families. In the following two weeks the team tested and modified every aspect of the interactive until families and museum staff were satisfied. The final prototype was a mess of paper and tape—but visitors knew what to do.

In addition to refining the instructions, feedback from families also shaped the format and functionality of the interactive. Kids told us to make it more gamelike and to add a scorecard; parents wanted more information so they could answer questions and engage with their kids; and families even requested that we include more recruiter questions. Staff followed up on all these suggestions and created a more engaging interactive that both kids and adults find fun and informative. The process was so painless and successful that asking a few families for feedback on labels, programming, instructions, and just about anything the museum produces is now standard operating procedure.

The practice of prototyping was even embraced by the museum's youth staff members. A group of high school students who worked at the USS Constitution Museum during the summer as interpreters for summer camp groups found a problem in an exhibition. Staff invited visitors to climb on the yard and shorten sail but did not explain what knot to use, thus making the interactive much less active. So the students decided to remedy the problem. They practiced tying knots and teaching kids to tie knots, then wrote down the steps and took pictures of the process. Sharing this activity with young and old visitors alike brought them back to the drawing table for modifications. The students worked with the exhibits department to create a figure in the exhibition that provides directions for tying the knot before kids climb aloft. The experience of developing an exhibit element, prototyping it, testing it, and modifying it gave the students a much greater appreciation for museum exhibits. It also yielded a product that has served 350,000 visitors. The fun of letting kids take charge is that you never know where you will end up, but kids will usually surprise and inspire you.

Media Prototype

Collaboration with kids can extend even to the development of media pieces. At the USS Constitution Museum, staff tested a future "Battle Theater" presentation that included graphic language about war. First staff members made a rough audio recording of a draft script, and then they identified images to accompany the recording. One cold December Saturday, staff gathered families from the galleries with the promise of hot chocolate. After the families viewed the test version, follow-up in-

FORMAL EVALUATION[7]

Exhibition evaluation is a process seeking answers to specific questions. Evaluation can happen at any stage of a project, and many different techniques may be used, such as observation, prototyping, tracking/timing, sweeps, and surveys.

- **Front-end evaluation** happens at the beginning of a project, when themes and story lines are still under development. Questionnaires, interviews, and focus groups can help determine what kinds of information visitors want to know and common misconceptions that may need to be addressed.

- **Formative evaluation** is testing a simple prototype or early version before creating an expensive final exhibit element. Feedback on a draft script, a simple interactive or instructions, can catch any design or content problems before the final (and more expensive element) is fabricated.

- **Summative evaluation** looks at the completed project and determines whether the major goals of the project have been achieved, and it provides guidance for future projects.

terviews revealed that the language and images in the original test version were appropriate, nothing worse than kids were already exposed to on television. The feedback quelled staff fears, forestalled hours of meetings, and led to the quick development of the full "Battle Theater."

The final, more polished version included many more images than were in the original test version. Through observations and interviews with visitors, staff discovered that the enhanced presentation was now too graphic for our youngest visitors, but that parents appreciated the honesty of the presentation. A few even said that it gave them an opportunity to talk with their kids about a difficult subject. Through tracking and timing studies, staff found that about 20% of families watched the entire nine-minute presentation and that kids sometimes forced parents to stay to the end. At the same time, visitors wanted to know in advance how long the presentation was, since many did not stay owing to time concerns. In the end, staff produced the "Battle Theater" in-house, with an audio track provided by a professional theater company. The long-range plan had been to hire a production company and invest significant funds to create a more polished final version. The audience evaluation gave staff the confidence to plan on changing just a few things and saved the budget nearly $50,000.

Summative Evaluation: The Power of Audience Surveys

How kids and adults use your finished exhibition may be quite different than you expect. Your dialog with your audience should not end with the exhibition opening. Plan to use summative evaluation to determine the effectiveness of your final installation. Spending modest amounts of money to change a few text panels or even to reedit a media piece is an investment in the life of an exhibition.

Observing kids and families for a simple tracking and timing evaluation study is easy, informative, and objective. It requires minimal training, so everyone from frontline staff to your board president, interns, and volunteers can participate. With a floor plan of your exhibition and a stopwatch, identify locations where you can observe kids and families entering your exhibition. Visitors should be able to identify observers either by uniform or with a name badge; some institutions post a sign to inform visitors that observations are being conducted.

Where do kids stop in the exhibition? Is there an artifact that interests a percentage of them? The results may be fascinating. Once you have some basic information, try a little behavioral coding—for example, by placing a mark where certain behaviors occur, such as looking at an object, reading a label, calling over fellow family members, or participating in an activity. If kids are attracted to a particular object, can you expand on its interpretation? If there is a great object no one stops at, can you find a way to make it more appealing? If no one reads 95% of your text panels, consider removing a few. Once you know the average time kids spend in your gallery and what they do during their visit, you can determine the changes needed and then evaluate the success of the changes you made. Professional evaluators can help you to collect even more information and can provide an independent perspective.

Summative evaluation is an investment in the future. Tracking, timing, and exit interviews can lead to modifications in a new or existing exhibit, but they also provide important ideas to shape future planning. What you learn from speaking with kids and families becomes part of the ongoing knowledge of the staff and the institution as it continues to put the audience first. The lessons of working with children on one exhibition carry forward and inform the process of generating future exhibitions. The improvement of long-term exhibitions (informed by summative evaluation) is an ongoing process.

Conclusion

The *What If . . . ?* and *Dinosphere* exhibition development processes at The Children's Museum of Indianapolis took kids' contributions to a new level. Staff asked open-ended questions in the formative stages of exhibition development, allowing kids to truly shape the content. The use of kids' feedback early on not only informed the final exhibitions, it also formed the backbone of their content. Subsequent stages of exhibit development, including the selection of artifacts and word choices on labels, were all informed by conversations with kids. *Sensing Chicago* at the Chicago History Museum is another example of an exhibition truly shaped by kids. All phases of exhibit development included regular testing with kids, soliciting their feedback and shaping the project accordingly. Summative evaluation indicates that these exhibitions are extremely successful with their target audiences.

As schools and communities experiment with new in-school and out-of-school programs, they are looking for creative partnerships. At the same time, museums everywhere recognize the need to make connections with their communities. History museums in particular have an opportunity to create and to nurture a lively new dialog between kids and history by inviting their participation in the exhibition development process.

As history museums begin to collaborate with kids, this change in practice will likely influence more than just the projects we are currently developing. Opening this dialog has greater, long-term implications. These collaborative relationships will help museum staff see that there are no risks to letting kids into the exhibition development process. They are positive, helpful, honest, and instructive collaborators, and if we are good collaborators, they will make our projects more successful at reaching a younger audience. At the same time, kids will come to see history museums as places that look and feel nothing like a traditional history lesson. Indeed, they will see places that welcome them, that value them, and that are committed to them. This sort of collaborative relationship is a two-way street in which good ideas and good feelings move in both directions. The exhibitions that emerge from these relationships help to shift the paradigm from exhibitions created for kids to exhibitions created with kids.

NOTES

1. John Falk and Lynn D. Dierking, *Learning from Museums* (Walnut Creek, CA: AltaMira Press, 2000), 92–3.
2. Falk and Dierking, *Learning from Museums*, 97–8.
3. Cathy Donnelly described audience testing at the Indianapolis Children's Museum, personal communication with the authors, USS Constitution Museum, 2005.
4. Peter Alter, curator, Chicago History Museum, email message to John Russick, January 23, 2009.
5. The installation *A Sailor's Life for Me?* served as a prototype for the new permanent exhibition, *All Hands on Deck: A Sailor's Life in 1812*, which opened in the summer of 2009 at the USS Constitution Museum.
6. Minda Borun, "Prototype Template" (training materials, Museum Solutions, c 2003).
7. Minda Borun, "Evaluating Exhibits and Programs" (training materials, Museum Solutions, 2004).

PART II

Connecting Kids
to History

B y reaching out to children, history museums find themselves trying to connect the distant past to an audience whose own history may span less than a decade and who are focused on exploring and defining their own place and associations with the visible world around them. In "Helping Your Child Learn History" Elaine Wrisley Reed writes: "Your child is born into history. She has no memory of it, yet she finds herself in the middle of a story that began before she became one of its characters. She also wants to have a place in it."[1] History expands a child's story and challenges her to find a place in this new and unfamiliar narrative.

Comparing what a child does to what a historian does reveals viable approaches for connecting kids to history. Consider a day in the life of a child—children experience and investigate the world around them. They sniff out a pan of cookies baking in the oven; pretend to be a ship captain navigating their sofa boat across the choppy waters of the family room rug; or become a princess ruling a bedroom kingdom populated with stuffed animals as loyal subjects. These same activities could be described as identifying, analyzing, and interpreting olfactory evidence; exhibiting empathy and identifying with the lives of others through narrative; and considering and immersing themselves in the circumstances and the conditions that defined another time and place.

Chris Husbands, in *What Is History Teaching?*, offers insight into the work of the historian: "In the construction of historical understanding, the historian is not a cipher, but an active participant in the dialogue between the present and the past."[2] History is not simply uncovered, complete, and whole; rather, it is an active, rigorous, and complex process of identifying, analyzing, and interpreting sources to make sense of things we did not experience firsthand. For some reason though, when teaching or presenting history to kids, we displace the dynamic, inquisitive, and conversational nature of history by facts, names, and dates. It is no wonder that the subject has the unfortunate stigma of being boring to young audiences.

In the opening paragraph of Lewis Carroll's otherworldly story, *Alice's Adventures in Wonderland*, Alice sits on the bank of a river "having nothing to do: once or twice she had peeped into the book her sister was reading, but it had no pictures or conversations in it, 'and what is the use of a book' thought Alice, 'without pictures or conversations?'"[3] Although historians speak passionately about their craft, children are often left on the sidelines of the historical process as passive receivers of information and memorizers of facts. Children are naturally driven by their own curiosity. However, they are novices. They seek information from experts—older siblings, parents, teachers—to better understand their circumstances. Their continuous stream of questions characterizes their inquisitive nature: What is this? How does it work? Can I do that? Who are you? These and other queries allow them to make sense of and bring some type of order to their lives. In a similar manner, questions can be their entrée to the past: What was it like? In what ways was it different? How can I find out? In teaching history to children, both museums and schools need to leave the door open for such questions, avoiding the temptation to leap into the telling of history rather than allowing children's own inquiry and curiosity to lead them into the realm of the unknown, the unfamiliar, and the unseen. At the same time, children are drawn to life's experiences and trying them out for themselves. They are active, energized individuals, and meaning and understanding come through participation—by doing.

As a first step, museum professionals need to reconsider our notions of teaching and learning history. Grounded in the understanding of cognitive development and learning presented in the first part of this book, these chapters seek opportunities to connect kids to the process and product of history through conduits already accessible to them.

Although museums must provide pathways for kids to physically navigate museum galleries, they must also provide threads that draw children into a rich experience with the people, places, and events of the past. Leslie Bedford in Chapter 4, "Finding the Story in History," challenges history museum professionals to reconsider their notion of historical interpretation beyond an accounting of facts, events, and dates and to begin to conceive of history in the form of a narrative designed to engage kids' imaginations, emotions, and memories. Evocative objects, first-person accounts, and the exhibition environment itself can appeal to and lead kids through a story that takes them to places in time with which they have had no previous experience.

In Chapter 5, "Imagination—A Child's Gateway to Engagement with the Past," Daniel Spock asserts that the imagination is more than flights of fancy for the young but rather an interpretive tool that thrives on cognitive, affective, and kinesthetic stimuli. The challenge for the museum is to create history exhibitions that ignite the visitor's imagination through environments rich with sensory stimuli, props, and kinesthetic engagement. Spock argues that "the experience is the information," and museums must create history exhibitions that allow a child's imagination to try on and try out the past.

The characteristics of play become desirable and complementary traits of any museum visit—voluntary, pleasurable, and an end unto themselves. Jon-Paul C. Dyson extends an invitation to both the practitioner and the visitor to play in Chapter 6, "Playing with the Past." Dyson demonstrates how a child or any visitor can be a player in the historical process and in the museum experience. The various types of play foster historical thinking as children, through pretend play, imagine themselves in another place and time; act out the challenges and stories of others; and make comparisons of similarities and differences over time.

In Chapter 7, "A Sense of the Past," D. Lynn McRainey draws on all five senses for exploring the past. This chapter is constructed on the simple reality that kids acquire information in the same manner that historians do, through their senses. Whereas historians use their senses in combination with decades of historical training and insight, children are ready to apply their, albeit fewer, years of sensory-based experience to explore the past as well as the present. As historical evidence, the senses give the past a dimension; as an interpretive tool, the language of the senses offers children access to a familiar resource for meaning making. Sensory-rich environments transport children through time to places where they can use their own senses for making connections and for imagining themselves being there.

Whether it is the museum gallery, a historic site, or a child's own imagination, place is a powerful medium for connecting kids to history. In Chapter 8, "Are We There Yet? Children, History, and the Power of Place," Benjamin Filene foregrounds "here, now, and how" as means for establishing a child's place in time. The museum is both a destination for exploration as well as a point of departure as the imagination journeys to distant places in time. History, like children, can be grounded in the here and now, as tangible evidence of the past is seen around the corner or in a child's own backyard.

The chapters in this part illustrate that story, imagination, play, senses, and place are ready tools that both children and museums can use to bridge the gap between now and then. In this approach, children become actors in the stories, explorers of new places and times, agents of their own discoveries, and players in history and the museum experience. Within the historian's toolkit, museums can find new approaches to interpreting the past and connecting kids to history.

NOTES

1. Elaine Wrisley Reed, *Helping Your Child Learn History: With Activities for Children Aged 4 through 11,* ed. Jacquelyn Zimmermann, (Washington, DC: United States Department of Education, Office of Educational Research and Improvement, May 1993), www.kidsource.com/kidsource/content/history.html (accessed February 16, 2009).
2. Chris Husbands, *What Is History Teaching?: Language, Ideas and Meaning in Learning about the Past* (Buckingham, PA: Open University Press, 1996), 62.
3. Lewis Carroll, *Alice's Adventures in Wonderland and Through the Looking Glass* (Chicago and New York: Rand McNally & Company, 1932 [1916]), 13.

CHAPTER 4

Finding the Story in History

Leslie Bedford

In 1983 the U.S. Holocaust Memorial Museum opened *Daniel's Story: Remember the Children*, an exhibition for children that tells the story of the Holocaust through the eyes of a young boy. Several years later, Lauriston Marshall, the museum's former deputy director of exhibitions, recounted how one youngster had responded to the experience:

> Some of my best memories are watching young people react to the history exhibits that we've done at the Holocaust Museum. Watching their responses to [it]—because we do have some places where kids or families, or adults, if they choose to, can interact and write things. . . . And I remember, it kind of made me come unglued at the same time, when I saw a note that was written by, I think, a 10-year-old girl named Charlotte. . . . We get many, many, notes. But this one I remember in particular. . . . It was addressed to Daniel, the boy in *Daniel's Story*, through whose eyes you experience the history. . . . It said, "Dear Daniel, I feel so bad for you and your family and what happened to you. I wish I could bring them back. I think I've fallen in love with history."[1]

This chapter is about the place of story and storytelling in exhibitions such as *Daniel's Story* that are designed for children and families. Telling stories is something we do every day of our lives. But commonplace as it is, story is not a simple concept; familiarity with how it has been analyzed in both theory and practice can enrich one's work in exhibition development.[2]

Some Theory on the Meaning of Story

Most people use the terms *story* and *narrative* interchangeably, but scholars distinguish between the two. The *story*, fiction or nonfiction, tells what happened at some time to some one in some place. The *narrative*, sometimes called *narrative discourse*, is how the story is told or interpreted in a particular medium, such as a book, film, video game, newspaper article, painting, or exhibition. Whether one is analyzing or creating an exhibition, it is useful first to articulate the story—what happened, who the characters are, where it occurred, and what is its emotional value—and then consider how it could be told in ways appropriate both to the audience (in this case children and families) and to the exhibition format.

Narrative can also be a way of thinking about the world. Among a great many scholars who write about narrative (narratologists who work in the field of narratology), one of the most influential has been cognitive psychologist Jerome Bruner, who believes that narrative is an ineluctable part of being human. The storytelling habit begins with very young children and in adulthood becomes a primary way to making meaning of life. Recently there has been an explosion of interest in narrative in all fields, from adult development and psychology to law.[3]

Bruner distinguishes between two major modes of thought: the storytelling or narrative mode and the paradigmatic or logico-scientific mode. The latter draws on the Enlightenment's faith in the supremacy of reason and the possibility of transmitting knowledge independent of context. This is the domain of science, math, and logic—of observable phenomena answerable to discernible and immutable laws. The narrative mode, Bruner argues, is the one people use to make sense of their world; it is subjective, interpretive, qualitative, and contextual. Both modes are natural to human thought and both can and are used to convince others: "yet what they convince *of* is fundamentally different: arguments convince of their truth, stories of their lifelikeness."[4]

In *From Knowledge to Narrative: Educators and the Changing Museum*,[5] Lisa Roberts writes at length about how learning in the museum has changed from the transmission of knowledge from curator to the public to the sharing of narrative by educator and visitor. The key point for exhibition development is that narrative creates a conversation, leading to an opening up—rather than a shutting down—of the listener's mind. Garrison Keillor, the master storyteller of National Public Radio's "Prairie Home Companion," claims the listener is also active in the story:

> I find that if I leave out enough details in my stories, the listener
> will fill in the blanks with her own hometown, and if a Freeport
> girl exiled in Manhattan hears the story about Memorial Day,
> she'll put it right there in that cemetery with those names on
> the stones, and she may think of her uncle Alcuin who went to
> France and didn't return and get out her hanky and blow. I'm not
> the reason she's moved, he is. All I do is say the words: cornfield

and Mother and algebra and Chevy pickup and cold beer and Sunday morning and rhubarb and loneliness, and other people put pictures to them.[6]

In other words, storytelling, or the narrative mode of thought, is about *both* the storyteller *and* the listener (or viewer or visitor). Narrative stimulates personal interpretation; the person watching the film, reading the book, or experiencing the exhibition is engaged in his own kind of internal dialogue with the story. In this process of making meaning we create story out of story so that perceiving and creating become two sides of the same coin. British scholar Chris Husbands puts it succinctly: "The telling of stories calls forth further stories."[7]

Finally, narratologists talk about something called narrativity, or the power to evoke story in the listener's or viewer's mind. In other words, something does not have to be a formal story (with setting, action, characters) in order to generate one. A piece of music, a painting, even a beautiful sunset can evoke a narrative. And so can objects.[8]

In the following story an adult recalls his childhood encounter with a diorama that possessed considerable narrativity for him:

> The really great [diorama] was the jaguar stalking the big rodent. And I couldn't read that word when I was a kid of what the animal was. And it was supposed to be someplace like Venezuela, but I thought that jungles were all in Brazil, so I thought it had to be Brazil. But it was neat to me. It was like seeing another way to paint, or another way to make a picture at least, to create this environment. And you could stand in front of it and just make up a whole story about what the bird that was sitting on the branch was going to do next, where that jaguar had come from, and, you know, did this big rodent have a family somewhere and was it out gathering food? I mean, there was this whole thing that you could fill in yourself about it, but that was really exciting.[9]

Although no research currently exists on how objects evoke story for children in a museum setting, there is anecdotal evidence from, for example, the Brooklyn Children's Museum, which recently reinstalled its extensive *Collections Central* exhibition in its new building. As Curator of Collections Beth Alberty notes, objects can evoke story in several ways. For instance, they can:

> provide occasions for parents/grandparents and children to make stories together or to join their stories. Our collection of metal lunchboxes is an obvious example where parents recognize their

own childhood lunchbox . . . or share that with each other and their children, which leads to other reminiscences and sharing of parent/child childhood experiences.

Objects also become part of a child's ongoing personal narrative:

> They build on what the child is already creating in his mind: the story may be an ongoing one in the child's imagination that attaches itself to the object. . . . I keep thinking of a boy, perhaps 8–9, I overheard in the [reconstructed Brazilian fishing] boat—words spoken to himself that I wish I had written down—he was doing exactly what it was intended to promote: playing out a boating scenario, a disaster . . . which would be his ongoing story; another child might have an altogether different boating scenario.[10]

Story and Imagination

In filling in the blanks and creating story from story, people are using their imaginations, that uniquely human capacity that author J. K. Rowling calls "the fount of all invention and innovation."[11] There are several theoretical frameworks for clarifying how story and imagination relate. One of the most fruitful comes from the ideas of Kieran Egan and his Imaginative Education Research Group.[12] This school of educational thought and practice believes that we learn best by engaging our imagination, which Egan defines as "the capacity to think of things as possibly being so." Egan's work is based on a synthesis of two preexisting ideas—a reframing of the long-discredited concept of cultural recapitulation (each person learns by recapitulating the various stages of Western development) and Russian developmental psychologist Lev Vygotsky's notion of culturally and socially mediated cognitive tools. As Egan explains:

> It is not that something that occurred in cultural history causes an aptitude in every child to acquire knowledge in the same order, but rather that by acquiring specific intellectual tools, the modern individual generates similar kinds of understanding as existed for people using those tools in the past.[13]

According to Egan, there are five kinds of understanding—Somatic, Mythic, Romantic, Philosophic, and Ironic—each with distinct cognitive tools that the imagination employs to learn. The understandings are not hierarchical, biological, or inevitable; they appear and continue to develop through our ongoing interaction with our environments.

Adults possess all five. An acquaintance with these five constructs can be helpful in developing exhibitions for children alone or in groups with adults.

Somatic understanding, the earliest stage of human cognitive development, is about understanding experience in a physical, prelinguistic way. As our physical bodies interact with the environment, information comes to the brain through the senses, what Egan calls the body's toolkit, including rhythm and musicality, humor, emotional responses and attachments, gesture and communication, and intentionality. These are the tools that humans used before language was invented and still use in activities such as the performing arts.

Mythic understanding refers to understanding experience through oral language, which appeared with evolutionary changes in human physiognomy. The acquisition of language enabled our ancestors to discuss, represent, and understand even things not actually experienced personally. The tools of Mythic understanding include story structuring; jokes and humor; abstract binary opposites (for example, peace/war, parent/child, rich/poor); forming images; a sense of mystery; games, drama, and play; rhyme, meter, and pattern; and metaphor. Metaphor as a cognitive tool receives considerable attention from Egan and his followers. Metaphor involves talking about something in terms derived from something very different. It is a linguistic tool that is most evident in very young children but then begins to atrophy at age 8 or 9.[14] By generating, not simply articulating, relationships among disparate things or ideas, metaphor expands our understanding and reveals pathways to alternative interpretations.

Romantic understanding is about grasping experience through the tools associated with literacy. Children experience growing independence and separateness from a world that appears increasingly complex. They relate readily to extremes of reality, associate with heroes, and seek to make sense of the world in human terms. The tools thus include the sense of reality; a focus on the extremes of experience and the limits of reality; an association with heroes; a sense of wonder; knowledge and human meaning; collections and hobbies; revolt and idealism; context play and role-play; and narrative understanding. In *The Educated Mind*, Egan presents the concept of "humanized knowledge" as a key theme in Romantic understanding. As children focus on individuals and the emotions that inspire them to act in certain ways, they gain understanding of the emotions that humanity shares. Thus Charlotte, the visitor to the Holocaust Museum, could empathize with Daniel and experience the sadness and loss his story personifies.

Philosophic understanding refers to the management of experience through the theoretic use of language. Its tools include the sense of abstract reality; the sense of agency; a grasp of general ideas and their anomalies; the search for authority and truth; and meta-narrative understanding. This understanding is nurtured in upper secondary school and thus, as with *Ironic understanding*, the fifth type of understanding that Egan discusses, is more applicable to adults than to children.

In his many articles and books written for practitioners, Egan and his colleagues expand on what these tools mean for teaching and learning. Story is central to Imaginative Education; Egan's most popular work is *Teaching as Story Telling*.[15] In a recent article he and his co-author Gillian Judson explore the tool of story structuring that shows up in Mythic understanding. Story structuring "shapes experience and knowledge into forms that establish their emotional meaning, helping us understand how to feel about events."[16] The exhibition team can take advantage of this capacity by asking, What's the story on the topic? How can I make the factual content clear and bring out its emotional importance?

Because humans are natural storytellers, narrative applies not only to Mythic understanding but also to Romantic, because youngsters aged 8 to 13 thrive on real-life narratives, and also to Philosophic, because teenagers and adults create and appreciate meta-narratives about the world. These understandings build on one another; they do not disappear. For example, in talking about Mythic understanding Egan writes:

> these affective orientations to binary opposites are to become a part of a mature historical understanding. They are not simply childish and inadequate ways of thinking. They will later be controlled by more sophisticated "paradigms," but they will remain absolutely basic and essential.[17]

This insight provides a powerful set of strategies for engaging multigenerational audiences. It resembles the principles of universal design; for example, the opportunity to touch exhibition objects not only benefits visitors with limited vision but also enriches the experience for everyone else. Thus the narration of an epic struggle between the forces of Good and Evil—the Star Wars series, for instance—can engage the imagination of every age.

Egan's concern is with formal classroom education; he argues that engaging the learner's imagination furthers his grasp of every area of the curriculum. A different perspective comes from Chris Husbands, who analyzes the benefits and challenges of using storytelling specifically in the history classroom. He reminds his readers that "the relationship between history and story has always been a difficult one: the very definition of story shifts along the uneven border between fact and fiction, between truth and lies, between emotional and causal logic."[18]

Husbands supports using story to teach history but insists that teachers respect three critical standards in its application: "accuracy to what can be derived from historical evidence," "authenticity to period and character," and "openness to other versions of the story."[19] He concedes that the imagination shapes both the historian-teacher-storyteller's as well as the student-listener's understanding of the past:

> the boundaries between history and fiction are no longer clear or distinct, if, indeed the argument is that understanding the past is itself a creative act which can be rendered differently by historians, novels and poets, then the place of the imagination in the construction of historical accounts becomes central.[20]

Given this blurred boundary between history and fiction, a conscientious teacher should engage her students in examining stories critically in terms of what Husbands calls the "organizing principles—the ideas of causation, continuity, change—of complex historical discourse."[21]

Husbands inadvertently raises a common fallacy in exhibition development—the idea that the principles of teaching children in a classroom are transferable to exhibitions, environments where the learning is voluntary, ungraded, and often unfacilitated.[22] That said, storytelling can be both a compelling teaching method and a powerful interpretive tool for use in museum exhibitions. Bruner and visitor studies experts John Falk and Lynn Dierking all point to research showing that information received in story form is more easily absorbed and remembered. Throughout the process of exhibition development, the story is interpreted through a "creative act" of the imagination—by historian or curator, by exhibition developer and designer, and finally by the visitor. Visitors bring their own imaginations to the task of making meaning; just like the adults listening to Garrison Keillor or the boy looking at the diorama, they fill in the blanks and create story out of story.

To summarize, story or narrative is a foundational mode of thinking for children as well as for adults. It engages listeners' imaginations and emotions, and thus their memories. It can be an effective method of teaching and learning as well as a well-established mode for making sense of personal experience. Finally, the narrative mode of thinking is interpretive rather than logical. It speaks to a definition of learning that embraces individual meaning making, and thus its application to the medium of exhibitions requires a skilled and artful hand.

Theory into Practice: Examples from the Field

If there were a great many excellent examples of history exhibitions for young audiences, this book would not have been written. Nonetheless one can find a variety of approaches to storytelling that support and extend the preceding discussion of theory.

An excellent example of storytelling in a history exhibition for young people is the aforementioned *Daniel's Story: Remember the Children* at the U.S. Holocaust Memorial Museum in Washington, DC. The current and very popular version of *Daniel's Story* is actually its third iteration; a fourth traveling version is no longer extant. Versions one and two were done by the Capitol Children's Museum; the Holocaust museum team was able to use summative evaluation of the earlier version as well as their own honed instincts as storytellers, designers, child advocates, and Holocaust researchers to improve it.

One might examine *Daniel's Story* on several levels, including the process and leadership behind it, elements critical to its ultimate success as a narrative exhibition. More directly related to the subject at hand, the exhibition team employed a number of proven strategies—things that the field knows work—such as a handful of identifiable and evocative objects (a diary, suitcase, World War I medal); personalization of the story line through a young person with whom young visitors can identify; and a very careful use of exhibition text.

Much of the text is in the first person in the form of Daniel's diary. This is Bruner's narrative mode, the text as storyteller and generator of the imagination:

Dear Diary,

Things are beginning to change. The Nazis are taking over more and more. Many people are following their ways. Now some of my friends won't play with me because I am Jewish. I feel awful.

Daniel

Third-person text—the curatorial, omniscient voice more characteristic of exhibitions—is limited to periodic panels designed to move the story along by focusing on the core elements:

This is where Daniel and his family lived.

See how different it is from his home in Germany.

In addition, visitors can both touch most of the exhibition and experience the kind of "minds-on" elements that add depth and texture. For example, for me the ambient sound in the ghetto street of a

FIGURE 4.1. Two youngsters listen to a radio broadcast that a family of this period might have heard. Courtesy United States Holocaust Memorial Museum.

mother singing to her crying baby was particularly moving; someone else might choose to listen to a 1930s radio broadcast about Hitler's growing power.

In addition to these elements, the team made several critical decisions about narrating this story. The first was to preserve the original *Daniel's Story*, a fictional account that, although based on many true ones, was created expressly for the first version of the exhibition. Daniel is not "real," and his face is never shown; rather there are photographs of groups of boys, laughing or playing sports. These boys are not identified; one can essentially choose one's own Daniel. The text in the introductory area, entered through a heavy theatrical curtain, explains:

> This is the story of a boy named Daniel and how he survived the Holocaust.
>
> It is based on the stories of children who experienced the Holocaust in Germany, the Lodz Ghetto, and the concentration camp at Auschwitz.

Although *Daniel's Story* suggests a play, it is informed by the most rigorous of historical research and authenticity. The team imposed a critical rule on themselves: every single detail of every scene had to have a visual antecedent from the historical record. For example, the exhibition's ghetto is based on the Lodz Ghetto in Poland, where German Jews of this time and region were taken; the photographs taken by resident Mandel Grossman provided the details. The narrative thus conforms to Husband's three criteria for historical storytelling: accuracy, authenticity, and recognition of multiple interpretations.

Second, the team wanted to create a complete narrative, an arc that enabled visitors to make sense of a complicated piece of history; for example, the original version of the exhibition had relied on two settings (the family's late Victorian bourgeois living room in Germany and their impoverished room in the Ghetto) to explain what happened to Daniel and his family. The team responsible for the redesign thought this abbreviated narrative too confusing for young visitors; their version narrates the entire story of the family's move from their middle-class home (furnished in German modernist style to represent the period accurately and also to forge connections to a contemporary audience) and the streets of their town, to the Ghetto and their single and very destitute room, to the last section where, through barbed wire, one glimpses a vertical slice of a train—huge and terrifying—and a photograph of children being taken to the camps.

Short videos help narrate the story at two points: the beginning, where video provides a basic introduction to the period and Daniel and his family, and then again at the end, to explain what happened afterward. We are told that Daniel's mother and sister die and that he and his father survive. The voice-over closes with an older Daniel exhorting us to remember his story and to remember the children.

This narrative arc is punctuated by well-chosen objects: the WWI medal that Daniel had proudly received from his father shows up again in the suitcase that he will take to the Ghetto and finally lies abandoned on the ground by the camp train. Such objects work in ways similar to metaphor—the medal as the family's tragic transformation over time—and help generate story within story.

The role of exhibition design is to create or to enhance narrative without words. Designer Darcie Fohrman has been strongly influenced by stagecraft and used theatrical devices to provide the sensory and emotional context and movement to the story. Every surface has a texture—often provided by scenic paintings and two-dimensional cutouts such as that of the enormous camp train—and the colors, flooring, and lighting change with each scene. But because the exhibition was about Daniel's memories—he is telling the story looking back—the designer recast the details uncovered through historical research as if they were being recalled over time. For example, three of the four beds in the ghetto room are *trompe-l'oeil* so they would fade into the background, al-

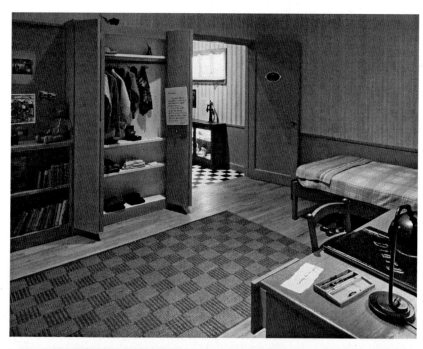

FIGURES 4.2 –4.3. Visitors travel from Daniel's comfortable and modern bedroom to the single room shared by his entire family in the ghetto. Courtesy United States Holocaust Memorial Museum.

FIGURE 4.4. The continuing appearance of a few iconic objects helps move the story along. Courtesy United States Holocaust Memorial Museum.

lowing Daniel—and the visitors—to focus on his. Thus in imperceptible but critical ways the visitor enters Daniel's memory and becomes an actor in his play, in the narration of this particular story.

Although the team determined that Daniel would be a fictional creation—and identified as such—youngsters continued to ask if he really existed, where he lived now, and so forth. This became a challenge for educational and floor staff, who went on to create supplementary materials to address this and other issues. It may be that no matter what the museum does, children of a particular age will insist on the real thing; for example, Egan's view of children ages 8 to 13, the period of Romantic understanding, is that they respond best to real people exemplifying heroic qualities and struggles.

But there is another issue at play, which is the one Bruner raises— the difference between truth and authenticity or lifelikeness. A good narrative has authenticity; we believe in it, because it resonates with our understanding of the world. This characteristic is also required of exhibitions, as they are also a storytelling medium, and it gives exhibition makers license, if not the obligation, to exercise their creative imaginations. The Holocaust Museum imposed rigorous parameters on their creative imaginations, but other stories may be less well researched or the teams less disciplined.[23]

The final critical decision about *Daniel's Story* involved establishing the exhibition's goals with regard to the historical content. As exhibition researcher Alexandra Zapruder described, "The Holocaust is difficult enough for adults and really *not* an appropriate topic for kids." [24] The challenge was to avoid both nihilistic pessimism and unrealistic optimism. The team decided that some of the family, but not all, would survive. And they anchored the ending, as they had throughout, in the particular, concrete details of Daniel and his family's story. They wanted the exhibition to be a "safe first step" that would provoke compassion and provide a foundation for future learning. It was not intended to teach the history of the Holocaust. As the story of Charlotte and her visit to *Daniel's Story* suggests, the narration of this difficult story succeeded wonderfully well.

Daniel's Story successfully achieves what many history exhibitions set out to accomplish—to translate a difficult adult story into a narrative for children or intergenerational audiences. This is the crux of the dilemma for many museums and a task requiring a range of expertise, time for try out and evaluation, and great sensitivity.

A very different example of how a museum chose to narrate an essentially adult story for children comes from the Oklahoma City National Memorial, the site of the 1995 destruction of the Alfred P. Murrah Federal Building and the deaths of 168 people (including 19 children). Here the museum decided to house the children's version in a separate room similar to a hands-on history space. Rather than telling the entire original story, the museum decided to focus on the positive aspects of this horrific event—the tree that survived the blast and, most importantly, the way the community and nation responded. There are places for youngsters to dress-up and role-play characters such as the ambulance drivers, nurses, fire fighters, and police who arrived to help. In other words, the children are free to create their own narrative of the story. One assumes that—depending perhaps on accompanying adults—the result may or may not bear any relationship to what happened in Oklahoma City, Oklahoma. If parents wish their children to know the original story, the museum has a large-format and beautifully illustrated book called *On American Soil: A Day to Remember* (2001).[25] Written to be read to children, it is available in the room as well as the gift shop.

A third example of an exhibition for children based on story is *Noah's Ark*, the space for young children and families at the Skirball Cultural Center in Los Angeles, California. If the goal of *Daniel's Story* is to provide a safe first step and foundation for future learning, that of *Noah's Ark* is to support the institution's mission of welcoming culturally diverse

FIGURE 4.5. The entrance to the ark transitions visitors into the story of the flood. Photograph by Grant Mudford. Courtesy Skirball Cultural Center.

communities and building community. The well-known story of the ark resonates with flood stories from around the globe and offers rich program possibilities; on two visits I heard the stories of first a Chinese and then an African flood. The exhibition is organized in three "chapters"—the storyteller's beginning, middle, and end—which defined the space and transitioned visitors from the approaching storm, to community life within the ark, and finally into a new and more hopeful world.

To what extent the average 4-year-old understands or connects to this story is problematic—and not yet formally evaluated—but probably not very important to the overall institutional goals. Essentially the story of the ark provides a marvelous conceptual umbrella for the design of an extremely creative and popular platform for various kinds of play, including storytelling. The exceptionally high quality of the design, including the magical work of puppet artist Chris Greene and the sculptural power of the immense wooden ark, bespeak both creativity and extensive resources not found in many places for very young children.

A different approach to story is to treat it as one of several different exhibition strategies. When the Boston Children's Museum installed *Endings: Death and Loss* in 1984, they employed multiple ways of helping youngsters make sense of this challenging topic, including television footage, live and dead animals, artifacts, and talkbacks. A story, "When Grandpa Died," was illustrated by designer Signe Hanson and narrated on two levels by developer Janet Kamien: the text for children to read or to have read to them was simple and straightforward ("one

FIGURE 4.6. A view of the new world concludes the flood story. Photograph by Grant Mudford. Courtesy Skirball Cultural Center.

day grandpa . . ."); a line oriented to adults followed below in smaller font incorporating suggestions for helping children cope with major loss. The story was further illustrated by miniature dioramas at child height that showed the embalming room, the wake, and the cemetery (including a cross section of the grave) and another artifact box holding a pocketknife left to the boy by this grandpa. These elements addressed the developmental level at which most children approached the topic of death—a deep curiosity about the concrete details.

I couldn't sleep.

Ricky couldn't sleep.

He remembered that he and Grandpa
were supposed to go to the farm together,
and now he was dead.

Where was Grandpa going, anyway?
Where was heaven supposed to be?
Could it be that Ricky really would
never see him again?

It was all so confusing, Ricky couldn't
even cry. He was wondering about that
when he fell asleep.

FIGURE 4.7. The exhibition *Endings: Death and Loss* included text on two levels. Courtesy Signe Hanson.

A similarly selective use of narrative characterized *Play Ball!*, a small exhibition at the Brooklyn Historical Society in the mid-1990s, which included the story of Jackie Robinson's courageous integration of the Brooklyn Dodgers. This incorporated the idea of two-level text, basing the one for children on Egan's Romantic level of understanding—that is, highlighting Robinson as a real-life hero whose story embodied a struggle between binary opposites. In addition to providing text at an 8-to10-year-old reading level, the exhibition offered a chance to "Stand in

Jackie Robinson's shoes and hear what he heard." As they placed their hands on the bat suspended from the wall, young visitors heard the terrifying boos and yells that greeted Robinson's first appearance, thus incorporating a bit of Egan's Somatic understanding.

Although designed for junior and senior high school students, rather than young children, the exhibition *Choosing to Participate* also illustrates storytelling as effective exhibition element.[26] Each element is a story narrated in ways the design team thought appropriate to the topic, audience, and space. For example, the story of the integration of Central High School in Little Rock, Arkansas, in 1957 is narrated through the personal experience of Elizabeth Eckford, one of the Little Rock Nine. As visitors enter her bedroom they see her newly ironed shirt-waist dress—well-known from media coverage of the event—hanging on the wall (next to an ironing board) and hear her, as an adult, narrating what happened.

The story of Cambodian-American Arn Chorn Pond also uses first-person voiceover as well as photographs, video, and an evocative passage of flute music to help narrate the story of his horrific experiences as a child soldier during the Khmer Rouge regime. Both stories would need significant reframing for younger visitors, but the first-person perspective and voice that generate empathic imagination, the strong visual and spatial design, and evocative prompts such as the flute melody worked for all ages.

These examples illustrate the variety of narrative modes that exhibitions can embrace.[27] Because they are three dimensional, exhibitions can offer opportunities for what has been called embodied imagination or exploration through the senses—a chance to see oneself in a costume, pick up a tool, lug a heavy sack, move through darkened spaces, or hear a melody. Because they often include objects, exhibitions can help tell or evoke story through artifacts. Because they are visual experiences, exhibitions can use images, color, and texture as narrative elements as the designers did in *Daniel's Story*. And because they are individual experiences, exhibitions enable each visitor, of whatever age, to create his or her own meaning out of the encounters.

A preference for story argues against the conventional wisdom that visitors need choices and dislike having to follow a single chronological line; this is an important point. However, not every story is a narrative. Too often history museums fall back on the story-like, what I once called "didactic wolves dressed in storyteller sheep's clothing"— exhibitions with titles such as *The Story of Colonial New England*.[28] These may be stories; there are characters, a setting and action. But they are not real narratives. They do not take the visitor to another place in his mind; they do not engage her emotions or imagination. A true narrative has to be true to its medium; for exhibition makers that means engaging all our senses, including the somatic or physical, speaking to our emotions, using the specific to generate connections to the familiar and universal, and telling us something about some one(s) we are going to care about. Something happens in the imagination in the face of a real story; it creates a new one.

Conclusion

What *Daniel's Story* and other effective exhibitions that use narrative successfully—whether as organizing principle or single strategy—teach us is that the best exhibitions draw as much on the arts as on education. The narrative mode is closer to art, especially literature and theater, to the emotional and the cognitive, than it is to conventional teaching. It is helpful to turn to educational philosopher John Dewey for his definition of an educative or meaningful experience, that is, one that builds on what came before and leads to future growth.[29] And for Dewey the purest kind of growth-enhancing experience was aesthetic: it happens in the act of engaging with a work of art—among which he would include the art-like such as a beautiful sunset—and leaves in its wake an awakened imagination. That is what storytelling can do. We know this from other narrative media; we need to realize it in exhibitions as well.

NOTES

1. This story and several others included in this chapter belong to a collection of some seventy-five stories narrated by museum professionals to Michael Spock and a research team at the Association of Children's Museums and American Association of Museums' annual conferences in Philadelphia in 1995. Some have been published, sometimes in more than one form, such as in individual journal articles, as chapters in books, or as part of a video (and accompanying teacher's guide) called *Philadelphia Stories: A Collection of Pivotal Museum Memories* (Washington, DC: American Association of Museums, 2000). Many of the interview transcripts remain unpublished. *Daniel's Story* is an unpublished interview from section 17, page 34 of Michael Spock's 1995 transcripts, herein referred to as "Philadelphia Stories: A Collection of 75 Interviews."
2. For an authoritative guide to the many issues involved, see Porter H. Abbott, *The Cambridge Introduction to Narrative* (Cambridge: Cambridge University Press, 2002).

3. Recently some scholars have argued that narrative is not innate but socially constructed. They suggest that new media are helping to shape a nonnarrative way of understanding, one that is more about webs and connections than beginning, middle, and end. Although this understanding corresponds to how children and adults, for instance, use web-based resources, possibly we construct and use modes of thinking that work in both ways. In any case, designers working with interactive media, such as video games, continue to work off a storyline. (See, for example, Christopher Stapleton and Charles Hughes, "Interactive Imagination: Tapping the Emotions through Interactive Story for Compelling Simulations," *IEEE Computer Graphics and Animation* 15 [Sept/Oct 2003].) With regard to young children, recent studies have suggested that some young children—for example, those who have not been read to by adults—do not use the beginning-middle-end narrative form at as early an age as Bruner and others have assumed.

4. Jerome Bruner, *Actual Minds, Possible Worlds* (Cambridge, MA: Harvard University Press, 1986), 11.

5. Lisa C. Roberts, *From Knowledge to Narrative: Educators and the Changing Museum* (Washington and London: Smithsonian Institution Press, 1997).

6. Garrison Keillor, "In Search of Lake Wobegon," *National Geographic* 198, no. 6 (2000): 109.

7. Chris Husbands, *What Is History Teaching?: Language, Ideas and Meaning in Learning about the Past* (Buckingham, PA: Open University Press, 1996), 51.

8. Places can also evoke story. Here is a story from the Spock collection of an adult recalling a childhood visit to an historic site: "And then when I was in fourth grade my fourth-grade teacher, Mrs. Nichols, took us on a field trip to [Letchworth] Park to see the home of Mary Jamison, who was a young girl who had been taken captive by the Iroquois Indians, and she had spent the rest of her life actually married to an Iroquois Indian and set up her home in [Letchworth] Park. And so there was a cabin where she had lived. And I had a fantasy from then on that I always wanted to be Mary Jamison and be kidnapped by the Iroquois Indians and taken away into a whole new lifestyle. And I always used to fantasize what it was like to grind corn and do all those things that Mary had to do" (Michael Spock, ed., *A Study Guide to Philadelphia Stories: A Collection of Pivotal Museum Memories* [Washington, DC: American Association of Museums, 2000], 28).

9. Michael Spock, from unpublished transcripts, "Philadelphia Stories: A Collection of 75 Interviews" section 17, page 25. Also published as Michael Spock, "Tales of Alonetime and Owntime in Museums," *Journal of Museum Education* 25, no. 1 (2000): 15–9.

10. Beth Alberty, email message to author, October 8, 2008.

11. "The Fringe Benefits of Failure and the Importance of the Imagination," J. K. Rowling's speech at the 2008 Harvard University commencement, where she received an honorary doctorate, can be found at http://harvard magazine.com/commencement/the-fringe-benefits-failure-the-importance-imagination (accessed September 3, 2009).

12. The most thorough explication of Egan's theory can be found in *The Educated Mind: How Cognitive Tools Shape Our Understanding* (Chicago: University of Chicago Press, 1997). But he has written many other less academic works that can be very helpful to museum professionals. These can be found on his website (http://www.educ.sfu.ca/kegan/) or that of the Imaginative Education Research Group (http://www.ierg.net/).

13. Egan, *The Educated Mind*, 30.

14. According to research by Ellen Winner and Howard Gardner, these children begin to reject metaphors, saying, for instance, that colors cannot be "cold" (quoted in Egan, *The Educated Mind*, 54–5).

15. Kieran Egan, *Teaching as Story Telling: An Alternative to Teaching and Curriculum in the Elementary School* (Chicago, IL: The University of Chicago Press, 1986).

16. Kieran Egan and Gillian Judson, "Of Whales and Wonder," *Educational Leadership* 65 (2008): 22.

17. Kieran Egan, *Accumulating History: The Philosophy of History Teaching* (Middletown, CT: Wesleyan University Press, 1983), 74.

18. Husbands, *What Is History Teaching?*, 47.

19. Husbands, *What Is History Teaching?*, 50.

20. Husbands, *What Is History Teaching?*, 59.

21. Husbands, *What Is History Teaching?*, 51.

22. Many children visit museums in school groups, which are typically led around by a docent or an educator. Others visit with their families or adult caregivers. Although in both cases the learning is mediated by adults, the experience is very different from learning in a classroom.

23. For example, in 1996 an exhibition about Brooklyn's emerging Chinese community at the Brooklyn Historical Society included an object theater called *Between the Bridge,* which narrated a story about a Chinese immigrant family living in Sunset Park. The story was crafted by a playwright out of scores of oral histories; it was authentic, but it was not true. And unlike *Daniel's Story*, the setting was minimalist and theatrical—a black box where objects were lit and unseen characters spoke.

24. Alexandra Zapruder, personal conversation with author, July 14, 2008.

25. Oklahoma City National Memorial Education Committee, *On American Soil: A Day to Remember* (Oklahoma City: Oklahoma City National Memorial Trust, 2001).

26. *Choosing to Participate* was created in 1999 for the national educational organization Facing History and Ourselves. It toured the country for several years and was updated and reopened in 2008. It can be seen online at http://ctp.facinghistory.org/ (accessed September 15, 2009).

27. Alexandra Zapruder, personal conversation with the author, 14 July, 2008.

28. Leslie Bedford, "Storytelling: The Real Work of Museums," *Curator: The Museum Journal* 44 (2001): 33.

29. Dewey elaborates on what he means by a educative experience in several of his writings; see esp. John Dewey, *Experience and Education: The 60th Anniversary Edition* (1938; repr., West Lafayette, IN: Kappa Delta Pi, 1998).

CHAPTER 5

Imagination—A Child's Gateway to Engagement with the Past

Daniel Spock

In 2006 the Minnesota History Center opened an exhibition called *Open House: If These Walls Could Talk*. The exhibition chronicles the lives of a diverse group of families who all happened to live in one actual, ordinary house over 118 years. Part of the experience involves making comparisons between the various families and their experiences over time. As it turned out, one common thread that our research turned up was the practice of keeping chickens. The German, Italian, and, most recently, Hmong immigrants who lived in the house all raised and butchered chickens in the basement, a fact recreated in meticulous detail in the exhibition. One day, I saw an older man, whose feed cap, beard, and suspenders telegraphed his agricultural roots, leaving with a boy I took to be his grandson. The old man looked at the boy and said, "How's about every time you wanted a McNugget, *you had to kill a chicken?*" The boy stopped and got a faraway look in his eyes as he struggled to imagine this.

Imagination is the human capacity that put the muse in "museum." From the times of the earliest *Wunderkammer,* a sense of wonderment is the quality of thought and feeling that museums have sought to inspire in museumgoers of all ages. As early as 1957, the dean of heritage interpretation at the National Park Service, Freeman Tilden, surely sensed this quality as he urged the field to *provoke* rather than to *instruct*—a principle, rooted in his direct observations of how the process of interpretive engagement with the public actually works.[1] But imagination is a diverse and slippery thing. Under its broad aegis, imagination, a process of transformative ideation, expresses itself through a dizzying variety of human activities. Truthfully, it is far from a matter of habit in history museums to see imagination in all of its complexity and richness; even less so is it perceived as the most powerful tool in the museum toolbox for creating engaging learning experiences of all kinds. On some level, all of us think we know what imagination is, but few of us have stopped long enough to examine the profound effect a museum visitor's imagination might have on the tradecraft of museum work. Still less is a child's imagination given proper, if any, consideration.

It is a fact that the past must be imagined in order for it to be experienced. Indeed, the past does not actually exist in the present, either for those who have experienced the events of the past directly or those who have not. To conjure up the events of the past in the imagination, to the extent that this is enjoyable, is the essence of what it means to enjoy history for children and historians alike, though, naturally enough, historians have elaborated from this basis to a far greater degree. Still, more even than the skills of reading and writing, analysis and scholarship, imagination is the primary act of thinking historically. As such, imagination stands as the primary fountainhead through which history proceeds, a fact surely intuited by the ancient Greeks when they named Clio as the Muse, and therefore the source of inspiration, for history. It is also the most natural and appropriate starting place for a child to cultivate a sense of meaningful engagement with the past.

In order to set a general context for the power of the imagination, I attempt to interweave mutually supportive strands, each one an aspect of imaginative thinking relevant to history museums: forethought, or the capacity to anticipate the future and its alternative possibilities; imagining the past, particularly *what it was like* to experience it; the creation of meaning through imagination; imaginative roleplay and make-believe; the human predisposition to imaginative empathy; and the encoding of imagined meanings in memory—what I broadly call learning. Necessarily, I'll attempt to paint this composite portrait of the imagination before illustrating the practical applications with some examples. As we will see, experiences that bring us closer to imagining for ourselves *what it was like* in the past prove to be the most engaging for young and old, a fact that helps explain the comparative popularity of the context-rich living history programs in stark contrast to the more austere history museums generally.[2] Perhaps even more than adults, children must actively rely on the imagination to make sense of the world around them, and this is a natural point of engagement for a child.

The Ubiquity of Imagination in Play

Children everywhere engage in imaginative play. Although there are certainly proven ways that a child's imagination can be stimulated (and thwarted), observers of children have noted that children normally participate in activities involving the imagination quite naturally as they mature. What has been disputed, however, is the value of the imagination to children in the natural course of their development. In particular, the Western canon has a deep current of ambivalence toward the imagination and imaginative play, which has tended to undercut the legitimacy they might have as tools for learning or thinking. Plato was famously inclined to see the imagination as an inferior mental activity, painting it as antithetical to reason, a stigma that has been persistent ever since. In the twentieth century, influential theorists of the human psyche ranging from Freud to Piaget were still inclined to see the imagi- nation as a rather primitive, irrational specter, necessarily dominating the early life stages perhaps, but a stage that any normal person could be expected to grow out of on the path to becoming an adult.[3]

Although most Western cognitive theorists have generally credited imagination for its necessary role in creativity, many have also heaped scorn on the imagination the more it indulges the end of the spectrum of pure fantasy for its own sake. The strong utilitarian strain in our intellectual culture hasn't found much practical value in the sort of ser- endipitous musings that, superficially at least, appear to be cut off from any objective reality.

More recently, imagination's mixed reputation has begun to change for the better. A number of converging lines of research and thought, ranging from learning theory to neuroscience to psychology, are tak- ing a more nuanced and complex look at the role of imagination in the human mind. In the process, imagination is being seen not so much as an outlier to normal cognitive thought processes but as an integral com- ponent of them. Child psychologists Dorothy and Jerome Singer note that, although Freud theorized that human fantasies could be reduced to sexual and aggressive urges, this reduction could never really explain the full range of human drives encompassing curiosity. They also note that Piaget emphasized a developmental progression toward abstract reasoning, but with this emphasis he discounted the persistence of the imagination in adults as surely as he paid short shrift to the reasoning capabilities of children.[4] Educator Kieran Egan quotes the poet William Wordsworth's insight that imagination is nothing more than "reason in her most exalted mood" and asserts that "[Wordsworth's] view is making slow headway against the commoner, and cruder, notion of [imagina- tion and reason] being competitors for the dominance of the mind."[5] To draw an analogy, a holistic understanding would see the exercise of a person's imaginative "muscle" in any respect as beneficial to strength- ening cognition more broadly. It is all part of flexing the mind's think- ing capability. For example, developmental psychologist Paul Harris has suggested that the human capacity to imagine the future as a variety of possible alternatives (forethought) may be linked to the evolution of anticipatory strategies essential for survival, just as it is surely linked to creative problem solving.[6] In this sense, strategic risk taking and reasoning itself are products of imaginative thinking, not antithetical to it.

As we shall see, the imagination is also certainly involved in the mechanisms of empathy because it is in fact impossible to comprehend the motivations and feelings of others without the exercise of the imagination. Empathy is, by definition, the way in which we imagine what it might be like to be another person.

The combination of these patterns begins to suggest some intriguing implications for imagination as it relates to teaching and learning in the self-directed learning environments of museums and historic places. Critically, it also heaps ever more doubt on the traditional, unidirectional pedagogy that sees learning as merely a process of absorbing, retaining, and regurgitating information, a model in which the imagination is too often viewed as an unwelcome distraction to the business at hand. Once we begin to see the imagination as an essential and natural part of our cognitive hardwiring, it's not long before we have to see learning as a far more complicated and expansive business than we ever thought possible, and a richer vein for museums of all kinds to tap.

Imagining Meanings from "Blooming, Buzzing Confusion"

As a boy, I remember asking my father, "Were you in the Civil War?" When he laughed that off I asked, "Then did it happen when you were a little boy?" In particular instances, I noticed that historical hairstyles for men and boys ranged dramatically in length from my own early 1960s crew cut. In 1963 or 1964 long hair on men seemed extremely exotic, and it was the kind of thing I really noticed, for me it was one of the things that, like the black and whiteness of historical photographs, defined the strangeness of the past. To make sense of it, I first imagined a general trend over time toward shorter and shorter hair. So, I reasoned, things might progress like this: first there were cavemen (I had seen them in the diorama at the Ford Rotunda at the New York World's Fair), then the three musketeers, then the blue coats who fought the red coats, then the Civil War, *followed by the Romans,* whose hair was only a little longer than mine. My father corrected me on that misconception and other imaginings of what I called "the olden days."

Naïve childhood schemas are amusing enough, but they also tell us something about how we as human beings wrest meaning from what William James called, when imagining an infant's perception of the world, the "blooming buzzing confusion" of raw experience.[7] The philosopher John Dewey might have said that my childish curiosity arose from being "unsettled" (Why, apparently, did men and boys in the past have hair so much longer than mine?) and that my natural impulse was to apply some orderly explanation to this otherwise provocative impression, a provisional sort of understanding that Dewey would have termed *operational*.[8] In this same way, a child makes do with some explanation or other until some contradictory experience unsettling enough comes along to trigger the motivation to supplant it. As we mature, the operational part of this process becomes ever more critical. In some areas of knowledge, operational understandings ossify, appropriately or not, into rigid perceived "truth." At other times life experience would seem to teach us, sometimes in delightfully surprising ways, at other times rather traumatically, that things are not what they initially seemed to be.

Surely some may find this next assertion heretical, but I feel it is better to encourage a child's speculative faculties and fantasies about the past as an impetus to lifelong learning than it is to quibble too much over the facts at early contact. Children have the rest of their lives to sort facts from fantasy. In their visits with us, children find their experiences more memorable and positive when they are fully engaged in active, imaginative thinking. As adults, most of us know that sorting fact from fantasy is what life is all about as we plan for retirement, choose a car, or decide which political candidate we should vote for. The most important thing, more even than learning how to do the sorting, is to learn to enjoy the sorting process itself. Dispositional enjoyment such as this is the best insurance that a child will grow up to be a thinker, learning to think for the pure enjoyment of it. More narrowly, a set of positive feelings about history museums and sites provides some impetus for children to count history as one of their interests in life, a set of many things, we hope, about which they associate learning with pleasure. Indeed, this sort of delight in the discovery process inherent to museum-going I argue is one of the critical affective indicators to look for as a sign that visits will accumulate in meaningful ways to a child.

Encoding Meanings in Memory

Without memory, there can be no learning. From a neuroscience perspective, the mechanics of how we are able to remember are still very elusive. As I have already suggested, behaviorist "information-processing" notions, reducing the brain functions of memory to a file-drawer model of information storage and retrieval, are simply no longer adequate to explain the complexity of human memory. Harvard psychologist Daniel Schacter asserts that there are distinctly different variants of informational memory, each with its own functional characteristics and, according to evidence, involving distinctly different interactions of brain structures. Of episodic memory (the most relevant category for us), which, Schacter says, "allows us explicitly to recall the personal incidents that uniquely define our lives," he goes on to say:

> The idea of remembering as "mental time travel" highlights something that is truly remarkable: as rememberers, we can free ourselves from the immediate constraints of time and space, re-experiencing the past and projecting ourselves into the future at will. What we ordinarily think of as an exotic feat that could be accomplished only in science fiction is something which we all engage in each and every day of our lives.[9]

Schacter's analogy of remembering as "mental time travel" certainly fits a description of imagination. Interestingly, recent neuroscience research in studies by Schacter and others indicates that imagination of the variety that seeks to anticipate the future activates the same structures of the brain as long-term memory, suggesting that memory and forethought may be aspects of the same cognitive processes. To the extent that memory is fundamental to learning, this relationship reinforces the idea that the imagination exercises the memory and vice versa. As Susan Gaidos recounts it in *Science News*, in his research Schacter sought to test his hypothesis that "perhaps the overlap between memory and imagining could be explained by memory's 'constructive' nature. Rather than pulling up a file, like a computer, human memory strings together all the bits and pieces—place, people, sounds—needed to re-create an episode."[10] Research by Kathleen McDermott at Washington University seems to bolster Schacter's idea, Gaidos reports, and another study by Eleanor Mcguire and her colleagues at Wellcome Trust Center for Neuroimaging has elaborated on the importance of spatial memory to this process of imagining and remembering. Gaidos writes that "[Mcguire] proposes that this scene construction is a key part of retrieving past experiences in any memory process, including navigation, planning for the future, daydreaming, and mind wandering." Mcguire says, "We think scene construction underpins not just autobiographical and spatial memory and imagination, but a whole host of other critical cognitive functions."[11]

As we can see, if these researchers are right, the "encoding" (Schacter's term) of memory is not only a multisensory process, transcending word-based information, but, equally significant to the act of remembering, also relates to those aspects of the experience that trigger memory recall—triggers that can be activated by stimuli in any of the senses. See museum visits in this light and suddenly the value of the spatial museum environment comes into sharp focus. The environment itself, along with the elaborated network of imagined, evocative associations it entails, is information. The constructive nature of memory, as articulated here, also strongly supports the constructivist museum learning theories of George Hein and others who have argued that knowledge must be constructed within the minds of learners.[12]

If imaginative play prospers in certain environments better than it does in others, on a continuum, environments that contain a poverty of sensory features and where coercive controls are in place tend to limit the scope of flights of the imagination, whereas high-context environments redolent with variety, a high degree of sensory features and props, particularly those zones where free play is sanctioned and relatively unstructured, seem to spur the imagination.[13] Perhaps most problematic, imaginative play takes time. In the hyperstructured world of today's children (and their museum visits), the unbounded time necessary for the development of unencumbered flights of fancy is the scarcest commodity. Designers, therefore, should consider whether a space affords comfortable and easygoing dwell time for both children and their adult companions.

When we watch children in museums who are truly engaged, we see imagination in action. Children respond to, and remember best, rich, multisensory environments, because they are naturally predisposed to engage with the kinds of places that stimulate imaginative thinking. In the process, they will seek out familiar things, the memory triggers that readily connect to their prior experience of the world, but they will also show fascination for new, unsettling things. As this natural attraction relates to history places, children will respond to the activities and settings that give them the most evocative flavor of what it was like to live in the past in ways that are at once affective, cognitive, kinesthetic—on the whole, imaginative.

The Kinesthetic Attributes of a Child's Imaginative Play

The conscious or unconscious imaginative process of conjuring up what it was like to live in the past is a process that involves the entire body, a complex of kinesthetic sensations. This process is particularly enhanced through role-play, games, and imaginative enactments of all kinds. If the emotional/cognitive hook for a child is to imagine what it was like to live in the past, this process is greatly intensified when a child is allowed to move from a relatively passive physical position as a receptor of a story to the active position of being able to enact a role. This explains the universal popularity of dress-ups, recreated games, and work activities of the past as a ready means for a child's engagement.

Take for one example, the USS Constitution Museum in Boston—at the dockside of "Old Ironsides." Some of the more engaging features of a visit there involve a set of very simple elements. One may discover, for instance, that children served on the warship as "powder monkeys," boys whose job it was to carry gunpowder from the ship's magazine to the gun crews. To better understand this experience, not only can a child try on a child's period uniform, but he can also climb into a ship's hammock. (The Museum of Science and Industry in Chicago allows a similar experience through a snug simulated submarine berth.) It's easy for an adult with decades of life experience behind him to dismiss the value of such a simulation. But one must appreciate the absolute novelty of this experience for a child. Conjure up the pungent smell of pitch, the surround of a gently creaking, rolling ship, rank upon rank of canvas hammocks swaying in a low, oaken interior full of strange new things, all things that can be experienced in the actual vessel and providing an immersive feel for what this experience might have been like for a boy, and the totality constitutes a powerful diversion from the familiar everyday world. But what really makes this experience sing is that there are enough hammocks for an entire family. And the masterstroke is that the staff have ingeniously provided answers *on the ceiling* to the very questions children are most likely to ask, so parents can simply look up while lolling there.[14]

Imagination and Props

According to some studies, children, as early as preschool age, seem to prefer props and simulations that take on a higher level of authenticity.[15] In other words, children set a high bar for the play experience by desiring things that look and feel more "real." This is part of what explains why the activity at the Chicago History Museum, where one can become a giant hot dog with all the trimmings, is so delightful. Although the outward display of imaginative simulation becomes, perhaps, more literal-minded (and less outwardly creative) with age, some experts have suggested that, rather than growing out of our capacity and desire for imaginative play as we mature, what is happening instead is an ever more elaborate fantasy life that, on a continuum, be-

FIGURE 5.1. Among a number of successful role-play activities in *A Sailor's Life* For Me?, a particularly compelling example is this sail-furling challenge. Photograph by Greg Cooper. Courtesy USS Constitution Museum.

comes more internalized.[16] Notable exceptions are those instances such as reenactment, pageant, masquerade, or other such meticulous rituals wherein a person may play the past in the company of others who wish to play it with them. For an extreme example, if one looks at the Civil War reenactor as a fully fledged pilgrim in the realm of imaginative play, one need only look to the exhaustive pursuit of accuracy in every prop detail (the reason so-called hard core reenactors are also commonly known as "thread counters") to understand how compelling the impulse for verisimilitude may become.

Think about how alien an experience it is to a child to try to master writing with a quill pen, to scrape rawhide until it is soft, to grind seeds into flour, to keep a hoop rolling down a dirt lane, to feel the chafe of rough wool against the skin, or lie down in a colossal hot dog bun. Even the smells of barnyard animals or the soot of an iron forge provide an immediacy to the senses that is utterly foreign to so many of today's children raised in cities and suburbs. Both the work and play of the past are redolent with possibility. These experiences are not informational in common didactic terms, but they are transformational in the sense that they allow a child to access the past in the most profoundly personal ways—through the complete sensorium of the entire body—imagining for oneself how someone once experienced living in the past. For the child, the experience is the information.

FIGURE 5.2. In *Sensing Chicago*, the heightened realism of the giant hot dog bun and garnishes intensifies delight in the imaginative play activity. Courtesy Chicago History Museum.

Empathy as an Imaginative Act

At an exhibition called *Tales of the Territory* at the Minnesota History Center, three schoolgirls press the button at the door of a recreated Dakota bark lodge. The button activates a life-sized, ghostly image of a Dakota girl who is about the same age as the students. Maza Okiye Win describes her life in the Minnesota Territory of the 1850s. Her story shifts in mood as she describes the changes that have been imposed on her family since the Dakota made a treaty with the *wasicu*, the white men. In the end, she relates her sadness saying simply that she feels "something is missing." The girls have been watching with rapt attention and, although the story is a fairly long at six minutes or so, they have lingered to hear the whole thing. What's behind this prolonged engagement? What is it about this girl and her story that has captivated this group of visitors? It's what we might broadly call empathy, a function of the imagination and one of the most powerful and compelling points of engagement and learning in the spectrum of history-based experiences.

Empathy is relevant here in at least two critical respects. First, as I have suggested earlier, empathy is a product of the imagination. In other words, one must *imagine* what it would be like to be another person, since actually being another person is obviously a physical impossibility. Second, empathy is an essential component in our social nature, since the reciprocal sharing of ordinary human social interaction requires some degree of appreciation of another person's needs, desires, and motiva-

FIGURE 5.3. Audience research revealed this exhibit element featuring a young Dakota girl in a bark lodge to be the most memorable feature of *Tales of the Territory*. The girl's poignant story about the consequences of treaties elicits feelings of empathy in viewers. Courtesy Minnesota Historical Society, www.mnhs.org.

tions. In this way empathy is the moral glue that binds our normative social interactions, the essence of the principle contained most famously in the Golden Rule. It's the way we identify with the lives of others in the storytelling of fiction, film, biography, and the myriad vehicles of new media; empathy is what makes us actually *care* by engrossing us in the details and dilemmas of the lives of other persons.

Studies indicate that children with a deeper sense of empathy perform better in school, have more friends, and are more likely to be perceived as leaders by their peers. By contrast, a poverty of empathic development in children has been traced to situations commonly regarded as negative influences: indifferent or abusive parents and/or caregivers, prolonged exposure to callousness or cruelty, and/or sharp experiences of trauma. As Kathleen Cotton puts it in her review of the literature on childhood empathy, "Empathy is coming to be regarded by more and more educators as a key attribute of a successful learner."[17]

Empathy and Identity

Surely our sense of identity is the product of our own imaginations, but a check against a purely solipsistic sense of the self is the social sphere around us—the realm of other human beings, who remind us of other contingent realities, who reinforce our self-image, or who call our self-image into question. This relationship connects to the core idea behind *social comparison theory* as elaborated by Leon Festinger. Festinger posited that people have an innate drive to look to outside images (including other people) in order to evaluate one's own abilities and opinions. Significantly, our comparisons are more positive when we perceive a similarity of the Other to ourselves.[18] If empathy is commonly understood as our way of understanding others, its less heralded function, then, is as a mechanism for how we reflect on ourselves. After all, much of what we come to understand about ourselves comes into relief only through our attempt to understand others and our own place in relationship to them, including people of the past. This explains why, both in visitor conversations that we have recorded in the galleries of the Minnesota History Center and in exit interviews, we find a steady stream of spontaneous comparisons between personal experiences and the depicted experiences of the people of the past.[19]

The evidence leads me to the conclusion that the empathic response is a mental process for making sense of the world, a biological filter through which we interpret our experience of life and our place in the scheme of things. If we see this need as, in fact, innate to children, then we can perceive also the natural hook in it for generating engagement with the past in ways that are useful for history museum applications. Indeed, so natural is a child's desire to relate her experience to the experiences of others around her that we can readily see her behavior represented in the imaginative, imitative roleplay of make-believe.

How Empathy Is Used to Engage Children in Storytelling

In a short amount of time, normally well before the age of 24 months, children begin to sense an affinity with other children. Who among us hasn't noticed a preverbal infant staring in fascination when another infant comes into view? Or crying simply because another infant cries nearby? This affinity is expressed naturally enough, apparently confirming Festinger's observations, with comparisons of the self to those who are most similar—which is to say other children of about the same age, gender, and so on. This natural connection is a fact intuitively exploited by the purveyors of every medium of storytelling known to humankind. These comparisons that children make aren't merely cognitive but involve great rushes of feelings, and the more stories evoke these feelings, the more compelling they are. For a set of familiar examples, think of Disney films. The plot vehicles of many of them are strikingly similar: a happy child figure (Bambi, Dumbo, Pinocchio) is traumatically separated by circumstance from one or more parental figures. The precise parts of these films where this loss occurred (Bambi's mother killed by a hunter, Dumbo's mother imprisoned, Pinocchio led astray and wandering lost in the world) are the most terrifying (belying Disney's wholesome image), because they are expressive of a child's terror—the loss of the love and protection of the parents (or guardians). It was no doubt a part of Walt Disney's genius that he understood a child's impulse to empathize so completely with another child's losses and triumphs. Children powerfully *identify* with the distress of other children just as they also identify with seeing the exultations of other children's victories and play.

Empathy as a Child's Bridge to the People of the Past

The same child-to-child empathic principle goes for children and their experience of the past. The fantastic success of the Pleasant Company's American Girl line of dolls and accessories is but one recent example of connecting a child's capacity for empathy directly to a clever and compelling product and, by extension, that product's association with the historical past.

To further illustrate the point, at the Minnesota History Center we conducted a visitor research project on the previously mentioned *Open House* exhibition. As part of the research methodology, we recorded conversations between visitors as they passed through the exhibition. In one section of the exhibition visitors can gaze up a recreated attic stairway while a multimedia presentation, incorporating theatrical lighting, sound effects, and eyewitness narration, dramatizes the fire that ultimately destroyed the attic. The story of the fire is told by a woman who escaped the fire, and she recalls the distress she experienced when she discovered that her baby brother was left behind. She also describes how the repairs after the fire changed the roofline of the house, a fact that is underscored with "before and after" pictures at the attic door. We recorded this excerpted conversation between a mother, age 39, and her 8-year-old son at this part of the exhibition.

Boy: Mom, did they forget a baby upstairs?

Mom: Well . . . [static] somebody went after it I think she said.

Boy: Did it say that?

Mom: They said that the roofline . . . yeah.

Boy: Wow. Did they say that?

Mom: There must have been tons of research.

Boy: Mom, can you see if they say that?

Mom: Well, yeah. Come here, they show the picture of—see how it used to look?

Boy: Yeah . . .

Mom: The roof is kind of tall, you can tell there's a little room on the third floor and then here later in 1974 it said that three years after the fire the rooflines were much lower.

Boy: Mom?

Mom: Yeah.

Boy: Do they know how the house caught on fire?

Mom: It doesn't say.

Boy: Oh . . . So this could be . . . did they say that the baby survived . . . Mom?

Mom: Yeah.

In museum storytelling, indeed, in any form of storytelling, this anecdote illustrates a child's empathic identification through the exercise of the imagination, as a road to engagement with history. But the attic conversation is illustrative in other key respects. The parent emerges as a critical interlocutor, the interpreter who guides the child toward some kind of meaningful answer. Rolled up in this particular exchange we see the child's preoccupation with the fate of the baby interlaced with the mother's preoccupation with the evidentiary and more abstract exhibition content of changed rooflines. But in the strange interplay of these two individuals talking past each other, learning takes place nonetheless, the details emerge in the dialogue. Experienced museum educators call this intergenerational learning. But what has been less clearly understood is the degree to which empathy generates the conversational spark. The child must know what became of the baby.

Imaginative Role-play

When we think of role-play, we history people naturally go to the vaunted dress-up box. Of course, this is because dress ups work exceptionally well as engagement tools (other than the fact that they require a great deal of upkeep and restocking, and hats, sad to say, are always out of the question because of the danger of head lice). But there are many ways that museums can expand the repertoire of make-believe role-play activities that extend beyond try-ons.

At Mill City Museum, the Minnesota Historical Society exhibit designers created a number of role-play activities in order to engage kids with the processes of flour and lumber milling. In one such activity, the exhibit team recreated the Mississippi River landscape in downtown Minneapolis in miniature scale as a "stream table" activity. Water is streamed through the landscape, and children are allowed to experiment by diverting water down various canal networks through trying combinations of damming and opening and closing various sluice gates. At the end of these canals, the water drops through waterwheels of different designs representing the different hydropower technologies available to the millers of the nineteenth century. The object is, simply, to get wheels spinning, ideally, as many as one can manage at once—emulating the actual challenges milling engineers faced. A relatively open-ended activity, it can take twenty to thirty minutes to master completely, or one can get a sense of things in a few minutes. Besides being open-ended and playful in its variety, the simulation also has the advantage of incorporating real water with all of its pleasurable wetness. This process brings to mind a marvelous observation by Henry David Thoreau, who once noted in his journal:

> I have no doubt that a good farmer who, of course, loves his work, takes exactly the same kind of pleasure in draining a swamp, seeing the water flow out into his newly cut ditch, that a child does in its mud dikes and water wheels. Both alike like to play with the natural forces.[20]

Similarly, we created another stream table down which children can drive simulated logs to lumber mills, and, in another lab environment altogether, children can turn millstones to pulverize real wheat berries into flour or knead bread dough. Throughout the museum, these simulations are also made available to be experienced in actual form, at actual scale, through collections objects. One can even take in the real river landscape from an observation deck—the same view from on high. The end result is a pleasing set of multisensory simulacra that are reinforced several times in multiple exhibit media.

The key consideration here, as always, is to bring children into imaginative contact with what it was like in as close an approximation as is, if not possible, at least necessary to engross them. To feel the irresistible power of the flowing water as it rushes down to turning a wheel is infinitely more memorable, even in a miniature simulation where one must extrapolate by imagining, than it is to see it only from a distance or to read or listen to an abstract description. For a child the first step to understanding the concept of industrial scale waterpower is to personally feel the power of water and the delight this engenders. Not surprisingly, in a summative evaluation, the "Water Lab" rated as one of the most memorable features of the museum visit. But the empathic and affective mainspring of the activity is not found in the poignant compassion that the term *empathy* usually evokes but rather is captured completely in Thoreau's observation—a sense of satisfaction in a challenge undertaken and a job well done, mirrored in adult and child.

Serendipitous Discoveries and the Imagination

As I have suggested, among the more useful adaptations involving the imagination are forethought or anticipatory strategies; for example, imagining the future and possible alternative outcomes resulting from actions taken. Museums are well-loved places partly because they play to a human delight in serendipity; they are places where people may enact these types of exploratory strategies in a low-risk, and hence enjoyable, environment. Likewise, anticipation of the suspenseful promise of the discovery not yet made is, of course, an underpinning of even the most serious adult intellectual pursuits. The puzzling out of solutions to high-risk problems naturally engenders a great deal of anxiety, but in a low-risk, simulated context quite the opposite is true, and the activity can be gamelike and very enjoyable.

At the Boston Children's Museum in the late 1960s an exhibition called *Grandmother's Attic* demonstrated this principle. Designed around an attic environment that, presumably, would be familiar to a great number of children, the space was "seeded" with a great many curiosities from the past that children could discover by rummaging around in old trunks and suitcases. The walls were festooned with all sorts of hanging antiquities, like a miniature Soane's Museum. Virtually all the objects could be handled. There were vintage magazines and comic books, an eighty-year-old encyclopedia, anachronistic clothes to try on, historical toys, a military uniform, ink-stained school desks and primers, household tools, such as a primitive carpet sweeper, rug beaters, a chamber pot and washstand, a coffee grinder, and the like. There were sleds and a baby carriage. There was an immense globe tattooed with strange nations and colonies that no longer existed. There were several antique dollhouses loaded with tiny figures of people and pets and miniature bearskin rugs, pantries brimming with glistening food, and Victorian bric-a-brac. But, apart from the things in this "attic," what really defined it was the open-ended nature of the space as a discovery environment. A child was free to explore it to whatever degree was preferred. Of course, parents and staff were there explaining things, too, and, significantly, there were plenty of places for people to sit. On the whole, it was an inviting and pleasant space to hang out in as a family.

It was this example, along with many others, that would inspire the Minnesota Historical Society to create the *Open House* exhibition referenced earlier in this chapter. Although *Open House* departs in a number of critical respects from *Grandmother's Attic*, the exhibition still depends very much on the curiosity of visitors, children and adults alike, to reveal its embedded secrets, and very nearly everything is available to the touch. *Open House* also goes further than *Grandmother's Attic* in that all its stories are of real people, and many can be activated in the form of highly contextualized multimedia vignettes throughout the exhibition. By contextualized, I mean that triggered stories emerge from the places in the recreated home environment where the stories once happened: supper table stories are triggered around the supper table, a falling bed story causes the bed to fall, and so forth. Facsimiles of historical documents are also embedded throughout, records containing clues to the life stories of the families that passed through.

On a granular level, children are allowed to uncover fragments of the past and assemble them at will in the memory of their own experience in *Open House*, a process that is in itself enjoyable because the result of investigation rewards curiosity. But at a higher level, the activity also suggests a number of other implicit things: that the past is something anyone can discover, that there is history everywhere, that every family and every house has its stories and place in history, that history is composed of the many fragments people leave behind, and, a lot of the time, those fragments can still be found. At the highest level, children are able to play at being historians by engaging in an approximation of what historians do—immerse themselves in the lives of people and the circumstances of the past and use their imaginations to conceive of how it might have been. Part of the exhibition's appeal is voyeuristic, and the license to snoop and recreate the past through the imagination is certainly made possible by the low-risk setting of the museum.

Engaging the Imagination

For history museums that seek to engage the imaginations of children the following questions should always be at the forefront of their work:

- Are there stories here that children can readily relate to and identify with?

- Are the stories and their protagonists sufficiently dramatic or familiar to elicit an empathic response?

- Has care been taken to create environments for children that welcome playful activity, particularly in ways that allow them to experience and imagine with all the multisensory immediacy possible what the past was like?

- Is the environment designed to be used in sufficiently open-ended ways, accommodating a variety of flights of fancy?

- Are there experiences that involve suspenseful discovery, rewarding curiosity with delightful surprises?

- Have you attended to the social exchanges that are likely to occur between children and adults, and is the environment a comfortable one for facilitating these exchanges?

If these considerations are given full expression and articulation during an exhibit development process, museums can offer experiences that will afford the kind of imaginative flights that make the experience rewarding and fun for the most children.

NOTES

1. Freeman Tilden, *Interpreting Our Heritage* (Chapel Hill: University of North Carolina Press, 1957).
2. A 2008 report on the competitive landscape of museums, zoos, and botanical gardens places history museums dead last with average annual visitation at around 15,000. Richard K. Miller & Associates, *The 2008 Travel & Tourism Market Research Handbook,* Part 1, Chap. 4, "Tourism in Metropolitan Cities," 4.7 Museums (Rockville, MD: Research and Markets, 2007).
3. Paul L. Harris, *The Work of the Imagination* (Malden, MA: Blackwell Publishing, 2000), 1–7.
4. Dorothy G. Singer and Jerome L. Singer, *The House of Make-Believe: Children's Play and the Developing Imagination* (Cambridge, MA: Harvard University Press, 1990), 27. In this instance, the Singers cite psychologist David Rapaport.
5. Kieran Egan, *Teaching and Learning Outside the Box: Inspiring Imagination Across the Curriculum* (New York: Teachers College Press, 2007), 7–8.
6. Paul L. Harris, *The Work of the Imagination* (Malden, MA: Blackwell Publishing, 2000), ix–xii.
7. William James, *The Principles of Psychology* (Cambridge, MA: Harvard University Press, 1981), 462.

8. John Dewey, "The Pattern of Inquiry," in *Logic: The Theory of Inquiry*, (New York: H. Holt and Co., 1938), 105–22.

9. Daniel L. Schacter, *Searching for Memory: The Brain, the Mind and the Past* (New York, NY: Basic Books, 1996), 17.

10. Susan Gaidos, "Thanks for the Future Memories," *Science News*, June 21, 2008.

11. Gaidos, "Future Memories," 2008.

12. George E. Hein and Mary Alexander, *Museums: Places of Learning* (Washington, DC: American Association of Museums Education Committee, 1998).

13. Rosalind Charlesworth, with contributions by Dilek Buchholz, *Understanding Child Development* (Albany, NY: Delmar, 2003), 79–80.

14. Lynn D. Dierking et al., "Laughing and Learning Together: Family Learning Research Becomes Practice at the USS Constitution Museum," *History News* (Summer 2006).

15. Vonnie C. McLoyd, "The Effects of the Structure of Play Objects on the Pretend Play of Low Income Preschool Children," *Child Development* 54 (1983): 626–35.

16. Singer and Singer, *House of Make-Believe*, 251–64.

17. Kathleen Cotton, *Developing Empathy in Children and Youth*, School Improvement Research Series, Northwest Regional Educational Laboratory, 16, www.nwrel.org/scpd/sirs/7/cu13.html (accessed July 11, 2009). Cotton's review of current research on childhood empathy provides some great primary research sources for anyone interested in this subject.

18. Leon Festinger, "A Theory of Social Comparison Processes," *Human Relations* 7, no. 2 (1954): 117–40. Festinger was particularly concerned with upward and downward social comparisons, but it seems to me that all sorts of comparisons are evident in the processes of how people identify with others, and studies at the Minnesota Historical Society have captured this impulse as a common reference point in visitor conversations.

19. Daniel Spock, "A Practical Guide to Personal Connectivity," *History News* Autumn (2008). In this article I cite a number of the relevant visitor studies conducted at the Minnesota History Center since 1993.

20. Henry David Thoreau, *The Writings of Henry David Thoreau*, edited by Bradford Torrey (Boston: Houghton Mifflin and Company, 1906), 170.

CHAPTER 6

Playing with the Past

Jon-Paul C. Dyson

Play is vital to the work of all museums, especially those that hope to reach children. Play, after all, is what kids like best, and they spend a vast amount of their time playing by themselves and with others. Philosophers, scholars, and parents have long been aware of this, and they have come to realize that it is during play that children learn best, relate to others best, and have the most fun. A museum that does not allow, or even encourage, play will not attract children or educate them very well. Today, as children drive more and more of the decisions that family audiences make about where to go and what to do, a museum that does not appeal to children will rapidly lose audiences of all ages.

Museums have institutional and educational reasons for emphasizing play in their exhibitions. When Americans make decisions about what to do in their free time they increasingly pursue playful activities. For history museums, play should have a special place as a key tool of the historian. History is an exercise of imagination and empathy, and a good historian invariably plays with the past. Public history uses pageantry, pretend, and role-play. If history museums hope to continue to remind their audiences of the past, educate them about its workings, and inspire them with its messages, they must embrace play, especially in exhibitions geared toward children. Furthermore, children increasingly drive the decisions families make about what to do for entertainment, so if the experience is not playful and fun children will not want to take part. History museums, which have suffered severe drops in attendance over the last few decades, have been particularly slow to accept this reality and plan accordingly.

Yet it is not only institutional attendance but also commitment to mission and education that should drive a commitment to play in exhibitions for children. Developmental psychologists such as Lev Vygotsky have explained how important play is for "scaffolding" learning, allowing children to advance from one stage of knowledge to another.[1] That play is an effective tool for learning is true in the abstract, but it is especially true in the case of museums, where free-choice learning is encouraged.[2] In the case of a voluntary activity such as visiting a museum, there is no substitute for play as the learning medium, especially when appealing to children. Although children do not play in order to learn, there is no doubt that they learn when they play. Three hundred years ago, John Locke warned that when educating children, "none of the things they are to learn, should ever be made a burthen to them," but instead should promote learning through play.[3]

There also is a tremendous opportunity for play to be not only the means of interpretation but also the subject of interpretation. People like to learn about things that have meaning to them, and for children (and many adults) little has more meaning than play. Anyone who has visited a living history site with a child recognizes this fact; whereas most children's eyes glaze over when visiting the printmaking shop or the land surveyor's office, children eagerly play with the "old-fashioned" toys set out for them on the town green: the stilts, battledore and shuttlecocks, and hoop and stick. Children, like all people, are interested in learning about things they can relate to, so they are eager to learn about play of ages past. Play is the link that ties this generation of children to their forebearers. Luckily not only children but also historians have taken an increasing interest in learning about past play of children and adults.[4] How, where, when, why, and with whom we played are important subjects of historical inquiry today and present museums the opportunity to build history exhibitons that not only use play but also are about play.

The Meanings of Play

What is play? This question is not easily answered, because almost every scholar who studies the subject proposes a slightly different set of criteria to define and identify play. Play is one of those things that's more easily known than defined; we know it when we see it, and when we start looking we see it in many places. Indeed, the historian Johan Huizinga, in his seminal work on play, *Homo Ludens: A Study of the Play Element in Culture*, argued that the very basis of civilization and culture lies in play: "culture arises in the form of play . . . it is played from the very beginning."[5] Play scholar Brian Sutton-Smith, after more than a half-century of work on the subject, concluded that play is best understood not through definiteness but through an exploration of its ambiguities, its many faces. As he noted in *The Ambiguity of Play*, "We all play occasionally, and we all know what playing feels like. But when it comes to making theoretical statements about what play is, we fall into silliness. There is little agreement among us, and much ambiguity."[6] In short, most scholars and educators have found that play is more easily celebrated than defined.

And yet despite play's resistance to easy definition, one can follow Huizinga and other play scholars and postulate certain functional characteristics of play that help highlight the role of play in history museums. First, play is voluntary. As Huizinga notes, "It is never a task. It is done at leisure, during 'free time.'"[7] No one can ever be made to play. Mark Twain trenchantly observed in *Tom Sawyer*, "Work consists of whatever a body is OBLIGED to do, and . . . play consists of whatever a body is not obliged to do."[8] To play, a person must willingly agree to do so. Second, play is pleasurable; it is fun. Where there is no joy, no laughter, no smiling, then there is probably no play. Huizinga asserts that "it is precisely this fun-element that characterizes the essence of play."[9]   Third, play is its own end, and "the purposes it serves are external to immediate material interests or the individual satisfaction of biological needs."[10] This does not mean that players do not benefit from playing, but benefit is not the reason they participate in it. Children playing with blocks may be learning valuable geometrical, architectural, or social skills in the process, but that is not why they are playing. They are playing for the sake of playing with blocks. Fourth, play invites participants into a realm of time and space apart from the demands and concerns of the everyday world; as Huizinga notes, players enter into a "magic circle" in which the normal rules of time and space of life do not hold.[11] Finally, when players are in this magic circle, they abide by rules that all have agreed to, either implicitly or explicitly. When these rules are broken, or any of the other conditions of play are not met, then it is doubtful that people are still playing. Further, it is an easy leap to see that playing by rules is akin to thinking like a historian, imagining events and people in the past and doing so within the limits of historical circumstances.

In diagnosing the applicability of play to creating history exhibits for children, one should note that the characteristics of play are similar to those that characterize a good museum experience. For example, there are parallels between the tenets that Judy Rand lays out in her "Visitors' Bill of Rights" and the characteristics of good play. She asserts that visitors want to have choice and control—that they volunteer to participate, they are not coerced into doing so. Likewise visitors have the right to enjoyment, to have fun. And she notes that museums should give

guests the opportunity to enter into activities that take them away from the everyday world and revitalize them: "When visitors are focused, fully engaged, and enjoying themselves, time stands still and they feel refreshed."[12] In other words, let them play!

Although scholars have had trouble agreeing on a definition of play, they have had no problem naming the different types of play they see, and as a result they can identify key categories of the most common forms of play. This is not an exhaustive taxonomy of play. Instead these categories are common types of play that are found everywhere and that can help define what types of play work best in history exhibitions for children. *Pretend play*, also called *pretense play* or *role-play*, leads the list. Any adult who has watched children climb walls like Spider Man or cook a pretend dinner for two knows the power of their imagination when they are engaged in pretend play. Children at a history museum who are busy "working" in a pretend kitchen from the nineteenth century are in fact engaged in pretend play. Whereas pretend play is possibly unique to humans,[13] another type of play, *object play*, is found in many species. Cats bat balls, and so do children. Chimps throw things just as kids do. Children's natural interest in play with things explains why they so readily pick up objects, especially toys that many historical sites leave out, and begin fooling with them. Psychologists often differentiate between object exploration and object play, and the distinction is useful for history museums. When exploring, children want to know, What does this object do? When they are playing, they are more interested in learning, What can I do with this object?[14] This difference is crucial, because object play demands activity, something that history museums do not always encourage in children. Merely learning what tasks artifacts were used for is not engaging children in object play, but letting children actually do something with historical objects can be play.

In general, with these and other types of play, children are active. *Constructive play*, the use of objects to build, is one particularly active type of play, and history museums and historical sites have found ways for children to engage in this sort of play, often by giving children raw materials to make things.[15] This can be done through low-tech craft stations or architectural building areas using blocks, but it also can be done on computers as kids engage in virtual construction. *Physical play*, another type of active play, comes in many forms, including what might be called *locomotor play* (running, chasing, twirling, jumping) and rough-and-tumble play.[16] These are important forms of play for children, but not ones often encouraged in indoor history museums—although living history museums have had great success engaging children in physical play through the use of historic games, sports, and dances. *Competitive play* is another type of play that often gives birth to *game play*, in which players compete according to formal rules (although some games, such as games of chance, are not primarily about competition). Museums can invoke this sort of play by creating new games that teach historical content or by giving children a chance to play old games from the time period they are exploring.[17] *Collecting play* lacks the hard-and-fast rules of game play, but the spirit of the collector is a playful (and often competitive) one that children indulge in readily and that they can easily relate to in the context of museums, many of which are built from collections. *Language play*, *parent-child play*, *outdoor play*, and *technology play* are some, although not all, of the other categories of play that scholars have identified to describe children's play. Applying these various ways of playing to history exhibitions is relatively straightforward and gives history museums ample opportunities to devise highly interactive experiences.

Play changes as children age. Indeed, some of the most famous play research, from that done by the pioneering child psychologist G. Stanley Hall to the mid-century contributions of Jean Piaget and Erik Erikson to the tidal wave of recent research papers being churned out today by developmental psychologists, has concentrated on the developmental aspect of play. The literature on this subject, too vast to be adequately summarized, reveals that children first learn locomotor and object play, begin simple pretend play at about a year-and-a-half, and attain increasingly more complex levels of constructive, imaginative, and game play as they get older. Whom children play with (parents, peers, siblings) also changes over time, and the gender of the child has a major effect on how he or she plays. As noted elsewhere in this book, history museums benefit from knowing how children develop over time, and the fact that play differs so dramatically across the developmental spectrum means that history museums, when creating play-based activities, must define very clearly who the intended audience is for their exhibits, interactives, and environments.[18] If they do so, history museums can successfully create play-based exhibitions for children that will enhance their institutional, educational, and interpretive goals.

Play in the History Museum

History museums are already familiar with play, even if they do not know it, because most history museums began in play, and the history museum field has been periodically reenergized by the play impulse. Other elements, such as patriotism, civic pride, and education, have had a role, but most of the major history museums in the country were founded from a play impulse, usually as it was manifested in the collecting interests of the founder. Winterthur (founded by Henry Francis du Pont), the Shelburne Museum (Electra Havemeyer Webb), Mercer and Fonthill Museums (Henry Chapman Mercer), Greenfield Village (Henry Ford), Williamsburg (John D. Rockefeller), Genesee Country Village and Museum (John L. Wehle), and Strong National Museum of Play (Margaret Woodbury Strong) are all examples of museums that came into being because their founders loved to play. As Michael Kammen noted in his analysis of the role of the founders, these museums resulted from "the institutionalization of their avocations."[19] Collecting is a form of play that children and adults readily engage in and easily understand, and without it there would be few museums.[20]

If collecting is the form of play that has led to the creation of many history museums, the subsequent evolution of the field of public history suggests that role-playing has been the form of play that has perhaps most energized history museums. In fact, the use of role-play has a long history as a tool for giving expression to people of the past. The ancient historian Polybius, for example, noted that the Romans would make a mask of an important civic leader when he died,

> fashioned with extraordinary fidelity both in its modeling and its complexion to represent the features of the dead man. On occasions when public sacrifices are offered, these masks are displayed and decorated with great care. And when any distinguished member of the family dies, the masks are taken to the funeral, and are there worn by men who are considered to bear the closest resemblance to the original, both in height and in their general appearance and bearing. . . . It would be hard to imagine a more impressive scene for a young man who aspires to win fame and to practice virtue.[21]

In the early twentieth century, historical pageants became extremely important; one commentator of the time noted that these pageants were important as a form of "public play."[22] These forms of public play became institutionalized in the succeeding decades in living history museums that provided a backdrop for performers to act out the roles of historical characters, famous and obscure. Starting with the Essex Institute's John Ward House in Salem, Massachusetts, in 1909 and reaching its full bloom with Colonial Williamsburg in the 1930s, various historical sites began dressing guides in period costumes. Inspired by the development of the new social history, the historic farms movement, and historical archaeology in the 1960s and 1970s, some sites, led by Plimoth Plantation, adopted an even more radical form of playing the past, a first-person approach in which interpreters became historic characters and stayed in character throughout their interaction with visitors.[23] Still, despite this long-standing commitment to role-playing, there has always been a flaw in this sort of reenactment: although some children may dress up in costumes and begin to become players on the stage (Colonial Williamsburg, for example, rents out costumes), most visitors remain passive spectators. Play, by its very nature, is active, and if visitors are mere witnesses and not participants, they are not playing.

History museums must embrace the next stage in their playful evolution if they are to reach children. They must move from being places that were created out of the collecting play of the founder (the collection-based museum) or have harnessed the role-play of their employees (the living history museum) into institutions that encourage the play of their guests, especially children. This new model of playful museum has exhibitions that attract children, because it invites them to learn and experience through play. Playful components in such new museums are not merely add-ons, thrown in like the discovery rooms that some institutions have added. Instead, play is woven into every fabric of the exhibition experience. When exhibit designers want to make an interpretive point, they think first not of a label but of a play-based interactive. In doing so, they can develop guests' understanding of almost any historical subject, including the skill to think like a historian.

Training in Historical Thinking through Play

To understand how best to develop exhibitions that invite young children to engage history through play, one can begin by asking, What are the skills of a historian? Those who answer this question often focus on the highest-order skills, such as the ability of the historian to sift evidence, to weigh the differing arguments of competing theories, and to know the historiography of his or her field. But these come after children have mastered three key skills necessary to think historically: imagining, storytelling, and sequencing. Play provides the best means for children to learn how to do these.

Imagining is the first task of historians. They must empathize and imagine in order to visualize what people of another time were like and to enter into their lives, their feelings, their wants, their motivations, and their concerns. As John B. Poster notes,

> A sense of physical time is a necessary but not sufficient ingredient of a sense of the past. What is lacking might be termed historicality—a sense of existing in the past as well as the present, a feeling of being in history rather than standing apart from it.[24]

It is easy to forget that the ability to place oneself in another's shoes is the most basic of all historical skills, even more important than a sense of chronology. It also is a basic human skill, one that separates humans from the animals and one that develops in children from ages 18 months to 6 years but especially blossoms at around 3 years of age. Psychologists term this ability to recognize that other people think and feel and to enter into those thoughts and feelings *theory of mind*, and children practice it and master it through play, specifically pretend play.[25]

Jean Piaget postulated three phases of children's play development.[26] The first two relate to pretend play. In the earliest phase, the *sensorimotor stage*, the infant learns the properties of things, touches them, tastes them, drops them, and takes pleasure (even if no one else does) in hearing them crash (over and over and over again). But in the second stage, the *preoperational stage*, starting at about 1½ to 2 years, the child begins to engage in symbolic play, what is also called make-believe, fantasy, or pretend play. Museums are well suited to provide the settings, props, and costumes that allow children to engage in this play. Giving children the opportunity to role-play in this manner helps them develop a theory of mind that enables them to imagine other people's lives. At the Strong National Museum of Play, for example, a child experiences life in a nineteenth-century house in *One History Place*; at Old Sturbridge Village's *Kidstory* exhibition the child plays the role of a farmer or shopkeeper; and at Old Mystic Seaport kids explore three nautical playscapes: sailing ship, lobster boat, and fishing dragger. In these spaces the child, by role-playing, imagines what it would be like to be someone else of a different time or place and in the process sharpens the vital historical skills of imagination and empathy.

To facilitate this sort of make-believe play, museums can create dynamic, imaginative settings and provide objects that kids can use for pretense, for pretend play. These environments invite children to play and encourage them to don costumes and use toys as tools to imagine themselves in another century, crossing the prairie, or mining for gold. These settings need not be complex or expensive. Large museums might create elaborate stage sets for children to role-play in, but even the smallest museum can create a setting that invites kids to come and pretend and provide props for them to use to this end. As they play in these exhibits, children learn the first skill of a historian—the ability to imagine oneself as someone else, perhaps someone of another time and place.

Storytelling is the second vital historical skill that young children develop through play, and environments that encourage pretend play also encourage storytelling. Kids tell stories as they play; indeed, storytelling is a form of play. As the keen educational observer Vivian Gussin Paley notes, "Storytelling is play put into narrative form."[27] Stories are the basis of historical narrative, and children must acquire the ability to understand them and tell them before they can become historians. This is why the National Standards for History emphasize the use of stories and literature in teaching young children about the past. Stories help kids learn the basic organization of narratives—that a story has a beginning, a middle, and an end. Stories help kids see that people face challenges and must overcome them. Stories help kids begin to comprehend the vastness of historical time—"Once upon a time, long, long ago" is different from "yesterday," "today," or "tomorrow." Kids' temporal imprecision sometimes bothers historians, but through play they begin to learn that all stories, including historical narratives, have a beginning, a middle, and an end. Through stories kids begin to sort out the rhythms of time.

Children love stories, and they also love reenacting what they hear. This behavior is another reason why museum settings for role-play provide such an important opportunity for guests to learn historical skills. When role-playing, kids reenact the stories they have heard or the ones they know, and they retell them through their play. For example, when kids play with one of the train role-playing areas at Strong National Museum of Play they become the storytellers, giving stories a beginning ("Let's get our ticket for a train ride"), a middle ("Quick, get on the train. We're going across country"), and an end ("Hurray we're here—we've reached California"). Kids also love the opportunity to perform, and so museums can sharpen their storytelling skills by providing places for them to perform their stories for others. Simple theatrical stages, for instance, allow guests to act out stories they have in their minds, whether they are ones they brought with them or ones they picked up while at the museum. Most museums and historical sites are interested in giving children the opportunity to hear new stories, but they should be thinking much more seriously about how they can give children the opportunity to act out those stories through play. That is why Old Sturbridge Village's *Kidstory* exhibition is so effective: it gives visitors the opportunity to play out the stories they have witnessed taking place in nineteenth-century Massachusetts during their visit. They are far more likely to understand and to remember what it means to be a farmer, a homemaker, or a shopkeeper by being given the opportunity to play at what they have seen than if they had had no opportunity to reenact what they witnessed.

Play-based exhibits also can help kids learn a third vital historical skill, sequencing historical time. In Strong National Museum of Play's exhibition *Making Radio Waves*, for example, kids get to compare a radio studio from long ago with a modern version as they perform their own dramas and make sound effects using modern high-tech approaches and low-tech methods from the golden age of radio. Likewise, in Strong's *DanceLab*, kids catch the rhythm of time through changes in the music that plays as they dance, from the syncopated rhythms of the Charleston to the driving beat of a modern hip-hop dance number. Intergenerational conversations among kids, parents, and grandparents inevitably arise about differences in their dance, music, and life experiences. The

Concord Museum in the exhibition *A Main Street Point of View* used a tiered system of pictures that guests could pull out to show the same site through time. There are any number of ways museums can encourage children to compare old with new, old with older, new with newer, or then with now; if it is playful and captures kids' attention and allows them to begin to understand chronology and sequencing better, then the museum has gone a long way toward building kids' historical skills.

Imagining, storytelling, and sequencing are only three ways in which museums can sharpen young children's historical skills through play. Whatever the approach, however, there is always one common denominator—play. Children need to play in order to learn in a museum; through play, a museum can begin training them in the fundamentals of history. Likewise, as museum professionals come to accept and anticipate play as a positive and valued behavior in exhibitions, we can become adept at recognizing different types of play and developing future projects that encourage meaningful play.

Applying Play in the History Museum

Museums not only must use play to help kids to learn to think historically, they also can and should use play to broach historical topics in an accessible and appealing way. This sometimes means that the history of play itself is worth exploring in exhibitions. Since the 1960s, the new social history, the new cultural history, leisure studies, and sport history have revolutionized our understanding of how everyday Americans lived, thought, and played. As Roy Rosenzweig noted in his study of Worcester, Massachusetts, *Eight Hours for What We Will: Workers and Leisure in an Industrial City*, there had been "a general scholarly reluctance to take up seemingly 'nonserious' subjects such as play," but that changed as historians began to understand the crucial role play and leisure have had in American life.[28] Exhibitions such as National Baseball Hall of Fame and Museum's *Baseball as America* and the Berkshire Museum's *Kid Stuff: Great Stuff from our Childhood* demonstrate that Americans' play itself can be a powerful subject of exhibitions, engaging audiences, sparking conversations, and attracting crowds. Yet history museums need not reserve play for exhibitions about the history of play. Instead, the ability to play in the exhibition should be a feature of every exhibit, regardless of whether play is the subject. Play is applicable to almost any subject matter, and with almost any exhibit topic, one can incorporate playful components that will help kids to explore

FIGURE 6.2. Role-play helps children in the exhibition, *Kidstory*, imagine life in the past. Photograph by Ericka Sidor. Courtesy Old Sturbridge Village, Sturbridge, MA.

the subject with greater depth, power, and enjoyment than they would in more traditional settings. Given the many different types of play, one can identify many practical applications of play in history exhibitions.

As has already been noted, exhibit designers can easily incorporate pretend play, or role-play, into their exhibitions. For role-play to work, children need a setting that sparks their imagination, clothes or props that allow them to assume a role, and an activity that invites them to play. The setting can be just about any place. An exhibition on Indiana history at The Children's Museum of Indianapolis featured a log cabin; the Lied Children's Museum in Las Vegas opened a mining area; the *Kidstory* exhibition at Old Sturbridge Village has a nineteenth-century farm, home, and general store. These are all settings that spark kids' imaginations, not only because their backdrops inspire imaginative play but also because the designers of such areas carefully stocked them with clothes and props that encourage and facilitate the play. These props need not be many, because children require only an apron and some pots and pans to imagine themselves tending the hearth in a nineteenth-century kitchen, for example.

Kids will role-play only if they can do some activity, whether cooking a pretend meal, pretending to drive a train, or setting sail on a boat. The best activities are those that encourage kids to interact with one another and with the adults who come with them. The beauty of these environments is that they are easy enough to create for museums and historical societies of any size. The North Dakota Heritage Center, for example, made a horse from a barrel with four wooden legs, a rope tail, and a simple wooden head and placed it in front of a large mirror. Kids could not resist climbing aboard and imagining themselves riding as the horse transported them, if not physically at least imaginatively, through their play. It is a short step for children imagining themselves in a different era to begin noting contrasts and continuities between their own era and past times. Children's interest in pretend play peaks around ages 4 to 6, but it never truly disappears, as adults' continued enthusiasm for historical reenactments makes evident.

Physical, or locomotor, play provides history museums the opportunity to engage children in the past through the active use of their bodies. Recent historical research into the history of the senses in America has highlighted historians' attempts to capture more fully the many ways we experience the world, and physical play gives children the opportunity to experience the past actively.[29] Physical play is always popular with children. Kids love to move, and museums that find creative ways to engage this play in service of their mission are very successful. A museum devoted to nineteenth-century sailing, for example, is missing a golden opportunity to engage kids and let them really feel what it was like to be a sailor if it doesn't give them the opportunity to climb the rigging; the Chicago Children's Museum created a giant rope structure up the mast of a ship that kids climb. The Minnesota History Center similarly created a replica grain elevator that children could climb up, clamber through, and slide down. Physical movement need not be over wide spaces. The Minnesota History Center demonstrated the concept of horsepower by letting kids try to move the amount of weight a horse could move, and the National Museum of American History invited people to balance on a high-wheeled bike.

When children play with objects, especially when they make things through construction play using building materials, arts and crafts, or even computers, they gain a more concrete feel for the physical fabric of the past. One can always modify this type of constructive play to fit a particular historical setting or subject as well. Old Sturbridge Village, for example, carved foam blocks in the shapes of stones with which kids could build "stone" walls. Although the blocks were lighter than real stones, they presented the same challenge that New England farmers faced of how to stack irregularly shaped stones into neat walls. The Shaker Museum and Library in Old Chatham, New York, invited guests to try activities inspired by the Shakers' legendary commitment to craftsmanship: guests could fill sachets or weave the seat of a cane chair. The National Museum of American History's *Hands On History Room* had a spinning wheel for guests to use and try to spin wool. This form of constructive play can be equally applied to activities of the industrial revolution and those of preindustrial craftsmanship. Strong National Museum of Play has an assembly line where guests can construct a toy car while learning about such concepts as interchangeable parts, mass production, and speedup (which happens when a guest turning the crank on the conveyor increases the speed of the assembly line). Arts and crafts are opportunities for personal expression and can be easily adjusted to interpret almost any subject or historical time period as long as exhibit designers develop good places for guests to use them.

Living history museums commonly supply old-fashioned toys for kids to play with, but often modern toys can be used to connect children to the historical content being explored in the exhibition. For example, any exhibition about the history of transportation can offer model trains, boats, or cars for kids to play with as a means to gain a better understanding of the historical processes at work in moving people and goods. An exhibition on railroad history might have a Brio-style train table, as Strong does, for children to play with as they imagine trains transporting goods and people across country. Rochester Museum and Science Center has a model of the Erie Canal that demonstrates the functioning of the lock system. Small history museums can easily adapt many of these ideas. For example, a local history museum might put a map on the floor or on a table and invite kids to drive from place to place in town (whether they're driving toy buggies or toy cars). Many modern toys can be adapted for use in a way that encourages object play.

Game play can also be easily adopted or adapted to make historical points. Quiz games, for example, work well in many settings. Strong National Museum of Play created a game show on food history called "Family Food" that invited participants to compete against one another as they tried to answer questions about the history of food. Guests understand how to play game shows, so they easily grasped how to play this one. The USS Constitution Museum's exhibition *A Sailor's Life for Me?*, showed how sailors were selected for service on a ship by creating a simple quiz game using images on laminated cards that determined whether a sailor would be a good recruit or not—guests found fascinating such criteria as how many fingers a potential recruit had!

Serious subjects can be approached as playfully—and therefore as effectively—as light ones. The Children's Museum of Indianapolis created a variation of the popular "Oregon Trail" computer game, in which visitors navigated through a series of challenges to reach their destination, which was, in this case, not the West Coast but Indiana. For its exhibition *Say Ahh: Examining America's Health,* Strong modified the popular labyrinth game (in which players roll a ball bearing through a maze avoiding holes along the way) to show the many threats that nineteenth-century Americans faced to their life expectancy. Each hole in the game represented a potential life-threatening event, whether it was a farming accident or a cholera epidemic. The immense popularity of computer games such as Civilization and SimCity proves that subject matter is no barrier to gaming simulation; after all, who would have thought urban planning could so engage players? There are many possible games out there for museums to emulate, modify, or adapt to make interpretive points, just as there is no shortage of types of play for museums to use in their exhibitions. Exhibit designers should seek to use games that guests understand already or can pick up easily. Plenty of such games exist, and designers interested in creating exhibitions that use these games need only be creative, watch children play, and build exhibits that allow kids to play while they learn. Whether through game play, object play, physical play, construction play, or role-play, there are many ways that museums can integrate play into their history exhibitions for children.

Conclusion: The Play's the Thing

Museums begin in play, and when they stop embracing play they begin to die. This statement may sound alarmist, but it reflects the reality of museums' origins, mission, and purpose. Museums, including history museums, are almost always born out of a spirit of play, whether through a passion for collecting or out of a desire to imagine and to role-play the past. Museums are sustained by play and maintain their relevance to audiences by being playful institutions. Museums are not necessary; they are voluntary. People go to them because they want to, and the voluntary nature of play is one of its key attributes. Therefore, if museums want to have maximum appeal, they must be playful places.

History museums are facing a crisis of relevance. No longer do Americans automatically assume that history is important to constructing and maintaining their personal or civic identities. No longer are most people interested in learning from exhibitions that use the old means of dispensing information through ponderous labels and static graphics. Many history museums struggle to be both relevant and appealing, and as long as they remain unappealing they will never become relevant.

Declining attendance at most history museums points to a need for something different. A number of years ago, some museums began to reorient the way they thought of the people who came through their doors. They stopped calling them "visitors" and began calling them "guests." This was not merely a semantic change but reflected a new commitment to giving visitors experiences of the highest possible quality, just as a host in a home seeks to attend to his or her guests' needs. Perhaps today administrators of history museums need to think of the people who attend their institutions in a new way. Perhaps the people who walk through the doors of history museums, especially the children, are neither simply "visitors" nor "guests"—perhaps they are "players." When history museums invite audiences in to be players they will become engaging and attractive institutions for promoting historical learning. It is time to use play times to explore past times.

NOTES

1. Lev Vygotsky, "Play and its Role in the Mental Development of the Child," in M. Cole, ed. *Soviet Developmental Psychology* (White Plains, NY: M. E. Sharpe, 1977), 76–99 (reprint of article originally published in 1934).
2. On free-choice learning, see John H. Falk and Lynn D. Dierking, *Learning from Museums: Visitor Experiences and the Making of Meaning* (Walnut Creek, CA: AltaMira Press, 2000).
3. John Locke, *Some Thoughts Concerning Education* (1693), Section 73.1.
4. Recent historical scholarship about children's play includes Howard Chudacoff, *Children at Play: An American History* (New York: New York University Press, 2007); Steven Mintz, *Huck's Raft: A History of American Childhood* (Cambridge, MA: Harvard University Press, 2004); and Pamela Riney-Kehrberg, *Childhood on the Farm: Work, Play, and Coming of Age in the Midwest* (Lawrence: University Press of Kansas, 2005).
5. Johan Huizinga, *Homo Ludens: A Study of the Play Element in Culture* (Boston, MA: Beacon Press, 1970 [1950]), 46.
6. Brian Sutton-Smith, *The Ambiguity of Play* (Cambridge, MA: Harvard University Press, 1997), 1.
7. Huizinga, *Homo Ludens*, 8.
8. Mark Twain, *The Adventures of Tom Sawyer* (Hartford, CT: American Publishing Company, 1895, c. 1876), 36.
9. Huizinga, *Homo Ludens*, 3.
10. Huizinga, *Homo Ludens*, 9.
11. Huizinga, *Homo Ludens*, 10.
12. Judy Rand, "The 227-Mile Museum, or A Visitors' Bill of Rights," *Curator: The Museum Journal* 44, no. 1 (2001), 13.

13. For comparative discussions about pretense in humans and possible pretense in animals, see Robert W. Mitchell, "Pretense in Animals: The Continuing Relevance of Children's Pretense," in *Play and Development: Evolutionary, Sociocultural, and Functional Perspectives*, ed. Artin Goncu and Suzanne Gaskins (Mahwah, NJ: Lawrence Erlbaum Associates, 2007), 51–75; and Thomas Power, *Play and Exploration in Children and Animals* (Mahwah, NJ: Lawrence Erlbaum Associates, 2000), 215–94.

14. Power, *Play and Exploration*, 19–22.

15. For a discussion of constructive play, see George Forman, "Constructive Play," in *Play from Birth to Twelve Years: Contexts, Perspectives, and Meanings*, ed. Doris Bergen and Doris Fromberg (New York: Routledge, 2006), 103–10.

16. On physical play, see especially the work of Anthony Pellegrini, such as Anthony D. Pellegrini and Peter K. Smith, "Physical Activity Play: The Nature and Function of a Neglected Aspect of Play," *Child Development* 69 (1998), 577–98.

17. The study of competition (agonistic play) was at the heart of Huizinga's *Homo Ludens*, and Roger Caillois in his *Man, Play and Games* sought to correct and expand on Huizinga's concentration on competitive games. Roger Caillois, *Man, Play and Games* (London: Thames and Hudson, 1962).

18. For accessible overviews of key issues surrounding play development in children, see the following chapters in Bergen and Fromberg, *Play from Birth to Twelve Years*: Barbara P. Garner and Doris Bergen, "Play Development from Birth to Age Four," 3–12; James E. Johnson, "Play Development from Ages Four to Eight," 13–21; and M. Lee Manning, "Play Development from Ages Eight to Twelve," 21–30.

19. Michael Kammen, *Mystic Chords of Memory: The Transformation of Tradition in American Culture* (New York: Knopf, 1991), 320.

20. On the collecting impulse as play, see Paola de Sanctis Ricciardone, "Collecting as a Form of Play," in *Play: An Interdisciplinary Synthesis, Play & Culture Studies* 6, ed. F. F. McMahon, Donald E. Lytle, and Brian Sutton-Smith (Lanham, MD: University Press of America, 2005), 279–290.

21. Polybius, *The Rise of the Roman Empire*, translated by Ian Scott-Kilvert (New York: Penguin Books, 1979), 346–47.

22. Kammen, *Mystic Chords*, 278.

23. Warren Leon and Margaret Piatt, "Living-History Museums," in *History Museums in the United States: A Critical Assessment*, ed. Warren Leon and Roy Rosenzweig, 64–97 (Urbana: University of Illinois Press, 1989).

24. John B. Poster, "The Birth of the Past: Children's Perception of Historical Time," *History Teacher* 6, no. 4 (1973), 587–98.

25. See Peter K. Smith, "Evolutionary Foundations and Functions of Play: An Overview," in Goncu and Gaskins, *Play and Development*, 39–42, on the relationship between pretend play and theory of mind; Robert J. Coplan, Kenneth H. Rubin, and Leanne C. Findlay, "Social and Nonsocial Play," in

Play from Birth to Twelve, ed. Bergen and Fromberg, 75–86; Doris Pronin Fromberg, "Play's Pathways to Meaning: A Dynamic Theory of Play," in *Play from Birth to Twelve*, ed. Bergen and Fromberg, 159–66. On Theory of Mind, see Martin J. Doherty, *Theory of Mind: How Children Understand Others' Thoughts and Feelings* (New York: Psychology Press, 2009).

26. Jean Piaget, *Play, Dreams and Imitation in Childhood*, translated by C. Gattegno and F. M. Hodgson (New York: W. W. Norton & Company, 1951).

27. Vivian Gussin Paley, *The Boy Who Would Be a Helicopter* (Cambridge, MA: Harvard University Press, 1991), 4.

28. Roy Rosenzweig, *Eight Hours for What We Will: Workers and Leisure in an Industrial City* (New York: Cambridge University Press, 1983), 1.

29. For a discussion of the new sensory history, see "The Senses in American History: A Round Table," *Journal of American History* 95, no. 2 (2008), 378–451.

CHAPTER 7

A Sense of the Past

D. Lynn McRainey

The sound of the alarm, the chill of the early morning air, the taste of toothpaste, the smell of toast, and the sight of the approaching school bus—a child's sensory day is off and running. The senses are critical instruments for navigating life as children look, listen, feel, smell, and taste their way through each moment. When faced with an unfamiliar situation or surprise, the senses go on alert, collecting and processing new data to make comparisons and contrasts between similarities and differences of the known and the unknown. As you mature and accumulate life's experiences, the senses are also powerful stimuli for memory and transporting you back in time. The taste of macaroni and cheese, the feel of a wool scarf, the smell of the ocean, the sound of a forgotten melody, and countless other sensory triggers personal to each individual can catch you off guard as a moment from your own past comes vividly into focus.

This chapter explores the role of the five senses in interpreting the past and the present and in providing children with unique access to history. Although history museums have traditionally favored the tactile impressions from hands-on experiences, all five senses are viable tools for investigating the unfamiliar landscape of history and discovering unknown places, events, and times. The senses spark our curiosity about our present surroundings: What is that noise? How is it similar to or different from familiar sounds? How can I discover what it actually is? In a similar way, the senses can become a tool for expanding a child's curiosity about the past, leading them to consider, What was it like? How was it different? How can I find out? The senses emerge as an unexpected tool for accessing the past and connecting to the present.

Making Sense of Our Senses

What is the language of our senses? Before exploring the potential of the senses as tools for historical investigation and meaning making in museums, we need to consider the senses as tools for documenting the past and the present. A simple exercise is to consider the sensory landscape of your own past—the sights, sounds, smells, tastes, and tactile impressions that shape memories of childhood. My mind's eye sets these memories in a 1960s ranch house with a screened-in porch that my sister and I would sleep on in the summer. The feel of soft grass underfoot as we ran barefoot to a neighbor's house; the mid-day humidity contrasted by the chilling cool of entering the air-conditioned public library; and the crisp cotton of new summer pajamas. Sound penetrates these scenes with the squeals of friends in an evening game of kick-the-can; the piercing whistle of my father calling my sister and me home; or our new family console stereo playing our first album, *Magical Mystery Tour*. Smell infuses these summer scenes through the scent of chlorine in my hair from daily visits to the neighborhood pool and the pungent odors of endless livestock displays competing with the sweet fried aroma of corndogs at our annual pilgrimage to the state fair, marking the end of summer. And finally taste connects me to my paternal grandparents in North Carolina. When visiting them during summer vacation, we were treated to a typical Sunday spread of three meats—fried chicken, sliced ham, and a roast—with a bountiful collection of seasonal vegetables from butterbeans to field peas, and always a pot of rice and pitcher of sweetened tea. Though highly personal and probably resonant only for me and my immediate family, these examples illustrate the richness of the sensory landscape of "days gone by." As readers, the senses provide you access to an unfamiliar story (my childhood) by giving dimension and depth to this unseen place. These sensory impressions paint a picture of what it was like and encourage readers to consider how it was similar to or different from their own childhood.

Diane Ackerman in *A Natural History of the Senses* explores the unique characteristics, functions, and personalities of the five senses. The pleasures and challenges of each sense are captured in her eloquent essays on a range of topics from the songs of whales to personal stories of visiting the Exploratorium's *Tactile Dome*. Whether we are aware of it or not, our senses are constantly on duty collecting and directing to the brain vast amounts of information and data to be processed, interpreted, used, and stored. Ackerman also reminds readers of the complexity of this process. Waves of molecules set the ear into action, while light waves are the trigger for sight. Smell relies on five million waving neurons, while its sensory neighbor (and frequent collaborator), the mouth, houses the tongue and ten thousand taste buds. As Ackerman notes, while every other sense is associated with a key organ, touch sensations come from the skin that covers the entire body.[1]

It all has the feel of a Rube Goldberg machine with endless actions and reactions, stimulating and igniting neurons to send signals to the brain. Color and light; pitch, tone, volume, and frequency; texture, temperature, pressure, and weight; salt, sweet, sour, and bitter; and odor, aroma, and scent all provide a continuous stream of sensations to inform, engage, and stimulate the brain as we move through the familiar and the unfamiliar encounters of life.

Although distinctive in how they work, our senses are also great collaborators, filling in details for one another in supportive roles. In my first yoga class, I was introduced to ujjayi breathing, the slow inhale and exhale of air through the nose with a slight constriction of the throat to create an ocean-like sound in the back of the mouth. The instructor transformed breathing into a multisensory act, coaching the class to "see your breath, feel your breath, and hear your breath." No sense works in isolation, as evidenced by the close affinity of smell and taste, which share a passage in the back of the mouth.[2] As a multisensory experience, taste begins with the sense of sight in that you first eat with your eyes. Even before your taste buds are set into motion, taste is further heightened by the smell coming from the plate, its texture on your lips, and the sound of the food as you take the first bite.[3] In some cases, in the absence of a sense, we call on other senses to step in and fill the void. Art museums frequently encourage their younger visitors to "touch with their eyes" to prevent small hands wandering onto their collections. New to the profession and in my first position in an art museum, I decided to incorporate this clever message into my own tour for a group of energetic 4- and 5-year olds. I turned around to discover two of them actually placing their rapidly blinking eyes onto a large modern painting. Forbidden to use their hands, these children found another way to have a tactile encounter with the object before them.

Work, home, and leisure time are each distinct sensory spaces and experiences. We live in a sensory-rich world. Businesses, hotels, amusement parks, and retailers are turning to smell to create a mood, define their brand, and sell a product.[4] The senses also serve as a tool for creating experiences and reaching new audiences. For example, the French cosmetic company L'Occitane en Provence offers a four-day course for the blind in perfume making.[5] Martin Lindstrom in "Smelling a Branding Opportunity" explores the role of the senses and their "sensory touch points" as assets for defining and maintaining a brand identity from the brilliant red of the Coca-Cola label to the scent of a new car. He notes, "In fact, 75% of all our emotional connections are based on smell and yet, less than 2% of today's communication takes scent into account."[6] In *The Last Lecture*, Randy Pausch reflects on the powerful sensory stimuli of a single crayon in its ability to transport you back to childhood:

> I've often carried a crayon in my shirt pocket. When I need to go back in time, I put it under my nose and I take another hit. I'm partial to the black crayon and the white crayon, but that's just me. Any color has the same potency. Breathe it in. You'll see.[7]

In addition to its appearance, a place has other distinctive sensory characteristics that shape its identity. The senses infuse cyberspace as users share their sensory experiences to document exterior spaces of the urban environment. At the "New York Subway Smell Map," travelers identify (or alert) fellow commuters to the odors and scents found at different subway stations. Food, body odor, chemicals, perfume, and vomit are among the icons that populate and define each station's olfactory personality.[8] "Favorite Chicago Sounds" explains its intent is "to showcase unique audio portraits of Chicago and mirror what Chicagoans think about their city's soundscape."[9] Users post responses to questions: "What's your favorite Chicago sound? Where did you hear this sound? What's your favorite sounding place in Chicago?"[10] The urban environment offers pedestrians sensory encounters to identify, describe, and document for shared experiences and personal connections.

In *Eavesdropping: A Life by Ear*, author and poet Stephen Kuusisto, who has been legally blind from birth, compiles a collection of essays—his "auditory postcards"—that describe his travels and journeys.[11] As he "sight-sees by ear," Kuusisto refers to his approach as "creative listening" or "to listen with effort."[12] In one essay, "Intersection: New York City," he remembers standing on a corner at Fifth Avenue and Eighth Street to identify its distinct auditory characteristics.

> Along with the trucks you hear the bicycle deliverymen—you hear the chains of their bikes and the gritty noise of gears. There's a clatter of a loose manhole cover as a bus hits it. You notice a woman laughing on the far side of Fifth Avenue—she is a mezzo-soprano, loud and high and laughing to beat the band. And then she's gone.[13]

Although we encourage children to stop, look, and listen before crossing a street, how often do we ask them to do the same when in a new environment? Imagine what unexpected discoveries children could make if on family outings or vacations we all "listened with effort" and created our own auditory postcards to record the sounds (or even the smells and tastes) that define a place. On a recent visit to Colonial Williamsburg, I purposely used my senses to create two distinctive "postcards" of the Duke of Gloucester Street. My daytime postcard was populated with the swish of a costumed interpreter jumping rope, the clatter of horses pulling carriages, the feel of dirt underfoot, and the sight of the British flag. Walking down the same street at night a different sensory postcard emerged filled with the chill of the evening air, the glow of a bonfire and cressets, the approaching sound of the fifes and drums, and the feel of the crowd as we all move in procession down the street. Earlier in this chapter, the senses were tools for accessing my personal past. Now they become tools for exploring and experiencing a historical past.

On a National Public Radio *On the Media* segment, Brooke Gladstone reported on the *Moveable Type* installation in the *New York Times* lobby. In the interview, artist Ben Rubin describes the vanished sensory elements that once dominated the newsroom:

> There was the clatter of typewriters in the newsroom itself. There were the sounds of all the machinery from the teletype machines that would clank away with the incoming news from the wire services to the linotype machines that were slamming away, manipulating hot lead to make these printing plates, and then the printing presses themselves, which at a certain time of the night would kick in and start to rumble and shake the building. And you could smell it. You could hear it. You could see it.[14]

As a contemporary interpretation to this place lost to time, *Moveable Type* causes one to pause and consider, What other sensory experiences may be fading from our world? With the advancement of technology and cellular phones, the once ubiquitous phone booth is one example of a sensory experience (sight, sound, touch) that is now only rarely found on street corners. Another sensory experience that the media has forecast will possibly disappear are the shouts, hand signals, and postures of traders on the floor of the stock exchange. While these and other examples illustrate that the "now" is fading and some sensory experiences are lost to the past, they also remind us that like the present, the past was rich with sensory impressions.

Sensory History

First-person accounts provide vivid descriptions of past sensory environments. In 1835, Frederick Gustorf captured his impression of the prairie in details that appeal to readers' senses:

> The prairies in this state are charming—great stretches of flat
> land, covered with wild meadows that are hemmed by thin for-
> ests. The prairies are covered all summer long with flowers that
> change color every month—yellow, blue, then red. By wandering
> from one meadow to another, one encounters a series of surpris-
> es. Huge green surfaces of unbelievably high grass that waves in
> the wind like the sea against a wooded background, more beauti-
> ful than the English parks.[15]

Color, movement, and space are just a few of the sensory details that
prompt readers to consider, What was it like?

Trying to answer the same question, sensory historians grapple
with the senses' temporal and subjective nature. Like other evidence,
the senses are bound to a specific place and time. Unlike other two- and
three-dimensional evidence, sensory stimuli are fleeting and difficult to
collect and display as we would other artifacts. In "Still Coming to 'Our'
Senses: An Introduction," sensory historian Mark M. Smith asks: "How
might historians best excavate evidence for the sensory experience of
the past from written texts? . . . Can the sensory past be 're-created' or
is its experience anchored in the time and place of its production?"[16] In
exploring the "uses" of sensory evidence, Smith asserts that the present
prevents the historian from truly experiencing (or "consuming") sensory evidence in the same way as individuals did in the past. Smith
defines sensory history as "a habit of thinking about the past," and the
historian's task is about understanding how different people responded
to these sensory elements.[17] Like any source, the senses are not givens
but subject to time, place, and diverse perspectives of the individuals
who experienced them in the past and the individuals who want to understand them in the present.[18]

In *Sensory Worlds in Early America,* Peter Charles Hoffer offers a different perspective into the role of the senses as a tool for the historian.
He challenges historians to "reeducate" their senses to mine the sensory
evidence of the past:

> Might we filter out the clutter of modernity that stands in the way
> of every historical flight by using our senses like a child unbur-
> dened by the weight of modernity? Perhaps we can do this if we
> follow children and their parents to the living museums that dot
> our country.[19]

For Hoffer, part of the historical process is the historian traveling to
the site to absorb through his own senses the impressions of what it
was like.

These two different perspectives of sensory historians are used not to imply that this level of historical analysis be replicated for younger audiences but rather to illustrate the potential for the senses in interpreting the past. What museums can leverage is that the past was filled with sensory stimuli unique to a place and time and that people experienced that moment through their own senses. The senses are both evidence and a tool for investigation.

An effective approach for engaging children with the visual arts is to encourage them to imagine that they are walking into the scene and to describe what they might see, hear, smell, feel, and taste. When exploring the past, children are entering an unseen place. Rather than transporting children to somewhere in the past, exhibitions run the risk of presenting history as anywhere through generic galleries and spaces filled with objects on walls and in cases, void of context for a specific place in time. The places where these stories and events occurred lack distinctive characteristics, almost like empty stages with no settings. Although we invite children to wander through our galleries, our spaces sometimes lack the sensory stimuli to prompt them to imagine the past.

The senses create a depth and a dimension to the past that opens a child's eyes (ears, nose, hands, and mouth) to imagine what a particular place might have been like at a particular moment in time. Similar to the example of inviting children to step into a painting, museums can invite children to walk in the sensory shoes of the past. In creating history exhibitions for kids, museums need to mine the full potential of the sensory landscape associated with a specific place and time. Through these sensory encounters, children's senses and imaginations are stimulated. Questions about the past are expanded from who and when to consider, What did the North American prairie smell like? What did the Great Chicago Fire sound like? What was the weather on the day Abraham Lincoln delivered the Gettysburg Address? The past now has colors, aromas, noises, textures, and flavors—no longer an empty stage.

Musing with Our Senses

In "Museum Manners: The Sensory Life of the Early Museum," Constance Classen explores the museum experience through seventeenth- and eighteenth-century visitors' accounts of the Ashmolean Museum of Oxford (founded in 1683). She reveals that museum visits were sensory-rich experiences with curators "extending the courtesy" to guests (and one that was expected) to touch and handle objects.[20] She explains, "Part of the attraction of museums and of the cabinets of curiosities which preceded them, in fact, seemed to be their ability to offer visitors an intimate physical encounter with rare and curious objects."[21] Over time, as the preservation of collections became more of a priority, Classen describes museums as evolving into places of "sensory restraint." While she notes contemporary museums' efforts to become more interactive, Classen laments, "yet such exhibitions are still exceptions to the rule of sensory restraint which is generally expected to govern the behavior of museum visitors. Artefacts for the most part are only to be seen, not felt, smelt, sounded and certainly not tasted."[22]

"Governing the behavior" of children in museums is typically manifested through a stream of verbal commands such as, "look, don't touch" and "walk, don't run," not to mention the constant hushing to keep their voices down. Although children's safety and that of the collection are always a priority, messages to younger visitors may be unintentionally restraining a key cognitive tool—their bodies. In his research on the role of the imagination in learning, Kieran Egan explores cognitive development through five kinds of understanding—Somatic, Mythic, Romantic, Philosophic, and Ironic.[23] In Somatic understanding, the senses are part of the "body's toolkit" for a prelanguage child. In "The Body's Role in Our Intellectual Education," Egan and Anne Chodakowski explain, "Our senses are necessary for our initial understanding of the world and allow us to perceive and deal with a certain range and scale of the phenomena of our environments."[24] Children come to museum visits outfitted with their personal toolkit, their five senses. Rather than asking them to check their toolkits at the door, museums can create exhibitions and experiences that invite children to draw on their senses as a point of entry to this new world, the past.

Reinserting the senses into the interpretive experience affords both the visitor and the museum unexpected tools for accessibility. For children, the senses empower them to explore and be engaged; for museums, the senses transform our spaces into distinctive and inviting places of the past. When considering children's perceptions of history museums, the barriers we must overcome lie in the questions and thoughts of our younger visitors: Is this place for me? Why should I care? As an interpretive tool, the senses provide children access on multiple levels—cognitively, physically, and emotionally.

Museums are moving beyond displays that foreground sight to infuse the other four senses into their galleries and interpretive experiences. The Spring 2004 issue of *Exhibitionist* published by the National Association for Museum Exhibition focused on the senses and their potential for awakening the imaginations of museum professionals. Through the senses, museums are able to consider alternative ways for creating a mood, communicating messages, and integrating unique and unexpected experiences. At the Mill City Museum in Minneapolis, Minnesota, children discover the cultural and economic importance of flour by actually baking biscuits, preparing an ethnic dish, or making chocolate chip cookies. While an experience in its own right, the *Baking Lab* at the Mill City Museum creates a comforting mood for adjacent galleries on the history of the flour industry as the familiar aroma of these tasty treats permeates that space.

The Lower East Side Tenement Museum skillfully leverages sensory access to its primary artifact, the tenement building at 97 Orchard Street in New York City. Although guided tours are the sole means of experiencing this building, sensory stimuli offer a different type of engagement and personal connection with that place. A simple flick of the light switch in the main foyer surrounds you in darkness, illustrating what a resident would encounter on a daily basis prior to electric lights. As you ascend the stairs to the upper floors of this 1860s building, you grasp a mahogany banister that was touched by seven thousand residents before you. In the "Getting By" tour, a group of fifteen adults squeeze into the approximately eighty-five-square-foot kitchen of the German-Jewish Gumpertz family, who were residents of 97 Orchard Street from 1869–1886. Although temporal, your physical discomfort caused by the close proximity to other tour participants prompts you to imagine what it was like for a family of six to live in this confining space day after day. The faint scent of coal blankets the room. Darkness, a banister, space, and coal all define that place and stimulate your imagination to wander through it as a resident.

Museums in the 1990s were drawn to Howard Gardner's multiple intelligences and the range of learning styles, particularly bodily-kinesthetic intelligence. As a means for creative and physical expression, the body is a tool for understanding through role-playing, mimicking, and pretending. The unique characteristics of the hand offer a different type of tool in their ability to construct, operate, and manipulate objects. Diane Ackerman identifies the range of tasks our hands perform from the monumental to the mundane: "After all, the hand is action, it digs roads and builds cities, it throws spears and diapers babies."[25] Hands-on encounters were important first steps for history museums to reinsert tactile experiences into the interpretive process. The potential for touch in history museums took physical form in the *Hands On History Room* at the National Museum of American History (opened in 1993). A wall of mystery objects greeted visitors with an invitation to "try it out," setting the tone of the tactile-rich experiences that filled this space. Children experienced history firsthand through treadling a sewing machine ("More Work for Mother") or harnessing a mule ("The Mighty Mule"). Tactile experiences created a sense of authenticity through a range of tasks, chores, and challenges to be performed and mastered. At the USS Constitution Museum exhibition *A Sailor's Life for Me?*, kids are invited to "Get on your knees and scrub!" A sandstone block and sand (and a lot of elbow grease) put visitors to work in the dreaded holystoning task of scrubbing the decks. While quotes from the captain, the surgeon, and the sailors offer divergent perspectives, the participant's physical encounter creates a new level of insight into life on the ship.[26]

Another effective tactile experience that a history museum can leverage is the temperature and weather conditions of an event or a place. A bold design feature and a memorable moment in the traveling exhibition *Titanic: The Exhibition* is the wall of ice. The simple act of placing one's hand on this powerful design element transported visitors to the icy waters of the North Atlantic. The context of place is communicated through touch rather than words. The cold winter that George Washington and his troops experienced at Valley Forge is integrated into Mount Vernon's "Revolutionary War Theater" in the Donald W. Reynolds Education Center through snow falling on the audience. In the Minnesota History Center exhibition *Weather Permitting*, the emotional "feel" of being there is created in the "Get to the Basement" multimedia experience. Set in a 1960s-era basement, your heart races as lights flicker, radio announcements fade to static, alarms sound, and finally rumbling and shaking surrounds the space to replicate the series of tornados that hit Fridley in 1965.

Music is a rich and versatile tool for museums and communicates on multiple levels to visitors—intellectually, emotionally, and personally. Diane Ackerman describes how a song or a tune can evoke shared emotional responses among individuals, eliminating the need to communicate through spoken words: "What sort of response can a few notes of music awaken? Awe, rage, wonder, restlessness, defeat, stoicism, love, patriotism."[27] Visitors experience the affective quality of music in the Exploratorium exhibition *Memory*. This exhibition delves into the dimensions of remembering from physiological and neurological to its social and cultural contexts. In a section devoted to the senses, "Jukebox Memories" demonstrates sound's affinity to memory through playing the pop songs of the previous four decades.[28] Listeners to the "oldies but goodies" cannot stop their minds from racing back in time to make personal associations between the tunes and melodies to distinct events and places in their lives. The songs are stimuli for cross-generational conversations and sharing of memories about "when I was your age." In addition to bypassing the barrier of time, the affective qualities of music are also able to bypass the physical barriers of exhibition cases, platforms, and velvet ropes. To create a unique connection between its visitors and collection, the Natural History Museum of Los Angeles County asked, "What do collections sound like?"[29] The innovative project *Sonic Scenery: Music for Collections* commissioned contemporary musicians to create original compositions in response to the museum's collections. An innovative approach to the traditional audio tour, the diverse musical styles accompany visitors' exploration of the exhibitions. The didactic approach is replaced with musical interpretations that use digital rhythms, harmony, abstract sounds, and melodies to stimulate the visitor's imagination.

Through exploring the language of the senses, museums become fluent in a vocabulary that extends beyond the written word and reaches across boundaries of age, ability, gallery display cases, and even time. The universal language of the senses offers history exhibitions a new set of terms and tools to integrate into their interpretive approach—volume, temperature, darkness, sour, and stench are means for stimulating children's curiosity and communicating powerful messages about past places and times.

Coming to Our Senses

In developing a history exhibition for children at the Chicago History Museum, we defined a course that challenged our understanding of children as a core audience and the interpretation of history. We chose to foreground the target audience of 8- and 9-year olds and draw inspiration from their abilities, interests, and expectations. Through focus groups, audience research into developmental traits, and extensive testing and prototyping, team members benefited from our continuous interaction with children: watching developmental traits in action; hearing their exclamations of pleasures and their expressions of confusion; and discussing with them their interpretations and discoveries. In front-end focus groups for 8- and 9-year olds, children effortlessly identified a range of sensory impressions that painted a vivid and colorful picture of Chicago, a place that is multidimensional and, like them, full of activity, energy, and excitement.[30]

FIGURE 7.1. *Sensing Chicago* invites children to use their own personal toolkit to connect to Chicago's past and present. Courtesy Chicago History Museum.

Through this approach, the senses emerged as a powerful tool for connecting children to the city's history. As an interpretive approach, the senses supported gallery objectives—to have children see history all around them and at work in their own lives. History is everywhere, even in the foods we eat, the songs we sing, and in the air we breathe. As evidence, sight, smell, sound, touch, and taste illustrate Chicago's unique identity found in places and events that have shaped the city's past and present. As evidence and as an interpretive tool, the senses foster a positive interaction with history by drawing on what children bring naturally to any new experience—their enthusiasm, wonder, and curiosity.

In the exhibition *Sensing Chicago*, each sense has its own space serving as a familiar guide to lead children through the unfamiliar places and times of the past. The range of sensory-based activities appeal to children on multiple levels, inviting them to make choices, exhibit control, challenge themselves physically and mentally, and personalize their experiences through creative play and their own imaginations.

Both touch and sight bridge the distance between then and now by creating a sense of being there. In the "Touch" exhibit, children take a ride on a replica high-wheel bike and sit in the actual seats of Comiskey Park, the original home of the Chicago White Sox, to discover what it

FIGURE 7.2. Through green-screen technology, children insert themselves into distinctive Chicago moments and places. Courtesy Chicago History Museum.

was like. The bike's solid rubber tires rotate over a floor treatment that replicates the wooden blocks that once paved Chicago's streets. These elements come together to create a bumpy ride when a child climbs onto the bike and pedals. By sitting in the stadium seats from Comiskey Park, children activate an audio clip of the crack of a bat and the announcer calling out the play as a baseball is illuminated overhead. The thrill of "being there" is experienced firsthand through whole-body interaction with objects (a bicycle and stadium seats) in a specific context and setting in time (nineteenth-century street and Comiskey Park).

Seeing yourself in the past becomes another way to transport a child back in time. Eight- and 9-year olds (and really any child) love to see themselves and so never casually walk pass a mirror. Drawing on children's narcissistic tendency, the "Sight" exhibit employs green-screen technology to insert children into footage of iconic Chicago scenes featuring familiar elements such as train tracks, buildings, and people. Children select from four clips that invite them to ride the "L" to the Loop, fly over Chicago's skyline, run the Chicago marathon, and be blown away by one of the city's signature blustery days.

The "Smell" exhibit illustrates how scents define a place. Just as physical appearance changes with time, so does a place's olfactory characteristics. Although the scent of chocolate is still evident in some neighborhoods, it is also reminiscent of Chicago's past claim to be the Candy Capital to the World. Other scents of the past no longer exist, such as the smell of wild onion (the city's Native American namesake, Checagou) along the riverbank. To broaden children's sense of place through smell, a tabletop map of Chicago is embedded with seven scents for children to sniff. The activity challenges children to identify the different scents and to associate them with key events and their locations in Chicago's past and present. In addition to chocolate and wild onion, the aromas for smoke, sulfur, prairie grass, manure, and hot dogs become tools for connecting to the Great Chicago Fire, steel mills, early Chicago, the Union Stock Yard, and Wrigley Field. The activity creates an unexpected moment for children as they breathe in the pungent aroma of manure at the Union Stock Yard that stimulates squeals of surprise. The tabletop fosters a collaborative experience, allowing groups to gather around, encourage one another to "smell this," and share their discoveries—"this is my favorite!" The scents also prompt adults to share memories of smelling the stockyards as a child when the wind blew toward their neighborhood.

Sixteen colored spots cover the floor of the "Sound" exhibit, each activating a different sound when children step, hop, jump, and sometimes summersault onto them. A sequence of three images appears on the wall—the Union Stock Yard, the Great Chicago Fire, and a jazz club. To advance to the next image, a child must find the five sounds associated with that image. While trial-and-error initiates the experience, memory takes control as children remember which spot made what sound. One of the sixteen spots changes with each image to create a silly, unrelated auditory moment—a warbling opera singer, chirping dolphin, and squealing pterodactyl. Once a child or group of children has successfully activated the sounds associated with the three images, all sixteen floor spots are replaced with new sounds. Now, as each spot is activated, a contemporary sound is heard with a corresponding image appearing on the wall, creating a soundscape of Chicago today.

Since eating in the gallery was not an option, the team was challenged to define a sensory experience that illustrates Chicago's distinctive taste and culinary style associated with certain foods. In the end, the simplest concept emerged as the one that dished out the most impact. The imagination became the sixth sense to partner with taste—you are the hot dog! In the "Taste" exhibit, children lie in a 5-foot long cushion resembling a poppy seed bun. A collection of soft, pillow-like condiments ensures they are truly dressed Chicago-style. Friends and family members pile on yellow mustard, green relish, onions, tomato wedges, hot peppers, and pickle spear, with an oversized shaker of celery salt standing close by. In a ceiling mirror, children take in their image as a Chicago-style hot dog, and history never looked more delicious.

All the senses come together at a media kiosk, where children create an electronic Chicago postcard. Children select images representing the five senses and drag them into the letters of the word "Chicago." The postcard is personalized with the user's face inserted into the "o" and their name in the upper-left corner. The user has the option to e-mail the postcard home or to a friend, and all postcards become part of a queue projected onto the gallery wall. Each child who visits the gallery leaves his or her mark and personal sense of Chicago.

Summative evaluation of *Sensing Chicago* confirmed the types of interactions and behaviors that sensory experiences generate—social, sensory, and imaginative. The evaluation study used a mixed-method approach that included self-administered exit surveys; tracking and timing; observations and intersect interviews; and depth exit interviews using picture sorts. Visitors expressed surprise in being able to use their senses, appreciating the novelty of the experience: "This was a fine way to discover history" one parent commented.[31] Social interaction among groups was demonstrated through conversations about the activities and content. Participants were eager to share their sensory experiences with other members in their group. At the map in "Smell," children frequently tried to trick their parents or siblings into smelling the stockyard scent, coaxing group members to "come smell this." The senses sparked memories and conversations as adults shared where they once sat at the Comiskey Park photo blow-up in the "Touch" exhibit or, at the smell map, remembering a relative who once worked at the steel mill. Collaboration among group members was evident at a number of activities. At the "Sight" exhibit, enthusiastic group members coached and cheered one another to flap their arms and fly over the city or to hold onto their imaginary hats and one another so not to get blown away. The film footage at "Sight" and the hot dog bun at "Taste" encouraged children to act out a variety of roles. Unexpected outcomes were frequently observed through creative play when children crafted their own experiences for fun and individual expression. The floor treatment at the stadium seats in "Touch" resembles a baseball diamond. Children have been seen playing their own pretend game of baseball, with one child pitching an invisible ball and another child swinging an imaginary bat and running the bases.

Conclusion: Is History Senseless?

Why turn to the senses to connect children to history? In *Releasing the Imagination: Essays on Education, the Arts, and Social Change,* Maxine Greene describes the teacher as someone who creates learning environments that challenge children to move beyond the routine into a journey or a search: "To see oneself on a strange island, clearly, is to imagine oneself in another space, looking at an unfamiliar world. To poke around is to investigate that world, to pay attention to it, to think about it."[32] The past is an unfamiliar world to children, and history exhibitions can offer environments for exploration. To "poke around" is what children do naturally. Sensory stimuli become guides for inviting children into the unknown places of the past and spaces of our museum galleries while also giving the past an unexpected richness and dimension. Drawing on their own sensory toolkits, children become active participants as their senses enable them to explore and to make discoveries. Sensory experiences awaken children's eyes, ears, nose, mouth, hands, body, and imaginations to overcome their anxieties about this unknown place, their preconceptions about history, and the distance between then and now. Through the senses, children are able to find answers to their questions: What was it like? How was it different? How can I find out?

As museum professionals, we have thought long and hard about the same questions. History exhibitions filled with sensory stimuli can signal to the child to stop and take notice, similarly to how poet Stephen Kuusisto describes his own discoveries absent of sight: "I have been lucky sometimes to find places where I could work by ear and pause for whole moments, receiving treasures of sound and sense."[33] At the end of this sensory exploration, we return to the questions of our younger visitors to a history museum: Is this place for me? Why should I care? As an interpretive tool for a history museum, the senses stimulate emotions and memories; extend access to unfamiliar places and times; and invite participation. Through the senses, the past becomes accessible to the newcomer and is filled with unexpected possibilities. History now makes sense.

NOTES

1. Diane Ackerman, *A Natural History of the Senses* (New York: Vintage Books, 1990), 77, 200.
2. Howard Hughes Medical Institute, ed. "Hearing, Seeing, and Smelling the World" (Chevy Chase, MD: Howard Hughes Medical Institute, 1995), www.hhmi.org/senses/ (accessed September 8, 2009).

3. Ackerman, *Natural History*, 142.

4. Elizabeth Lee, "Dollars and Scents," *Atlanta Journal-Constitution,* August 22, 2004, MS1. ("The world is getting smellier" Lee explains in "Dollars and Scents.")

5. Lori Aratani, "Visually Impaired Teen Puts Nose to Future," *Washington Post*, January 18, 2008, www.santafenewmexican.com/Teen/Visually_impaired_ teen_puts_nose_to_future (accessed September 8, 2009).

6. Martin Lindstrom, "Smelling a Branding Opportunity," *Brandweek*, March 14, 2005, 26.

7. Randy Pausch with Jeffrey Zaslow, *The Last Lecture* (New York: Hyperion, 2008), 165.

8. Gawker.com, "Smell of the City," New York City Subway Smell Map, http:// gawker.com/maps/smell/ (accessed September 8, 2009).

9. Experimental Sound Studio in partnership with Chicago Public Radio, Favorite Chicago Sounds, "What We Do," www.favoritechicagosounds.com/ aboutus.php (accessed September 8, 2009).

10. Experimental Sound Studio, Favorite Chicago Sounds, "Participate" www.favoritechicagosounds.com/participate.php (accessed September 8, 2009).

11. Stephen Kuusisto, *Eavesdropping: A Life by Ear* (New York: W. W. Norton & Company, 2006), auditory postcards, xii; sight-sees by ear, x; creative listening, xi.

12. Kuusisto, *Eavesdropping*, xiii–xiv. Kuusisto writes in his preface: "As a final point (and still in the sphere of biography), I like this remark by Igor Stravinsky. He once said, 'To listen is an effort, and just to hear is no merit. A duck hears also.'"

13. Kuusisto, *Eavesdropping*, 81.

14. David Carr, interview by Brooke Gladstone, "Moveable Type," *On the Media*, National Public Radio, May 30, 2008, www.onthemedia.org/ transcripts/2008/05/30/06 (accessed September 8, 2009).

15. Frederick Gustorf on September 12, 1835. From *The Uncorrupted Heart: Journal and Letters of Frederick Julius Gustorf, 1800–1845*, ed., with introd. and notes by Fred Gustorf, trans. by Fred and Gisela Gustorf (Columbia: University of Missouri Press, 1969), 52–3.

16. Mark M. Smith, "Still Coming to 'Our' Senses: An Introduction," *The Journal of American History* 95, no. 2 (September 2008): 379.

17. Mark M. Smith, "Producing Sense, Consuming Sense, Making Sense: Perils and Prospects for Sensory History," *Journal of Social History* 40, no. 4 (Summer 2007), 842.

18. Smith, "Producing Sense," 846.

19. Peter Charles Hoffer, *Sensory Worlds in Early America* (Baltimore, MD: Johns Hopkins University Press, 2003), 8.

20. Constance Classen, "Museum Manners: The Sensory Life of the Early Museum," *Journal of Social History* 40, no. 4 (Summer 2007), 899.

21. Classen, "Museum Manners," 896–97.

22. Classen, "Museum Manners," 895.

23. For a more in-depth discussion about Kieran Egan's kinds of understanding, see Chapter 4 in this volume, "Finding the Story in History" by Leslie Bedford.

24. Anne Chodakowski and Kieran Egan, "The Body's Role in Our Intellectual Education" (Imaginative Education Research Group, March 27, 2008), 3 http://ierg.net/assets/documents/publications/IERGBodyrole.pdf (accessed September 8, 2009).

25. Ackerman, *Natural History*, 116.

26. USS Constitution Museum, Family Learning Forum, "Holystoning the Deck: Visitors May Challenge You," http://familylearningforum.org/about-the-project/usscm-prototypes/holystoning.htm (accessed September 8, 2009).

27. Ackerman, *Natural History*, 214.

28. Michael Pearce, "Exploratorium Memory," *Are We There Yet? Conversations about Best Practices in Science Exhibition Development*, ed. Kathleen McLean and Catherine McEver (San Francisco, CA: Exploratorium, 2004), 74.

29. Jane Pisano, director and president, Natural History Museum of Los Angeles County, press release for *Sonic Scenery* exhibition, http://stage.nhm.org/site/sites/default/files/pdf/press/archive/2006_NHMPressRelease_SonicScenery.pdf (accessed September 8, 2009).

30. Minda Borun, "The Chicago Historical Society Children's Gallery Focus Group Report" (unpublished report, Philadelphia, PA: Museum Solutions, 2004).

31. Cecelia Garibay, "Chicago History Museum *Sensing Chicago* Evaluation" (unpublished report, Chicago, IL: Garibay Group, 2007), 39.

32. Maxine Greene, *Releasing the Imagination: Essays on Education, the Arts, and Social Change* (San Francisco, CA: Jossey-Bass, 1995), 24.

33. Kuusisto, *Eavesdropping*, xiv.

CHAPTER 8

Are We There Yet? Children, History, and the Power of Place

Benjamin Filene

History is about perspective, looking back to recognize that nothing under the sun is truly new. History is about empathy, seeing the humanity in distant figures and bringing their experiences to life. History is about context, recognizing that our actions are shaped by systems of power and constraint bigger than any single individual.

Kids are terrible historians. Ask any (honest) parent: perspective, empathy, and sense of context aren't the qualities that distinguish our children. Babies arrive with a gaping, cawing need to be the center of the world—in a good way. Healthy kids sense that time began the day they awoke and that life revolves around them and their needs. If it doesn't, they're programmed to let you know that it should. People in their immediate circle constitute the entire world; everyone else is peripheral at best. Even when they begin to form mental pictures of territory beyond their view, kids continue to see their own experience as the reference point for all that has come before and after. They expand their sense of the world by building concentrically, keeping themselves and their attendants securely at the center of their domain.

This narrow, self-absorbed, presentist outlook would seem to be a disaster for historically minded thinking, right? Perhaps not. In their self-centeredness, it turns out, young people are not so different from the majority of museum visitors and, truth be told, historians. Everyone makes history personal; some are just more open about it than others. Young people's relatively narrow worldview is potentially an opportunity more than an obstacle.

If the classic admonition to writers is to "start with what you know," to history museums it might be "start where they are"—make history come alive for visitors by connecting it to the world in which they already have personal investment. The strategy that hits closest to home, literally, is to build from visitors' sense of place—their relationship to their physical surroundings, to the geographical area they call their own, to where they have built their lives and where, in their mind's eye, they return in identifying "where I come from." Adults often build connections to multiple places over the years. But what does place mean to kids? And how can museums use that sense of place in their exhibitions to connect kids to history?

In the most rigorous geographic sense, children tend to be quite fuzzy about place. If I remind my kids that I'll soon be leaving for my trip to Memphis, they'll look at me with puzzlement and say, "But I thought you were going to Tennessee." With their limited life experience—their narrower window of context—children understandably are less able to register political boundaries or to grasp geographic scale. Just as "yesterday" for a 5-year-old might be 2 hours or 2 months ago, Egypt could just as easily be a nap-in-the-car-seat away as an ocean apart.

But kids do have a very strong sense of their immediate surroundings. They are keenly aware of home and of the world around it. Think of the enduring popularity of Richard Scarry's Busytown books.[1] As much as these stories are about vocations, they equally are about geography: the world just outside your door is a hive of activity, Scarry's bustling drawings show the child. Come explore! they beckon.

The Fort Lauderdale–based theme park Wannado City converts the Busytown idea into a three-dimensional experience. Children ("kidizens") choose a profession, don the uniform of their job, and walk the streets of a town made just for them (they can explore unaccompanied if age 8 or over). Throughout the day they earn and spend Wongas™ (the official Wannado City currency), which they deposit and withdraw at two bank branches and at State Farm® ATMs across the city. "At Wannado City," says the park's website, "kids can be whatever they want to be—right now. From paleontologist to news reporter, to everything in between, kids try out tons of grown-up jobs in the first indoor city just their size."[2] In his book *Madlenka,* author Peter Sís beautifully conveys children's sense of occupying a world within a world: "In the universe, on a planet, on a continent, in a country, in a city, on a block, in a house, in a window, in the rain, a little girl named Madlenka finds out her tooth wiggles." The girl rushes out to share her excitement with her square block of Manhattan and its international array of merchants. In Sís's full-page drawings, the geometry of Madlenka's city literally centers around Madlenka, and her tooth is world news.[3]

Educator David Sobel notes that children struggle with what he terms "outside in" approaches to geography—curricula that begin with remote or abstract concepts of place, such as the seven continents or the solar system: "Instead of connecting children to place, this approach alienates them and cuts them off from their local environments. The

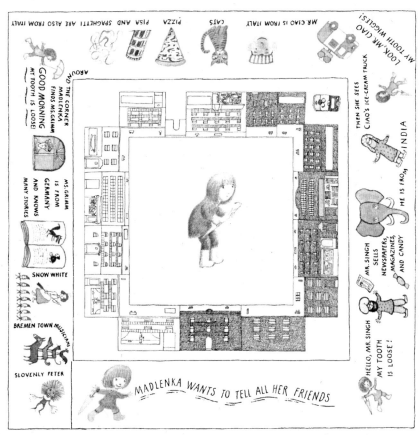

FIGURE 8.1. In author Peter Sís's drawings, the geometry of Madlenka's city literally centers on Madlenka, and the loss of her tooth is world news. Illustration from *Madlenka* by Peter Sís. Copyright © 2000 by Peter Sís. Reprinted by permission of Farrar, Straus and Giroux, LLC.

inadvertent hidden message is: *Important things are far away and disconnected from children; nearby things, the local community and environment, are unimportant and negligible.*"[4] Sobel favors an "inside out" or "small world" approach for kids that builds from their surroundings: "Asking first graders to make maps of their neighborhoods makes sense; asking them to make maps of the continents puts the cart before the horse."[5]

Kids may not chart place as a geographer would, but they do know where they are. How can young people's awareness of place help museums show kids where they (and we as a society) have been? How can it teach them history? That deceptively simple challenge contains within it a fundamental question, What counts as history, and how do museums teach it and kids learn it?

Becoming Places to Learn

In just a single generation, museum workers have witnessed a dramatic expansion of museums' sense of possibility and responsibility. As Stephen Weil has pointed out, one can chart the rising tide of expectations through the American Association of Museums' (AAM) blue ribbon reports. Even a few decades ago, the notion that museums could be educational institutions was not firmly established. Museums existed to create aesthetic experiences that transported visitors beyond humdrum realities. In 1973, Weil recounts, a group of prominent museum educators threatened to secede from AAM in disgust over the organization's disregard for their efforts. By 1984, though, with the report *Museums for a New Century*, AAM asserted "A New Imperative for Learning," calling for "a new approach to the place of education in the functioning of museums." The 1992 report *Excellence and Equity* asserted "unequivocally" that there should be "an educational purpose in every museum activity." In more recent years, museums seemingly have set their sights even higher: *Mastering Civic Engagement*, a 2002 AAM report by another group of museum luminaries, argued that museums could be powerful agents for social change. In the volume's lead essay, author Ellen Hirzy envisions a museum that "becomes a center where people gather to meet and converse, a place that celebrates the richness of individual and collective experience, and a participant in collaborative problem solving. It is an active, visible player in civic life, a safe haven, and a trusted incubator of change." As Weil summarizes, in three decades museums have shifted from seeing themselves as providers of diversionary "refreshment" to offering "education" to fostering "communal empowerment."[6]

Even as the museum community's sense of responsibility and purpose has expanded, its faith or interest in a museum's ability to convey factual knowledge has decidedly narrowed. When researchers began to look in detail at how visitors actually behave in museums—as opposed to how curators hope they will behave—they found that mastering content was only one among many concerns and preoccupations of museum-goers. As visitor-studies pioneers John Falk and Lynn Dierking have noted, a museum visit is a multifaceted experience, one that extends from the parking lot through the exhibitions, the museum café, and the gift shop and is shaped by visitors' preconceptions and interests. "Museum professionals," Falk and Dierking write, "want to know what visitors have learned, but have traditionally used a narrow definition of learning. They examine what visitors have learned from exhibits and labels, for example, which is an important aspect of the museum experience, but only one aspect." Falk and Dierking find that visitors "perceive their museum experiences as a gestalt." Museum-goers build experiences by making a series of choices shaped by the expectations they bring to the visit and their impressions of the environment around them: "Whatever the visitor does attend to [in the museum]," Falk and Dierking conclude, "is filtered through the personal context, mediated by the social context, and embedded within the physical context."[7]

At every point in their journey through the museum, visitors absorb messages and make meanings. Indeed, influenced by constructivist learning theorists such as George Hein, exhibition developers have begun to recognize that visitors constantly take learning in new directions that reflect personal interests, preconceptions (or misconceptions), and mental maps of the world. Hein writes:

> Museums are not efficient places for traditional "school" education, learning specific facts and concepts, because people don't spend enough time and are not there primarily for that purpose. . . . For visitors to have a positive experience, their interaction with the contents of the museum must allow them to connect what they see, do and feel with what they already know, understand, and acknowledge.

Visitors, in Hein's conception, "learn by constructing their own understandings."[8] Anthropologist Grant McCracken notes that a museum visitor is increasingly like a consumer, "accustomed to being treated as the arbiter of his or her own choices. . . . Visitors bridle when, wittingly or not, the museum insists they are subordinates."[9] As sites of voluntary, informal learning, then, museums operate differently than do traditional classrooms. Visitors are in the driver's seat as they navigate the learning environment of the museum.[10]

The implications of this reconception of museum learning are tremendous. History ceases to be an inert collection of names and dates and becomes a series of processes and habits of mind. Success is measured not by the amount of content absorbed but by the visitor's ability to deploy it in his or her own life. Accuracy as a buzzword is replaced by relevance. For young people in particular, history shifts from being a body of facts to being an historical outlook built on a core set of awarenesses:

- precedent: someone came before me;
- change: the world has not always been as it is;
- agency: people shape the world around them;
- perspective: historians assemble the past from evidence, and different people piece it together differently.

If the goal is to encourage students to adopt a way of thinking about the world, teaching in the museum depends more on engaging the learner than on assembling an airtight body of information. "The emphasis should be on method, not content," museum educator Elaine Davis asserts. History becomes open-ended, not a closed case, and teaching becomes a process of building trust and creating partnerships. "Dialogic practice and shared authority," Davis writes, "are essential to the intellectual growth and autonomy of the individual."[11] Young visitors need intrinsic motivation to study the past; a feeling of safety in taking intellectual risks; and a sense of personal investment as they build links between past and present, Self and Other.

Here is where museums and the power of place thrust themselves into the forefront. A sense of place is a uniquely effective tool for engaging young people in the historian's habit of mind. In trying to inspire kids, museums can draw on their own status as alluring places in young people's eyes; on kids' recognition that museums can be places of departure to parts unknown; and on the power of stories rooted in local places to make history concrete and personal for young audiences. To understand how museums can fully connect kids to history, we need to explore these three strategies.

Museums as Destinations

If museums think at all about themselves as places, they tend to do so in terms of tourism—our building will draw visitors looking for some place to show Aunt Gladys when she comes to town. But with children, especially, a museum's physical environment can be a pedagogical tool. Museum buildings are places that capture children's imaginations and can make them ready to learn. As Barbara Piscitelli and David Anderson found in their study of 4- to -6-year-olds, "children perceived museums as settings that were exciting, happy, and provided opportunities to learn and gain many ideas." As Piscitelli and Anderson also noted, children closely observe the museum spaces around them: "Children's visual recall and verbal descriptions of their previous museum experiences were remarkable in their accuracy in depicting actual exhibits and architectural features of museum settings. . . . [Their memories] showed astonishing accuracy for spatial relations, scale, shape and size."[12] Children engage museums as places and actively absorb messages from the physical environments they encounter there.[13]

Children's books again capture young people's perspective, the sense of wonder they bring to museums. In Lois Wyse's *How to Take Your Grandmother to a Museum*, the book's take-charge narrator calls her grandmother: "'Grandma,' I said. 'This is me. I want to take you to an Interesting Place. . . . I want to take you to the Museum of Natural History.'" At the museum, the girl expertly leads her grandmother through the galleries, sharing her excitement and her feeling of mastery of the space:

> "To Africa," I said. "Follow me!" We took a shortcut through Asia and turned left at Central America. Grandma was so amazed she wasn't sure where to look first. It's a good thing I was there to be her guide.
> "This feels like a safari," she said.
> "They're all real animals, not paintings," I explained. "These kinds of exhibits are called dioramas."[14]

The young visitor relishes the feeling that this museum—and her grandmother—are very much her own.

In *From the Mixed-Up Files of Basil E. Frankweiler*, when a child needs a home away from home the logical destination is a museum:

> Claudia knew that she could never pull off the old-fashioned kind of running away. . . . [H]er leaving home would not be running from somewhere but would be running to somewhere. To a large place, a comfortable place, and preferably a beautiful place. And that's why she decided upon the Metropolitan Museum of Art in New York City.[15]

For kids, museums are truly "destination vacations" in their own backyards, places that feel safe and familiar and that, at the same time, inspire awe.

Taking Off

Even as children embrace museums as destinations, they also appreciate them as points of departure. Museums are places where kids go to transport themselves to *other* places. *Under the Dock* at the Boston Children's Museum used ambient sound, aquaria, videos, and kid-sized crab costumes to invite children to enter the marine world beneath the surface of Boston Harbor.[16] Indeed, journeys of the imagination in museums do not necessarily depend on high-tech renderings of distant lands or razzle-dazzle hands-on activities. Piscitelli and Anderson found that children's "salient recollections of their visits to museum settings centre on experiences which appeared to be non-interactive in nature," particularly "large-scale exhibits" such as dinosaurs and life-sized models.[17] Smaller scale displays can be transporting, too. The dioramas at the American Museum of Natural History (AMNH) in New York allow young people to imagine that they have traveled to the African Savannah or the Alaskan Peninsula. These installations are magical places within a place. It was not just Ben Stiller's goofy hijinks that made my 11-year-old love the film *Night at the Museum*, in which the AMNH's dioramas come to life. The movie (based on a 1993 children's book by Milan Trenc) animated for her the fantasy implicit in the dioramas: What if you could actually enter the world the exhibits depict?[18] Museums, then, can build a sense of place by taking young people beyond the "real" world—back in time, to a different region or country, or to a place of the imagination.

Personalizing Place

Even as we celebrate museums' potential to deliver flights of fancy, in thinking about how to engage young learners in history we must return to the core of the notion of place—our physical surroundings. When museums tie history to specific locations in the contemporary, everyday world, they offer young people personal connecting points to the past and a window into the historian's craft. The premise behind this approach seems simple, but it is not at all straightforward: young people care more about the past if they can link it to their own lives and the places they call their own. The American Revolution seems less remote if students can imagine residents of their own town mustering to join the fight or weighing the benefits of siding with the British against their neighbors. The Great Depression hits home when students look at welfare relief rolls from their city or see a photograph of bread lines on Main Street.

History is not usually taught this way in secondary schools. Teachers often start as far away as imaginable from the students' lived experiences—John Locke's social contract for example—and either stay at this remote distance or, perhaps, gamely try to paddle back to terrain that might seem recognizable to the students: the social contract, natural rights, the Declaration of Independence, the First Amendment, (whew!), your right to criticize the principal in your school newspaper. In most history classes, larger-than-life figures act on the world stage, whether the Hall of Mirrors or the halls of Congress. Obligatory units on state history tend toward a similar approach, just shifting focus from the White House to the state house. Is it any wonder kids find history distant and bewildering?

Historians have spent decades trying to bring history down to earth. Since the 1960s, the "New" Social History has pursued the stories of ordinary people. Many of the pioneering works of the field, significantly, bore in on specific places, recreating the inner workings of individual communities.[19] Committed to "challenging the traditional ways that people learn about the past," the American Social History Project produced a textbook that tells the tale of the nation "from the bottom up," from the perspectives of working people. First published in 1989, the two-volume *Who Built America?* is now in its third edition.[20] In the 1990s, the National Standards for History likewise worked to make history more accessible to students. It emphasized skills over rote memorization, the need to study multiple perspectives and diverse people in the past, and the importance of student engagement. The voluntary standards include a unit on "The History of Students' Own State or Region" that invites teachers to use primary sources to "describe local community life long ago" and to "examine local architecture and landscape."[21] In that spirit, some model projects developed curricula in which students do original research on local history. In Georgia, Keeping and Creating American Communities, a project funded by the National Endowment for the Humanities, has spurred high school students to research, write, and advocate about their local cemeteries, endangered historic landmarks, and the promises and perils of urban sprawl.[22] The National Parks Service's "Teaching with Historic Places" website offers teachers lesson plans that connect one hundred historic sites to classroom subjects.[23]

To some extent, then, secondary schools have broadened their conception of history and deepened their connection to place. But their progress in this direction remains halting and marked by obstacles. Innovative teachers face the challenges of confinement in classrooms, pressures from standardized tests, and backlash against deviations from the traditional historical narrative. For the overwhelming majority of students, history remains something that happened somewhere else.

History museums face some of the same pressures and obstacles as teachers. As local or regional institutions, however, they are much more intrinsically rooted in place. They would seem to be well positioned to show young people that history is all around us. The appeal of historic sites, certainly, rests on the notion that "history happened here." Children may have little interest in the grand political arc of history, but they are fascinated by the idea that people came before them, and they love standing in their shoes. Kids ask, Is this where they ate breakfast back then? Did they sleep in this bed? Did someone die in this room? Young people fuzzy on the details of the Civil War respond to the notion that they are walking the same ground on which Gettysburg soldiers fell. Living history sites particularly try to capitalize on the "you are here" feeling. Colonial Williamsburg invites visitors to take "a trip to a different place and time." Children can rent eighteenth-century-style costumes and walk the streets that "re-create a living, changing town where people worked, dined, shopped, and visited."[24] The immigrant stories at Ellis Island and the Lower East Side Tenement Museum gain immeasurable poignancy from the fact that they are told in the spaces where they actually happened. Historic sites offer the allure of geographic authenticity: on this actual ground, real people from the past made history.

Many museums that do not literally recreate the past nonetheless take advantage of the power of their historic locations. In 1999, Old Salem (North Carolina) rebuilt a log church on the site where enslaved African Americans had worshipped; however, instead of reconstructing the church interior, the historic village uses the space to showcase contemporary artists' interpretations of slave life, including audio recordings in which actors present first-person stories about slavery in the village.[25] Although the interior space in no way attempts to be historically accurate, it gives visitors the powerful experience of hearing the stories of enslaved people on the same ground where they lived their lives. The National Mississippi River Museum in Dubuque, Iowa, does not have historic buildings in its complex, but it, too, builds on the power of place, chronicling the mighty force that flows right outside its walls. Corporate museums often create gleaming high-tech installations that nonetheless draw on a sense of place. The appeal of the Louisville Slugger Museum, the World of Coca-Cola, or the Hershey Museum depends in part on locality: learn the story of the products you love *right here* where they are being made.

Industrial history museums have been particularly adept at working within former factory sites to bring manufacturing history to life. In the Museo Del Acero in Monterrey, Mexico (opened 2007), visitors learn the history and science behind steel production by exploring exhibits installed within a seventy-meter-tall blast furnace. Visitors listen to oral interviews with former workers, slide down a cutaway model of a furnace, ride an ore lift to the catwalks atop the site, and watch a sound-and-light show about the manufacturing process.[26] The complex of museums in Lowell, Massachusetts, likewise uses historic structures to house contemporary exhibit experiences relating to the histories of those buildings. In Lowell, the Boott Mill boarding house includes an exhibition on *Mill Girls and Immigrants*, and the Boott Cotton Mills Museum showcases an operating power loom and other interactive exhibits; the Tsongas Industrial Center bills itself as a history center where "students learn about the American Industrial Revolution through hands-on activities and by experiencing history where it happened."[27] Similarly, the Mill City Museum in Minneapolis, Minnesota, was built within the ruins of the landmark Washburn A Mill. The museum uses interactive exhibits—including a water lab, a baking lab, and a moving freight elevator housing a multimedia show (the "Flour Tower")—to involve young people in industrial history.

Building Place

But can exhibitions connote place when their locations are *not* any place in particular—when seemingly (in Gertrude Stein's formulation) there is no there there? Children's museums often manufacture environments that engage young people. The grocery store, the restaurant, and the bus are all staples of the industry. The Minnesota Children's Museum invites children to don brown costumes and enter an ant hill. Almost always these settings are generic, places that could be anywhere or nowhere, and rarely do they look back in time.

Many history museums, however, have successfully created a sense of place, seemingly out of nothing, within their galleries. Often they do so by making visual references to local places beyond the museum's doors. Such exhibits rely on associations with sites that visitors bring with them, either from first-hand experiences or from virtual, media-driven exposure. *Brooklyn's History Museum*, a 1989 long-term installation at the Brooklyn Historical Society, built its exploration of the borough's history around five icons of the place and its past, each of which was mocked up in large scale in the gallery: the Brooklyn Bridge, the Coney Island Cyclone roller coaster, the Ebbets Field dugout, the Brooklyn Navy Yard, and the *Honeymooners* stage set. Each icon anchored a broader theme: the bridge opened onto an exploration of Brooklyn's transportation history; the roller coaster was a setting for discussion of leisure history.[28] The Chicago History Museum's *Sensing Chicago* (opened 2006) likewise spotlights icons of place: kids bump over old Chicago's wooden streets on a high-wheel bike, sit in seats from Comiskey Park, smell the Chicago Fire, and, through interactive technology, see themselves run the Chicago marathon and ride the "L" train.[29]

Do children get place-based allusions of this sort? No doubt most young Brooklynites recognize the bridge, but some probably don't; and they may or may not place the Cyclone, still thrill-riding after all these years. Likewise, most Chicago youth have associations with the "L" and some, but not all, have heard stories of old Comiskey Park (torn down in

1991 and replaced by U.S. Cellular Field). Even so, these "places" in the gallery—even those that existed beyond living memory—make history less abstract. They provide settings for the past and, implicitly, offer context for the oral histories that recollect what it was like to work at the Navy Yard or stroll the Coney Island boardwalk with the Cyclone's lights above. For children too young to grasp the geographic references, the settings nonetheless reinforce the idea that the past surfaces in the places of everyday life—that history is *everywhere*. As the *Sensing Chicago* website says in its invitation to young visitors, "Use your five senses to explore Chicago, uncover the past, and discover that history is all around you."[30] History gains tangibility by being set in place.

Indeed, even exhibits that do not depict iconic locations have deployed place to powerful effect. The Minnesota Historical Society used a single ordinary house as a frame for a set of stories. *Open House: If These Walls Could Talk* (opened 2006) focuses on an unremarkable house in St. Paul (472 Hopkins Street) and the fifty families who have made it home—from the German immigrants who built it in 1888 through the Italians, African Americans, and now Hmong who succeeded them. With its tight focus, the exhibition is about the richness of a single place and the concentric boundaries within which people live: visitors explore how families built lives within the four walls of 472 Hopkins Street, within the circle of railroad tracks that bounded their neighborhood and within the broader boundaries that defined them as Germans, Hmong, Minnesotans, and Americans.[31] The exhibition shows how residents turned "this place" into "our place" and invites visitors to explore their own set of connections between family, home, and self.

Open House could not use the real house in the gallery; the structure is being lived in, two miles from the Minnesota History Center gallery.[32] Nonetheless, the exhibition's designers felt it was essential to create a sense of "house-ness" in the museum. The exhibition is built around a series of rooms, each of which represents a different time period and tells the stories of a different set of families from the house's history. Visitors enter the front door of 472 Hopkins and step into the 1890s sitting room of the German residents; they then move through installations such as a 1930s kitchen from the Italian era and a 1960s backyard (set for a birthday party) before ending at a contemporary living room setting that profiles the latest Hmong occupants. Since the rooms are impressionistic installations, not artifact-based re-creations, visitors are free to touch everything—to stand on the city map embedded in the floor on the front porch, to open the kitchen stove (which triggers an audio story about raising chickens in the basement), and to sit at the

FIGURE 8.2. In *Open House: If These Walls Could Talk*, visitors approach a façade representing 472 Hopkins Street as it looked when it was built in 1888. A panel presents the exhibition's premise ("One house"; "50 families"; "118 years"; "Explore"). Courtesy Minnesota Historical Society, www.mnhs.org.

dining room table (which launches audio and images that surface in the plates). Formative evaluation showed that young people accepted the premise instantly: this place was a house, and they were free to explore its nooks and crannies (people over thirty were more inclined to keep their hands behind their backs unless given cues encouraging them to touch). Summative evaluation suggests that the sense of being in a domestic space prompts visitors to make associative connections between the past and their own experience.[33] Interestingly, the summative evaluation also shows that visitors explore the space at a more considered and deliberate pace than in other comparably sized installations.[34] Impressionistically, the gallery seems to suffer less damage than do others in the History Center. Could it be that young people sense the space's "houseness" and therefore treat it with more respect?

Here and Now

By itself, then, place matters in the museum gallery. The most powerful evocations of "here," however, connect it with an oft-overlooked partner, "now." Here and now would seem to be natural bedfellows, but

FIGURE 8.3. From the 1920s onward, first-person voices tell the stories in *Open House*. Visitors who sit at the dining room table are rewarded with a surprise—images surface in the glass plates and audio tells stories of family dinners during the house's Italian era. Courtesy Minnesota Historical Society, www.mnhs.org.

FIGURE 8.4. Set to represent a 1960s–70s neighborhood birthday party, the yard in *Open House* features a mural painting that gives the feel of an outdoor scene. Visitors play hopscotch and Pin the Tail on the Donkey, try their hands at the clothespin drop, and pull down the kite to read about the Krismer family's kite-flying exploits. Courtesy Minnesota Historical Society, www.mnhs.org.

their union has usually been anathema to professional historians and teachers alike. Academic historians are terrified of "presentism"—the charge that one's scholarship has been tainted by contemporary concerns. Traditionally, an historian is supposed to examine evidence and use the tools of the discipline—not subjective interests—to interpret and evaluate. History can be relevant to the present but not shaped by it. In the name of this dispassionate ideal (coupled with the pressures of the school calendar), history has often been taught in ways that divorce the past from the present. Again, think of how most secondary school students encounter American history. The teacher bravely starts the year by introducing hunter-gatherers, moves on to Pilgrims and Puritans, accelerates through the cotton gin and the Civil War, careens through World War I and the Depression, and sputters out sometime shortly after World War II, decades before the students' parents were born. History remains mired farther back in time than students can conceive.

If academics fret about bringing history too close to today, museums worry about how to make their subject relevant to contemporary audiences. One museum administrator explained low visitation to me lamenting, "History is too much about the past." Yet despite their desire to close the gap with visitors, museums themselves often contribute to the distancing of the past. How many state history museums have permanent "overview" installations that start with the Ice Age? (One state museum begins with the Big Bang.) Some museums don't feature an image of a single living person in their galleries. The "pastness" of the past need not be disguised, but if we truly expect young people to connect history to the present we need to show them it can be done. Again place offers a way in. Young people who may have no understanding of historical causation or precedent nonetheless grasp intuitively the notion that there are layers of the past beneath us. Think of the universal appeal of archaeology among children (and in children's museums). With the tag line "now you're in *their* world," the Children's Museum of Indianapolis features a dinosaur dig and a working paleontology lab.[35] Just as there are layers of earth, there are layers of time, and children are fascinated by the notion.

Children's books again illustrate the point. Nadia Wheatley's *My Place* richly charts the life and livelihood of one spot in Australia, moving backward from 1988 to 1788; Bonnie Pryor's *The House on Maple Street* traces three hundred years of history in one neighborhood, a story that culminates with two girls digging up an arrowhead and a broken china cup in their yard; *A Street through Time*, by Egyptologist Anne Millard, offers cutaway views of buildings in a single spot, moving from a nomadic outpost to a farming community, a medieval castle, a bustling merchant quarter, and finally contemporary office buildings.[36] In one of my most rewarding teaching experiences at the Minnesota Historical Society, as part of a four-week curriculum called "History Happened Here," I took fourth-graders from a Hmong charter school on a walking tour of the retail district a block from their school building in St. Paul. Armed simply with city directory listings from 1900, 1940, and 1960, the children excitedly charted how the space that now housed an Asian grocery and a tortilleria used to be a Swedish Baptist Church and how another building had evolved from drugstore to barbershop to jeweler to, now, a Western wear outlet.[37]

How can history exhibitions help young people draw connections such as these within museums? Mainly, museums simply need to start making the effort to highlight history in the world around us. At the Bob Bullock Texas State History Museum, *Forgotten Gateway: Coming to America through Galveston Island* (2009) features "Then and Now" stations that show newspaper headlines relevant to each section's historical themes: not just then (in the 1920s) but right here and now, immigrants are dying trying to get to America, are working in cramped quarters for less than minimum wage, are terrified of deportation.[38] *Sensing Chicago* purposely features historical icons that still exist in the city today. From the start, an essential part of the plan for *Open House* involved representing contemporary immigrants: it was essential that the walk through time that begins in 1888 continue up to the present. The exhibition set out to emphasize that the issues immigrants faced in the past—fleeing home, making a new start, raising children, wrestling with memories—are still with us. On the table in the 1930s-era kitchen sits the citizenship exam, along with recollections from the Italian residents about how terrifying the test was and how important it was to pass it; on the table in the 2005 living room sits the citizenship exam, along with recollections from the Hmong residents about how terrifying the test was and how important it was to pass it. Including a contemporary Hmong family signals that these relative newcomers, too, are part of the city's history. To young people in particular, following the house's story to the present makes a bigger point: history is all around us and within all of us.

And How

In striving to activate young people's historical sensibility, a powerful partner to "here" and "now" is an approach that we might call "how"—inviting kids to take part in the history-making process. In the same way that the *Whodunit* exhibition (opened 1993) at the Fort Worth Museum of Science and History brilliantly involved young people in the science of criminology, history museums have the potential to involve kids in the process of historical detection. Exhibitions that draw on the closely observed details of place offer opportunities to show how historians construct history and to encourage visitors to try out the research tools themselves.

One strategy is to give visitors, young and old, access to the primary sources that historians used to assemble the exhibition's stories. *On Gold Mountain*, an exhibition at the Autry Museum of Western Heritage (opened 2000), was based on author Lisa See's meticulous research into six generations of her family's history in both China and San Francisco. Visitors explored a series of environments, from a trans-Pacific steamship to a San Francisco restaurant, each of which contained family photos, documents, and records. Toward the end, the exhibition shared with visitors the genealogical methods that See used to uncover these sources and build her stories.[39] In the Valentine Riverside Museum's *Windows on Richmond* exhibition (1994), visitors looked through viewing devices to compare the contemporary James River landscape to historical photographs taken from the same vantage point.[40] *Open House*, too, encourages direct engagement with primary sources. Instead of giving visitors a master narrative, the exhibition asks them to piece stories together by exploring rooms salted with family photos, public records, letters, and oral recollections. Pulling open bureau drawers reveals pages from a high school yearbook; cranking a sausage grinder spins out a quotation from an oral history (about curing meat); opening the refrigerator door shows beer bottles with photos of the house's brewery workers and milk bottles with reminiscences about refrigeration; looking closely at a worker's uniform reveals that sewn across it are words from his death certificate ("contributory cause of death: age and hard work"). Such explorations invite cross-generational conversation. They enable grown-ups to answer the young person's query, Is this true? and they visually demonstrate that history is stitched together from multiple sources.

Some exhibitions directly cast young people as historians. In *Mysteries in History* (opened 1985) at The Children's Museum of Indianapolis, children examined evidence from the past within nineteenth-century-style log cabins and shops on a 1900s main street.[41] The National Museum of American History's *Within These Walls . . .* (another exhibition that traces a house's residents through time) adopts the mystery metaphor in the how-to section of its website. Likening houses to a time machine, the site exhorts, "Whether you own your own house, rent it, or live in an apartment, . . . you and your family can become house

detectives and discover the history of your home."[42] At the Outagamie
County Historical Society (Appleton, Wisconsin), *Time Capsules: History Goes Underground* (opened 1995) encouraged an historical mindset by asking young people to imagine themselves as *future* historians.
The exhibition asked children to vote on whom they thought historians would remember one hundred years from now (Green Bay Packers
quarterback Brett Favre consistently topped the list) and to write letters
to future Wisconsinites. Working from a sense of place, museums can
involve young people in the process of historical inquiry, of gathering
and evaluating evidence, and recognizing multiple perspectives.

Appealing to place, then, enables museums to address young people
where they are. Instead of dismissing the self-centeredness and presentism of youth, place turns these qualities into departure points. It
validates kids' worldview and, at the same time, offers humility. On
the one hand, recognizing the power of here, now, and how allows museums to exalt young people's powerful place in history. History happened right *here*—in your backyard. History matters right *now*—your
own life is history. You can learn *how* to do history—be the historian
detective. On the other hand, the lessons of here, now, and how gently
put young people *in* their place, in the way that all good history does.
Others were here before you. Others will come after. History is an evershifting mass of assertions and uncertainties. What a place to be.

NOTES

1. E.g., Richard Scarry, *Busy, Busy Town* (Racine, WI: Western Publishing Co.,
   1994); Richard Scarry, *What Do People Do All Day?* (New York: Random
   House, 1979 [1968]).
2. Wannado City, "Welcome to Wannado City" and "Plan Your Visit," www.wanna
   docity.com/grown_ups/index.php (accessed June 2, 2008); www.wannado
   city.com/grown_ups/planvisit.php (accessed November 24 2008).
3. Peter Sis, *Madlenka* (New York: Farrar, Straus and Giroux, 2000), 2–4.
4. Emphasis in the original. David Sobel, *Mapmaking with Children: Sense of
   Place Education for the Elementary Years* (Portsmouth, NH: Heinemann,
   1998), 7.
5. Sobel, *Mapmaking with Children*, 5–6. This "inside out" approach is not
   without its detractors. In the 1990s, advocates of national history standards
   criticized social studies curricula in which children focused on their local
   communities, deriding the approach for diluting history education. "From
   kindergarten through fifth grades," writes historian and former Assistant
   Secretary of Education Diane Ravitch, "children studied a curriculum
   consisting of 'me, my family, my neighborhood, my community, my
   town, my state, and my nation.'" Ravitch decries this "expanding horizons"

approach as "content-free, vapid, [and] trivial": "Typically, social studies textbooks for the elementary grades consisted of little more than stories about shopping in a generic supermarket, meeting a generic police officer, and learning how families eat dinner together" (Diane Ravitch, "History's Struggles to Survive in the Schools," *OAH Magazine of History* [April 2007]: 31). Ravitch envisions reversing the order of these concentric circles: "The core ring will be the skills and ideas that everyone in the nation (and the world) needs to know. The next ring will be peculiar to the state (reflecting its history, geography, and regional concerns). And the third will be local (supplying whatever the community cares deeply about). (Diane Ravitch, *National Standards in American Education: A Citizen's Guide* [Washington, DC: The Brookings Institution, 1997 (1995), xxviii]).

Defenders of "expanding horizons" counter that problems with the approach stem primarily from the unimaginative way it has been implemented in some schools—the generic approach that Ravitch herself decries. Many educators feel that there is room to do sophisticated work that begins with a tight local focus. Theorists also note that the "inside-out" and "outside-in" strategies need not be irreconcilable: students can be taught to tack back and forth between small- and large-scale concerns in a "think global, act local" approach. See David Hutchison, *A Natural History of Place in Education* (New York: Teachers College Press, 2004), 41, 44.

6. *Museums for a New Century: A Report of the Commission on Museums for a New Century* (Washington, DC: American Association of Museums, 1984), 54, 63; Ellen Cochran Hirzy *Excellence and Equity: Education and the Public Dimension of Museums* (Washington, DC: American Association of Museums, 1998 [1992]), 3; Ellen Hirzy, "Mastering Civic Engagement: A Report from the American Association of Museums," in *Mastering Civic Engagement: A Challenge to Museums* (Washington, DC: American Association of Museums, 2002), 9; Stephen E. Weil, "From Being about Something to Being *for* Somebody: The Ongoing Transformation of the American Museum," in *Making Museums Matter* (Washington, DC: Smithsonian Institution Press, 2002): 32–4.

7. John H. Falk and Lynn D. Dierking, *The Museum Experience* (Washington, DC: Whalesback Books, 1998 [1992]), 84, 93, 4.

8. George E. Hein, *Learning in the Museum* (New York: Routledge, 1998), 153, 179.

9. Grant McCracken, "CULTURE and Culture at the Royal Ontario Museum, Part 2," *Curator* 46 (October 2003): 423.

10. In recent years, many historians and educators have argued that traditional classrooms, too, should grant more active agency to learners and allow for more collaboration and dialogue between professor and student. See, e.g., Sam Wineburg, *Historical Thinking and Other Unnatural Acts: Charting the Future of Teaching the Past* (Philadelphia: Temple University Press, 2001); Winnie Wade, Keith Hodgkinson, Allison Smith, and John Arfield, eds., *Flexible Learning in Higher Education* (London: Kogan Page, 1994); Peter

Filene, *The Joy of Teaching: A Practical Guide for New College Instructors* (Chapel Hill: University of North Carolina Press, 2005).

11. Elaine Davis, *How Students Understand the Past: From Theory to Practice* (Walnut Creek, CA: AltaMira Press, 2005), 112, 161–2.

12. Barbara Piscitelli and David Anderson, "Young Children's Perspectives of Museum Settings and Experiences," *Museum Management and Curatorship* 19, no. 3 (2001): 277–8.

13. Museums that consider the educational implications of their physical space have often been influenced by the child-centered Reggio Emilia approach to early childhood education. To Reggio practitioners, "the environment is the third teacher" (after the child's classroom instructor and parents); see Louise Boyd Cadwell, *Bringing Reggio Emilia Home: An Innovative Approach to Early Childhood Education* (New York: Teachers College Press, 1997), 99. As educator Lella Gandini describes, every aspect of Reggio schools— "the color of the walls, the shape of the furniture . . . the arrangement of simple objects on shelves and tables"—is designed to foster "encounters, communication, and relationships" (Lella Gandini, "Foundation of the Reggio Emilia Approach," in *Next Steps toward Teaching the Reggio Way: Accepting the Challenge to Change*, ed. Joanne Hendrick [Upper Saddle River, NJ: Pearson, 2004], 16–7). The goal, writes educator Karen Haigh, is to create space that provokes "a sense of wonder, exploration, and socialization, and that fosters connections with nature and culture. The environment is seen as living and forever evolving" (Karen Haigh, "Reflecting on Changes within Our Learning Environments at Chicago Commons," in Hendrick, *Next Steps*, 200). Inspired by the Reggio approach and the Reggio Emilia-sponsored traveling exhibition "The 100 Languages of Children", the Children's Museum of Minnesota created an installation in which first- and second-graders expressed their views of the Mississippi River through the arts, including "dance, story, painting and a three-dimensional model of the city that traces the path of the river through the city of Saint Paul" (Minnesota Reggio Network, *The 100 Languages of Children*, www.mnreg gio.org/hundred.html [accessed December 1, 2008]). For discussion of how the Reggio approached shaped the philosophy of staff members at the Kohl Children's Museum (Wilmette, IL), see Fran Donovan, "Using the Reggio Approach in a Children's Museum," in *First Steps toward Teaching the Reggio Way*, ed. Joanne Hendrick, (Upper Saddle River, NJ: Prentice Hall, 1997), 181–95.

14. Lois Wyse, *How to Take Your Grandmother to a Museum* (New York: Workman Publishing Co., 1998), 8, 22–3.

15. E. L. Konigsburg, *From the Mixed-up Files of Basil E. Frankweiler* (New York: Atheneum Books, 1967), 5.

16. Diane Willow, "Exhibitions as a Context for Engaging Young Children and Families with the Ideas That Technology Can Reveal," *Exhibitionist* 27 (Spring 2008): 80.

17. Piscitelli and Anderson, "Young Children's Perspectives," 269, 275.

18. For a poetic description of how exhibitions transport the young imagination, see Felice Holman, "Museum," in *Behind the Museum Door: Poems to Celebrate the Wonders of Museums*, ed. Lee Bennett Hopkins, (New York: Abrams Books for Young Readers, 2007), 16.

19. For example, John Demos explored everyday life in Plymouth Colony (*The Little Commonwealth: Family Life in Plymouth Colony* [New York: Oxford University Press, 1970]); Kenneth A. Lockridge looked at Dedham, MA (*A New England Town: The First 100 Years, Dedham, Massachusetts, 1636–1736* [New York: Norton, 1970]); Stephan Thernstrom focused on Newburyport (*Poverty and Progress: Social Mobility in a Nineteenth-century City* [Cambridge, MA: Harvard University Press, 1964]); Paul Boyer and Stephen Nissenbaum studied Salem (*Salem Possessed: The Social Origins of Witchcraft* [Cambridge, MA: Harvard University Press, 1974]); Paul E. Johnson apprenticed himself to Rochester (*A Shopkeeper's Millennium: Society and Revivals in Rochester, New York, 1815–1837* [New York: Hill and Wang, 1978]); and Roy Rosenzweig pursued Worcester (*Eight Hours for What We Will: Workers and Leisure in an Industrial City, 1870–1920* [New York: Cambridge University Press, 1983]).

20. Christopher Clark and Nancy Hewitt, *Who Built America? Working People and the Nation's History, Volume One to 1877*, 3rd edition. New York: Bedford/St. Martin's, 2007.

21. National Center for History in the Schools, "K-4 Content Standards," http://nchs.ucla.edu/standards/;http://nchs.ucla.edu/standards/standardsk -4-1-2. html (accessed June 3, 2008).

22. Keeping and Creating American Communities, http://kcac.kennesaw.edu/ (accessed June 3, 2008).

23. "Teaching with Historic Places," *History Education News* 1 (May 2008), 5. See also www.nps.gov/history/nr/twhp/ (accessed August 14, 2009).

24. *Official Guide to Colonial Williamsburg* (Williamsburg, VA: The Colonial Williamsburg Foundation, 2004 [1998]), 7, 1.

25. Old Salem Museums and Gardens, "Plan Your Visit," www.oldsalem.org/index.php?id = 151 (accessed June 3, 2008).

26. Sanya Pleshakov, "Museo Del Acero," Exhibit Files: A Community Site for Exhibit Designers and Developers (Web site hosted by Association of Science-Technology Centers, Washington, DC, October 8, 2007, modified October 19, 2007) www.exhibitfiles.org/museo_del_acero (accessed July 22, 2009).

27. Tsongas Industrial History Center, "What Is the Tsongas Industrial History Center?" www.uml.edu/tsongas/index2.htm (accessed June 3, 2008).

28. For a description of the installation, see Michael Frisch, "Brooklyn's History Museum: The Urban History Exhibit as an Agent of Change," in *Ideas and Images: Developing Interpretive History Exhibits*, ed. Kenneth L. Ames, Barbara Franco, and L. Thomas Frye (Nashville, TN: American Association for State and Local History, 1992), 264–79.

29. Chicago History Museum, "Sensing Chicago," www.chicagohistory.org/documents/home/aboutus/pressroom/exhibition-releases/sensingChicago.pdf (accessed December 1, 2008).

30. Chicago History Museum, "Exhibitions," www.chicagohistory.org/planavisit/exhibitions (accessed June 4, 2008).

31. For information on *Open House*, see www.mnhs.org/openhouse/.

32. In contrast to *Open House*, the National Museum of American History's *Within These Walls . . .* exhibition is built around a real house, an artifact from the museum's collection. The house was collected by Smithsonian curators in the 1960s, who saved it from the wrecking ball and reassembled it in the museum's galleries as an example of eighteenth-century building style. Reflecting social history's influence, a 2002 reinstallation shifted the focus of the exhibit from architecture to people. The house remains, towering, in the gallery, but the new installation highlights five families who lived in the home. Since the house is an artifact, visitors cannot enter it. National Museum of American History, *Within These Walls*, http://american history.si.edu/house/home.asp (accessed June 4, 2008).

33. "Interaction with a history exhibition that includes and elicits storytelling is a process of a visitor placing themselves [*sic*] within place, time, and sense of self. This allows visitors to place themselves within the larger historical narrative, and both internal and external histories simultaneously acquire relevance, which is key to constructing personal meaning" (Kirsten Ellenbogen, Beth Janetski, and Murphy Pizza, "Summative Evaluation Report: *Open House: If These Walls Could Talk*," prepared for the Minnesota Historical Society [unpublished], 2006, 7).

34. Evaluators found the median time spent in the 5,200-square-foot exhibition to be 33 minutes (Ellenbogen, Janetski, and Pizza, "Summative Evaluation," 3).

35. The Children's Museum of Indianapolis, "Welcome to Dinosphere," www.Child rensMuseum.org/themuseum/dinosphere/index.htm (accessed June 5, 2008).

36. Nadia Wheatley, *My Place* (Brooklyn, NY: Kane/Miller Book Publishers, 1994); Bonnie Pryor, *The House on Maple Street* (New York: HarperCollins, 1992 [1987]); Anne Millard, *A Street through Time: A 12,000-Year Walk through History* (New York: DK Publishing, Inc., 1998).

37. "History Happened Here: Educational Curriculum That Brings History Home!" Minnesota Historical Society (unpublished), 2006.

38. For information on *Forgotten Gateway*, see www.forgottengateway.com (accessed May 31, 2009). The "Then and Now" strategy was presented at an advisory meeting I attended in Austin, TX, February 22, 2008.

39. The Autry Museum is now the Museum of the American West, part of the Autry National Center; see Autry National Center, "About the Autry National Center," www.autrynationalcenter.org/about.php (accessed June 18, 2008). James Hong, "On Gold Mountain: A Chinese American Experience," *Newsletter* (summer 2000), Chinese American Museum; Xiaojian Zhao, "*On Gold Mountain: A Chinese American Experience*" (review) *The Public Historian* 23 (spring 2001), 127–29. Like *On Gold Mountain, Open House* and *Within These Walls . . .* each ends with a "how to" section.

40. Henry Chase, "Past Due and On Time!" *American Visions* (June–July 1994), http://findarticles.com/p/articles/mi_m1546/is_/ai_15495026?tag = artBody; col1 (accessed December 2, 2008).

41. Cynthia Robinson and Warren Leon, "A Priority on Process: The Indianapolis Children's Museum and 'Mysteries in History,'" in Ames, Franco, and Frye, eds. *Ideas and Images*, 220–221.

42. National Museum of American History, "Clues within These Walls," http:// americanhistory.si.edu/house/clues/clues.asp (accessed August 14, 2009).

PART III

Creating History Exhibitions
for Kids

T hey prefer participating in an assembly-line activity to reading a label about an industrial process; they race from one eye-catching station to the next rather than methodically moving from gallery to gallery; they always travel in groups with an adult and have little disposable income beyond the means to purchase a souvenir pencil; and their behavior runs the spectrum from screams of delight to tears of anguish. On first read, the cognitive, physical, social, and emotional characteristics of this audience do not seem a match for a history museum. Why would a place dedicated to the interpretation of the past be interested in an audience who thinks their grandparents grew up with dinosaurs or their parents fought in the Civil War? Perhaps the answer lies in the question.

We know kids are curious about the past and their connection to it. We know that at different stages of development kids can grasp increasingly complex historical notions. We know that they can use their minds, bodies, and emotions to acquire ideas and information about the past. We know that kids can connect with historical people and places through stories and the tangible evidence of the past. And we know that kids can participate in the development of history exhibitions to make them work better for other kids.

The task is to make exhibitions that build on our knowledge of kids and our belief that they are a legitimate audience for history. However, history museums do not have a long tradition of developing exhibitions for kids. Too often our processes and products put adults first and consider children's needs later. A familiar scenario for reaching out to kids is to retrofit an adult-oriented exhibition with a printed scavenger hunt, a basket of toys, or a cart filled with objects to touch. Without the mind-set or the skill set to create exhibition experiences for kids, history museums are left wondering where to begin.

Today, terms such as accessibility, equity, visitor-centered, and universal design are found throughout the literature of our profession. These qualities take physical form in exhibitions that incorporate a range of interpretive elements. Font size and word counts, light levels and benches, and multimedia presentations are means for communicating messages, creating comfortable environments, and engaging visitors. Museums that embrace the idea of creating history exhibitions for kids are faced with the challenge of shifting their own practice and process to achieve this goal. What often eludes them is how to make this change when staff is untrained and the tradition of adult-centered exhibition development feels completely incompatible with the needs, interests, and abilities of kids.

To reach this audience museums must embrace new ways of conveying historical context and content. History exhibitions for children welcome wonder and curiosity, and the environments become spaces filled with surprises and play. History exhibitions for kids are primarily concerned with communicating content through experiences aligned with a child's abilities and attributes, and engaging younger visitors in the ideas that fuel historians, drive the historical process, and demonstrate that the past is valuable to us today. Familiar exhibition components and communication methods such as labels must be reconsidered when targeting younger readers. Objects must be interpreted through more creative methods than identification labels. At the same time, other resources can be leveraged in new ways. New technology provides access to content on multiple levels for kids already versed in high-tech communication methods. The visitor's entire body becomes a tool for engagement when the audience you seek learns with hands, head, and heart equally.

The chapters in this part of the book explore how the familiar interpretive tools of museums are being reconfigured to connect children to history. Andrew Anway and Neal Mayer, in Chapter 9, "Shaping the Space: Designing for Kids," pose a challenging question for the development of the physical space. In their exploration of the tenets of universal design they demonstrate that design is not responsible for accommodating disability, design defines it. As we create exhibition experiences, or when we design anything, we must recognize that the design can include or exclude anyone and everyone. If the design excludes, either by intent or by accident, it defines whom the exhibition and ultimately the museum is for. In light of this chapter, when museums suggest that not all exhibitions are for everyone, perhaps they will be challenged to consider, then, who is it not for? Who is not welcome here?

In Chapter 10, "Making History Interactive," John Russick demonstrates that history can be, and in fact is, interactive. Well-developed and -designed interactive experiences can better reflect the lives and experiences of people in history as well as the real work of historians as they formulate questions, search for clues, and solve puzzles. Interactives are one-of-a-kind, complex exhibition components that must be integrated into the exhibition-development process from the start, not just added on if time and budget allow. Russick argues that interactivity should be the central tool of history exhibition curators, developers, educators, and designers as they seek to connect kids to the past.

History museums largely define themselves by their collections. The materials they hold express their character and shape their identity. For some, the greatest challenge is to develop history exhibitions that successfully use these objects to help connect kids to the past. Mary Jane Taylor and Beth A. Twiss Houting bring decades of important research and insightful analysis to bear on the subject. In Chapter 11, "Is it Real? Kids and Collections" they demonstrate that children, and the families who come to the museum with them, can and do understand the power of objects when museums take the time to choose them wisely and make them cognitively inviting, physically accessible, and emotionally engaging.

Judy Rand in Chapter 12, "Write and Design with the Family in Mind" explores the many facets of label development beginning with understanding who the label is for and determining what function it will serve. Rand reveals that labels are much more than words alone. Carefully chosen words, thoughtful graphic design, and intuitive placement are all critical to the effectiveness of labels. Labels become the invisible guide for children's adult companions, assisting them in answering questions, sparking conversations, providing instructions, and communicating interesting information.

In Chapter 13, "In a Language They'll Understand: Media and Museums." Gail Ringel identifies three characteristics of kids that affect how, and perhaps why, media is a tool for connecting this audience to history. Kids live in a media-rich world, they can concentrate on a task for long periods of time, and their lives are fundamentally different from the adults who are charged with making exhibitions for them. Ringel argues that media programs draw on a child's inclination to have choices, demonstrate control, and master a new skill to provide emotionally and intellectually satisfying exhibition experiences.

Making successful history exhibitions for kids will require museums to embrace new approaches and new attitudes. But it will also force us to reconsider some old and familiar aspects of our work. For many, rethinking the way we work and who we do our work for will be the most difficult transition. As we reach out to this new audience, we will continue to use familiar tools to advance the process, such as design, interactives, objects, labels, and media. And these features of exhibitions will continue to provide context, communicate messages, offer points of connection, and encourage engagement, curiosity, and wonder. But these familiar tools will offer unfamiliar challenges and exciting opportunities as we seek to use them to connect the history that we love to an audience whose relationship to the past is unformed and uncommitted. If we embrace this challenge and build exhibitions that inspire young people to care about the past, we will make history.

CHAPTER 9

Shaping the Space: Designing for Kids

Andrew Anway and Neal Mayer

Introduction: What Does History Smell Like?

Experienced exhibition designers will tell you that there is no greater challenge than designing exhibitions for kids. The reason is simple. Most exhibitions for adults are *about* something—culture, science, history. Successful exhibitions for kids are primarily *for* someone—kids of varying ages and their caregivers. The advocacy implied in being for someone has fundamental implications for design. To be successful for kids, design must begin with the physical, cognitive, and developmental characteristics that make kids as an audience so diverse, interesting, and fun.

As we have learned in previous chapters, kids are immensely capable and their thought processes are delightfully unconstrained. They want to know about everything—how to measure the temperature of magma; how many helium balloons it will take to lift them into the air; why, if George Washington was the father of our country, he was also a slave owner; what it is like to be prey. They especially want to know what history smells like.[1]

History is an inquiry-based discipline that is founded on a process of asking questions, seeking answers, analyzing new ideas and information, and making new inquiries. Kids do this all the time. It is instructive to observe that kids possess, innately, some of the same essential skills of a trained historian. Since kids are natural questioners and history is a discipline based on inquiry, why is it that there is such a paucity of successful history exhibitions for kids? Perhaps it is because adults conceive of history as a series of proscribed linear events rather than an expression of an experience that is equal parts progression and serendipity. This chapter will explore how to design history exhibitions for kids by capitalizing on the skills and strengths kids bring to the museum experience from the start. A successful exhibition for kids will flow from an understanding of the cognitive and developmental characteristics of children, combined with their natural desire to investigate the world, to pay attention to it, to think about it.

FIGURE 9.1. A girl samples a history smell in the exhibition, *Sensing Chicago.* Courtesy Chicago History Museum.

Think Like a Designer

"I don't see much sense in that," said Rabbit.

"No," said Pooh humbly, "there isn't.
But there was going to be when I began it."

       —Winnie the Pooh[2]

How many times have you entered an exhibition gallery and, upon seeing some particularly inventive exhibit wondered, How did they think of that? The truth is that inventive design is almost always the result of a long iterative process in which numerous ideas are developed, tested, modified, sometimes discarded, and then finally materialize into the exhibit you see on the gallery floor. While this may seem like a sobering notion, it should come as some comfort to know that rarely does a great design happen simply because of the shear brilliance of the designer. Most often, great design is the result of intense collaboration by a talented team with clear goals over time.

 Some say design is a mysterious art practiced only by specially gifted and trained individuals. Another view is that we are all designers.

For example, you are designing when you decide to move your phone to the left side of your desk so that you can hold the handset in your left hand while you use your computer mouse with your right. You are refining your design when you decide to replace the corded phone with a hands-free device so you no longer need to hold the handset. Design is the thinking that leads to implementation of an idea that results in making something intentionally more successful. But for those who do not see themselves as designers, the process of design remains elusive. What are the sources of inspiration and insight a designer taps to invent designs that are simultaneously effectual and extraordinary? How does a designer know when he or she has it right?

Ultimately, an exhibition is a three-dimensional composition that evolves in many ways from many sources. Exhibition designers come from a variety of disciplines, but most often they come from the fields of architecture, industrial design, or theatre design. Depending on their training and personal inclinations, designers vary in their approach to the design process. Some consider space and physical form as a starting point for design; others consider the exhibition's subject first and let it drive the design. What is interesting is that designers can achieve success using both approaches by coaxing inspiration from the exhibition context, its content, and design precedence, and perhaps most importantly by observing and thinking about how the audience interacts with the world. Yogi Berra once said, "You can observe a lot by watching."[3] Sometimes design can flow from such elemental wisdom.

Universal Design

Everyone is a lot of people to design for.

—Joshua Rose [4]

Since the passage of the Americans with Disabilities Act (ADA)[5] in 1990 and the subsequent publication of the *ADA Standards for Accessible Design*[6] in 1994, designers have been required by law to become familiar with the tenets of accessible design. Until recently, compliance with ADA requirements was often *applied to* designs rather than *incorporated into* designs from the start. Now a much more enlightened movement has been powering design principles far beyond the minimal standards of the Americans with Disabilities Act. These principles, called "universal design," are based on a simple idea—disabilities are perceived by their context. Design has the ability to amplify or ameliorate a perceived disability by the context the designer creates.

UNIVERSAL DESIGN

Universal Design is defined by the North Carolina State University Center for Universal Design as "the design of products and environments to be usable by all people, to the greatest extent possible, without the need for adaptation or specialized design."[7] This definition includes seven principles:

1. **Equitable Use:** The design is useful and marketable to people with diverse abilities.

2. **Flexibility in Use:** The design accommodates a wide range of individual preferences and abilities.

3. **Simple and Intuitive Use:** Use of the design is easy to understand, regardless of the user's experience, knowledge, language skills, or current concentration levels.

4. **Perceptible Information:** The design communicates necessary information effectively to the user, regardless of ambient conditions or the user's sensory abilities.

5. **Tolerance for Error:** The design minimizes hazards and the adverse consequences of accidental or unintended actions.

6. **Low Physical Effort:** The design can be used efficiently and comfortably and with a minimum of fatigue.

7. **Size and Space for Approach and Use:** Appropriate size and space is provided for approach, reach, manipulation, and use regardless of the user's body size, posture, or mobility.

There is a tremendous power embedded in the idea that context is the primary definer of disability. This means a thoughtful design, one that takes into account the range of capabilities of all visitors, will offer access to the exhibition to the widest possible audience. A designer of a toddler exhibition creates a set of circumstances that never exceed the toddler's range of motion, strength, or balance, while at the same time challenges that toddler to explore the exhibit to the best of her abilities. Yet that same designer might create unnecessary accessibility barriers in an exhibition for adults by failing to take the same care in design as was taken in designing for small children. Here is a simple example. Have you ever been tired of standing in a museum and sought out a place to sit? How many times have you found a place to sit convenient to the place at which you had the thought about sitting? Has the lack of seating affected your ability to enjoy the exhibit and to continue to explore it? Now think about this. How many exhibits have you experienced that require you to see in bright light and see in dim light; hear in loud, multi-source audio environments and hear at low levels of audio amplification; transition from gallery to gallery via ramps and stairs with no perceptible difference in floor materials; read low-contrast, small-point fonts; use fine motor skills to manipulate trackballs, touch screens, flipbooks, knobs, and slides; and view collections in densely packed cases up to ten feet tall? Most likely you have experienced all of these. But if the designers of exhibits like these had applied universal design principles to their design thinking from the start, you would not have endured these challenges because the designers would have eliminated where possible, and minimized where practical, such barriers to the full exhibition experience for all visitors.

Among the great things about kids is that they come in all shapes and sizes and with a huge array of cognitive and physical abilities; in other words, they represent the full spectrum of human ability. Designers recognize the power of design to make exhibit experiences rewarding, engaging, and memorable for a range of physical and cognitive abilities. Active employment of universal design principles is one of the leading ways designers can ensure the maximum positive participation, in any type of exhibit experience, of the broadest possible audience.

The Power of Empathy

You can design and create, and build the most wonderful place in the world. But it takes people to make the dream a reality.

— Walt Disney[8]

In turning to the past, historians must bring a sense of empathy for the conditions of that particular moment and the perspectives of the individuals involved. Similarly, the designer draws on empathic associations. But whereas the historian looks to the past, the designer looks to the future, always considering the needs and abilities of individuals who will visit and experience a space that has yet to be defined or constructed.

Audience First

Exhibition design is a craft first and an art form second. Thus it has a singular purpose of communicating ideas to specific audiences through multiple points of engagement. How these points of engagement are conceived relates directly to the audience for whom the exhibition is intended. It takes much more than the designer's enthusiasm to generate triumphant visitor experiences. In order to be a success, exhibitions must satisfy the visitors' interests, needs, and abilities. The interests, needs, and abilities of children differ greatly from those of the people who are designing for them, so it becomes imperative for designers first to understand as much about the audience as they can from a developmental perspective, and second to begin to think and feel like a child.

For most exhibitions, the first question designers should ask is, For whom are we designing? While we know we will be designing for kids, an audience for whom there is a substantial developmental range, we also want to design experiences that work well for their caregivers. Increasingly, the aim of exhibitions targeting kids and their caregivers is for intergenerational interaction. Sometimes, though, exhibitions are designed to engage kids as a primary audience while providing a comfortable place for adults to relax and observe. The implication of this approach is that the designer may decide to create an environment that feels exclusive to kids, perhaps scaled to their size or set in an environment that is familiar to them but not to their caregivers. If it is a goal of the exhibition to promote interaction between kids and adults, then the designer may decide to create an exhibition that has some elements that resonate with parents—something familiar from their own childhood, or maybe an environment that would be considered novel to any group.

Establishing Design Criteria: Questions and Answers

When we have arrived at the question, the answer is already near.

— Ralph Waldo Emerson[9]

It is often said that great design is the answer to difficult questions—the more challenging the question, the more inspiring the design response. This axiom is particularly true of designing history exhibitions for kids. The very notion of history is a turnoff for some kids. It conjures up a universe of boring memorization and tedious facts that have nothing to do with kids' lives. So at their most elemental level, history exhibitions for kids have to deal with a question profound in its simplicity: How can history exhibitions for kids be made meaningful and fun?

If great design is the answer to challenging questions, then the whole design process is based on asking and answering questions. The more thoughtful these questions, the more useful the answers will be,

GUIDING PRINCIPLES FOR EXHIBITION DESIGN 1

Design flows from a project vision, a Big Idea, and goals.

Vision

All exhibitions begin with a vision. A vision sets out the large aims for a project and identifies the impact the exhibition will have on its intended audience. It answers the question, What are we trying to accomplish? A project vision is a required precursor to design. It will sprout within an individual or small team at first, but it will bloom only through the care and nurturing of the entire project team. The vision defines the purpose of the work but not the means to get there. Example: "To become a family-friendly history museum."

Big Idea

A Big Idea will be created by the project team to guide design. So what is a Big Idea? Beverly Serrell writes, "[t]he big idea provides an unambiguous focus for the exhibit team through the exhibit development process by clearly stating in one compound sentence the scope and purpose of the exhibition."[10] Designers use the Big Idea as a touchstone for design solutions. If an exhibition idea is not a natural fit within the project's Big Idea, then it should not be used. Example: "History is all around us." This Big Idea suggests a design that promotes observation and investigation of the echoes of history that appear ubiquitously in our everyday lives. The big idea is a tool for aligning project work.

Goals

Goals are the backbone of exhibition design. As we have seen in previous chapters, they must be carefully conceived and crafted to be useful. For something to be a goal, it must be measurable. Example: "To help kids to see the evidence of history in their everyday lives." The degree to which the exhibit successfully achieves this goal can be tested easily by asking kids questions about what, if anything, they can identify as part of history in their lives.

and the more likely they are to lead to successful design solutions. It is important to note that the process of asking and answering questions as a way to reach consensus for design solutions will produce unique results for each exhibition. Each team brings its own distinctive set of skills and experience to bear on every project and because each institution provides its own institutional culture within which the exhibition is developed. This process will guarantee a diversity of good answers to similar questions and thus wholly different exhibition designs, each with equivalent success at meeting their team's objectives. Nevertheless, the first question should always be, Who is this for?

What Do Kids Know and What Do They Want to Know?

Knowing how kids reason and learn is essential to knowing how to design for them. In addition to understanding developmental characteristics, the design team will want to know what their younger audience already knows about the intended focus of the exhibition. With this as a launching point, the designer can meet kids at their current level of understanding and move them beyond this point of initial engagement.

The answer to the question, What do kids already know (or think they know) about your subject? is the most pertinent to the exhibition designer, along with the answer to the corollary question, What else do kids know or care about in relation to this story? Armed with knowledge about what kids already know, designers can decide whether they need to create exhibition elements that are expository, bringing visitors to a common baseline of knowledge from which the exhibition can build. Getting visitors to engage with a story that's already known to and popular with them is different than getting them to engage with an unknown or unfamiliar story. To a kid, the story of a local sports hero may be more familiar than the story of a local mill owner who put the city on the map. We know from our own observations that kids are ultimately open to new ideas, but they hold onto their existing ideas dearly until they are given alternatives they deem to be of equal or greater value. For exhibition design, this means that a good place to start engaging kids is through things with which they are already familiar or in which they already have a demonstrated interest. For example, in designing an exhibition about civics and government, a design team may want to think about kids' interest in travel, their fascination with the presidency, and their existing knowledge of Washington, DC, as a way into an exhibition that reveals to kids their power and responsibility as citizens in a democracy.

What do kids want to know? What do they want to do in an exhibition? Kids' curiosity is as persistent as it is endless, so they want to know pretty much everything. As designers, we need to mine this curiosity as much as possible and leverage it as a tool for learning. Museum professionals understand intuitively that when children are engaged in an exhibition experience, they are collecting new information that will be assimilated into their worldview, if not during their visit, then soon thereafter. While adults certainly bring children to a museum with the expectation that there will be learning going on, this is not a kid's primary objective. Learning something new is a bonus when coupled with a positive, fun experience. Ideally, as kids go about the business of having fun, they will encounter information and experiences that relate to them personally—answering questions they might have asked, making sense of a subject from a kid-centered perspective.

What Will Be the Visitor Experience?

The museum experience is different from the school experience. Visitors choose to come to museums because they offer educational experiences that are informal and unique in the context of other leisure activities. Because so much learning is dependent on physical context, history exhibitions have an extraordinary opportunity to capitalize on their subject matter to create rich contextual presentations. To achieve this, it's appropriate to assess the visitor experience goals vigorously as part of the initial stages of design.

For example, kids experience the world with their bodies, minds, and emotions. Their exuberance for life is infectious. How can designers prepare space for kids that acknowledges their innate delight with themselves and the world around them, while helping them to focus on exploration and learning? Play is the way in which young children learn and older children engage subject matter best. Exhibitions that use play as a natural form of engagement overcome one of the initial barriers in history museums—the complaint that history museums are boring.

Time to Design

The fundamental failure of most graphic, product, architectural and even urban design is its insistence on serving the God of Looking-Good rather than the God of Being-Good.

— Richard Saul Wurman[11]

There is one primary rule of design: if the design is not helping to communicate an idea, it is helping to obscure it. Kids and grown-ups alike make use of all kinds of cues to understand any space they enter. As quickly as they can, they assess their options for moving around that space and they execute an arithmetic evaluation of who else is there, whether the space is comfortable, intriguing, or challenging, and how to get back out. If the space happens to be an exhibition, they also assess what it's about, what they can do or experience, and, especially, whether it's for them. The cues may be visual, auditory, tactile, and, in some exhibits, olfactory. Exhibition designers choose how these cues are delivered and the extent to which they help visitors make these assessments.

Manipulating Space

Placement of walls, cases, and objects affect what children can see from a given spot. These design elements define the context for what they do upon entering a space and where they may go after their initial assessment of what possibilities exist. With this in mind, designers can control—or at least suggest—a sequence of experiences that allow a story or experience to unfold in a particular way. Views and scale are principally important to kids and their caregivers. For kids, scale can be comforting and welcoming; for adults, unobstructed views allow them to monitor their kids without being overbearing.

Some exhibitions are best served by a linear, sequential arrangement; others are better served by a hub-and-spoke layout, with a central orientation or hub experience designed to launch the visitor into the exhibition. It is neither practical nor desirable to over orchestrate the visitor experience sequence. When entering a gallery, most visitors will proceed to the first exhibit they notice and go on from there. What makes a gallery design work is clear organization combined with a sense of comfort, confidence, and safety woven into design that is beautiful.

Control of Stimulus

The design team will want each element of the exhibition to be stimulating. Interesting objects, vivid graphics, captivating audiovisual programs, animated and interactive elements, and dramatic lighting are all ways to increase the sensory appeal of an exhibit. Of course, conflicting stimulus will be counterproductive, especially to kids, so designers need to be judicious in how they employ these techniques. For kids, stimulus needs to be varied and paced so that one part of the exhibition is not disrupted by another part that is so attractive it distracts from

---

GUIDING PRINCIPLES FOR EXHIBITION DESIGN 2

Know your space.

One simple way to envision space is to enlist the services of a shoe-box. Pick a box to represent the space for an exhibit. Then select objects that can be used for scale within the shoebox. If you have a shoebox that is approximately 7 inches wide by 12 or 13 inches long, its area is approximately 90 square inches. Change the scale by an exponent (10 to 1, or 100 to 1) and you can characterize this shoebox as representing 900 square feet or 9,000 square feet. If you place a jewelry box inside and it measures 3 inches by 3 inches, it becomes an exhibit component measuring 90 square feet or 900 square feet, depending on the scale you chose.

After manipulating your shoebox space model by placing a variety of scaled objects inside, try cutting an opening in one of the walls of your "gallery" as if to create a door or opening into another part of your museum. You will see a dramatic difference in the space relationship to the objects inside your box—they will seem to have more room around them and be less constrained by the shoebox walls. This exercise is a simple way to demonstrate the impact of large objects, exhibits and openings can have on the arrangement and feel of an exhibition. Remember to include shapes to represent people too—leaving room for groups of visitors is key to planning for kids.

---

the current experience. Particularly active spaces should be followed by more passive ones. If a design calls for a quiet space, perhaps a reading or video-viewing area, be sure that it can be bypassed so that visitors using it will not be disturbed by those just passing through. An experience map is a helpful tool for planning the sequence of techniques.

When designers think initially about an exhibition they think about the overall visitor experience rather than the design of individual exhibit components. In a practical sense, this means they are thinking about pacing, about the distribution of types of experiences and about the flow of emotional and cognitive engagement the experience can impart. This kind of thinking is what is meant by the term "experience design." A tool designer's use for this exercise is an experience map.

FIGURE 9.2. Space planning with a shoebox employs scaled inserts to approximate exhibit sizes and circulation areas. Courtesy Chicago History Museum.

An experience map can be as simple as a bubble diagram (Figure 9.3), loosely based on a thematic plan for the exhibition, or a detailed iteration of exhibits based on a fully fleshed-out version of a floor plan. In either case the experience map is a useful tool for evaluating the mix of experiences the design purports to incorporate and their likely resonance with the intended audience.

Leveraging Assets

In the world of marketing, assets combined with unique resources are what confer a competitive advantage. Museum assets consist of tangible things. For a history exhibition, the location of the space might be an asset, particularly if the subject matter is directly related to the site where the exhibition will be located. If place is an important part of a story, but the story happened far away, the design may incorporate some recreated environments, such as dioramas or scale models with media or a combination of these techniques to ground the story in a location.

Objects are another category of assets. If a museum is lucky enough to have real objects, they might comprise a powerful component of the display. If actual objects are not available (or even if they are, but visitors will not be allowed to touch them), designers can use replicas or

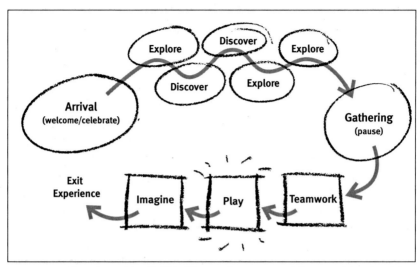

FIGURE 9.3. Experience Map Bubble Diagram is a great tool for organizing the visitor experience by thematic flow. Courtesy Andy Anway and Neal Mayer.

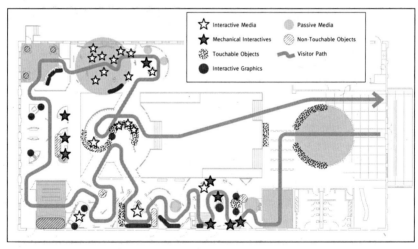

FIGURE 9.4. Experience Map Plan illustrates the pace and type of visitor experiences in a gallery. Courtesy Andy Anway and Neal Mayer.

props, especially working replicas that visitors can touch and manipulate. People can be assets too. For example, there may be people still living who participated in an historical event and can be incorporated into the exhibition through interviews and recorded oral histories to add dimension, relevance, and interactivity. When thinking about assets, imagine how they might be leveraged to make a story more dynamic, charismatic, and relevant to kids. People can be assets in other ways too.

Museum staff who are ready to meet the challenge of creating history exhibitions for kids are essential to the project. Team members must be committed to the task and possess an understanding of history that values the thoughts and feelings expressed by young children.

Using Color and Texture

Color, and to a more subtle degree texture, both influence the way an exhibit is perceived. Changing the color of a space, with paint, a simple wall covering, or lighting, is one of the least expensive ways to make a dramatic difference in how the space is perceived. Color is also an effective way to create organization in a space.

An exhibition can be "branded" by using a distinctive color palette. A relationship between dissimilar exhibit elements can be implied by using the same color or colors in each exhibit. Conversely, exhibit areas can be differentiated by using varied color palettes for each area. Remember that kids are no more drawn to primary colors than adults, so sophisticated color palettes in children's exhibitions can be effective. In addition to the basic characteristic of hue (red, yellow, blue, etc.) every color has two other characteristics. Value describes how dark or light a color is. Saturation describes how pure it is. The less saturated a color is, the more gray it is. Kids respond to color value and saturation in the same way as adults.

Texture can be used as a visual element in the same ways color can, but it is even more powerful as a tactile element. The use of texture as a tactile element enriches the experience for anyone, and especially for visually impaired kids and their caregivers. Texture provides tactile cues to changes in the exhibition environment and helps illustrate exhibition ideas in a literal sense. Think, for example, about describing what it feels like to ride a high-wheel bike over cobblestones in contrast with the experience of feeling the bike wheels bumping along over actual cobbles. The translation of a descriptive experience into one that transmits the physical characteristics of an historic experience will be more successful in attracting kid audiences and more successful in cementing the ideas of the exhibition through engaging sensory experiences that complement cognitive ones.

Choosing Materials

Strength, economy, durability, safety, sustainability, opulence—materials are chosen for a reason. Often there are conflicting considerations and designers must make compromises. Designing exhibitions for chil-

GUIDING PRINCIPLES FOR EXHIBITION DESIGN 3:

Budgets and schedules are tools not terrors.

With an honest understanding of budget and schedule, designers can feel free to design, certain in the knowledge that funds and time will be available to complete their work. Larger budgets do not always translate into better results, and budgets must be aligned realistically to the objectives of the exhibition and the realities of the conditions under which the exhibition will be created and installed. Contrary to popular belief, kids exhibitions are not less expensive than those tailored to adults, provided they each have similar design criteria.

Three factors determine the cost of fabricating exhibitions—the complexity of the design, the quality and variety of materials used, and the density of exhibits in a gallery. Like exhibitions for adults, exhibitions for kids use graphics and 3-D elements in concert to create the environment. Other costs to account for when planning exhibitions for children may include artifact displays, multi-media programs, computer interactives, and Internet access.

Exhibition costs are estimated in "dollars per square foot." Consider $250 to $350 per square foot (in 2010 dollars) a threshold for a good-quality exhibit with a mix of features, professional design, and quality production values. Exhibits with budgets below $250 per square foot are mostly graphic treatments with modest mechanical interactives and little or no multimedia. With budgets above $350 per square foot, exhibits may become more feature rich and include more sophisticated design elements, material choices, and audiovisual and/or computer interactive elements.

dren involves concerns that typically do not exist when designing for adults. Exhibitions for children receive harder use than most others. Generally speaking, the more successful they are, the harder they will be used. Because so many exhibitions are "hands-on," safety and cleanliness are concerns of caregivers and durability and maintenance are concerns of museum staff. Whenever possible, opt for materials that are resilient and easy to keep clean. Design exhibitions so that parts can be replaced without removing the entire unit from the floor.

Consider how the exhibition will look after months of use. Plastic laminates are durable and can be cleaned easily, but when they do wear or chip, there is no way to touch them up. Painted wood will wear, but can be touched up. Polyethylene (the plastic used in playground equipment) is very durable. It can't be painted, but the color is molded in, so even when the material is scratched or scuffed, it still looks good.

Conclusion: Design Is Iterative and Takes Time

The young do not know enough to be prudent, and therefore they attempt the impossible—and achieve it, generation after generation.

—Pearl S. Buck[12]

Exhibition design is a process in which ideas are generated, developed and tested, re-designed to satisfy new insights and understanding, and ultimately crafted into a detailed design specification for fabrication. The process, from start to finish, enlists skills ranging from free-form conceptual thinking to the selection of materials and finishes of every single surface and element in the exhibition. In order to begin this process, designers and design teams must generate a high volume of ideas that can be developed to a level that allows the team to evaluate their merit. Traditional brainstorming strategies are a good way for the design team to develop exhibit ideas rapidly. Of course, it is important to remember that ideas that gain traction in these early phases may fail to materialize as designed experiences.

Formal evaluation is one way to test exhibit ideas as they develop, but informal evaluation can be a useful tool as well. Museum professionals who have daily access to a new exhibition's potential audience have the opportunity to test ideas frequently through the presentation of progress drawings, models, and simple exhibit prototypes. Soliciting feedback from kids throughout the project will provide candid feedback on how new exhibit ideas and experiences resonate with them.

Designers of history exhibitions for kids face a complicated challenge. On the one hand they must overcome a cultivated resistance to history that some kids harbor as a result of classroom experiences and previous museum visits in which history was presented as dusty dates seemingly without relevance to their everyday lives. On the other hand, designers know history is so fascinating, so rich, so relevant, and so much fun, that they must grapple with how to connect the discontinuity of kids' perceptions of history with the reality of what an extraordinary visitor experience it can be. To do this successfully, designers know that history must connect to kids in meaningful ways and offer kids the opportunity to leverage strengths they already bring to the experience—an innate curiosity, the ability to focus intently on something that interests them, and the delight in mastering new skills and learning new things. Here are the ways we can ensure the rewards keep coming:

- Believe in the competency of kids.

- Design for differing ages, abilities, interests and learning styles—apply universal design principals throughout.

- Appeal to the full range of senses.

- Design for self-evident circulation, intentional lines of sight, and intuitive exit.

- Showcase stories—make kids part of the story through discovery-based interaction.

- Be authentic—make use of real objects, real stories, real people, and real places.

- Design from the perspective of one meter high.

An exhibition is more than a collection of individual exhibits, it is an *experience*. Many experiences are memorable. But the best museum experiences are memorable and meaningful. Our kid audiences reward us in enthusiastic and surprising ways when they engage with history exhibitions designed with them in mind.

NOTES

1. Minda Borun, "The Chicago Historical Society Children's Gallery Focus Group Report," (unpublished report, Chicago Historical Society, August 2004.

2. A. A. Milne, *Winnie the Pooh* (New York: Puffin Books, 1954), 124.

3. Yogi Berra and Dave H. Kaplan, *You Can Observe a Lot by Watching: What I've Learned about Teamwork from the Yankees and Life* (Hoboken, NJ: John Wiley & Sons, Inc. 2008).

4. Http://www.creativeworld.com.au/resources/design-quotes/ (accessed August 4, 2009).

5. Information on the act is available at: http://www.ada.gov (accessed August 4, 2009).

6. U.S. Department of Justice, ADA *Standards for Accessible Design*, Excerpt from U. S. Code 28, Part 36, Appendix A, rev. ed. (Washington, DC: Government Printing Office, July 1, 1994), http://www.ada.gov/stdspdf.htm.

7. Bettye Rose Connell, Mike Jones, Ron Mace, Jim Mueller, Abir Mullick, Elaine Ostroff, Jon Sanford, Ed Steinfeld, Molly Story, and Gregg Vanderheiden, *Principles of Universal Design,* Version 2.0 (Raleigh, NC: The Center for Universal Design at North Carolina State University, April 1, 1997), http://www.design.ncsu.edu/cud/about_ud/udprinciples.htm (accessed September 15, 2009).

8. Pat Williams and Jim Denney, *How to Be Like Walt: Capturing the Disney Magic Every Day of Your Life,* (Dearfield Beach, FL: Health Communications, Inc., 2004), 89.

9. Ralph Waldo Emerson, *The Topical Notebooks of Ralph Waldo Emerson,* vol. 2, edited by Ronald A. Bosc (Columbia, MO: University of Missouri Press, 1993), 371.

10. Beverly Serrell, *Exhibit Labels: An Interpretive Approach* (Walnut Creek, CA: AltaMira Press, 1996), 2.

11. Rob Carter, Ben Day, and Philip B. Meggs, *Typographic Design: Form and Communication,* 4th ed. (New York: Van Nostrand Reinhold, 1985); Web companion: www.typographicdesign4e.com/exploration_quotes.html (accessed August 20, 2009).

12. Pearl S. Buck, quoted in George H. Culp and Herbert N. Nickles, *An Apple for the Teacher: Fundamentals for Instructional Computing* (Monterey, CA: Brooks/Cole Publishing Co., 1983), 190.

CHAPTER 10

Making History Interactive

John Russick

Developing successful interactive experiences with history for kids starts with a commitment to understand young people and how they learn and a willingness to embrace new ways of developing and designing history exhibitions. This chapter explores how to engage kids with history content in exhibitions that are interactive. At its core are two questions: Can history be interactive? How can interactive history exhibits engage kids in meaningful ways?

The Basics

Kids: Kids learn through a combination of cognitive, emotional, physical, and social experiences. They use their senses, imagination, and play to experiment with and create an understanding of the past, present, and the future.

History: Young children can understand basic historical concepts, such as the ideas that the past happened before today, the past is both similar to and different from our time, and that we learn about our lives by understanding how people lived in the past.

Exhibitions: History exhibitions for kids need to be developed and designed to appeal to kids and engage their minds, bodies, and emotions through age-appropriate interactive experiences with historical content.

Interactives: In museums we often use the word "interactive" to describe the physical, emotional, and cognitive experience we hope visitors will have and to describe the exhibit itself, the element within the exhibition that is meant to engage visitors in meaningful activity. Although this can lead to confusion because we use the same word to describe both the exhibit and the engagement, the word interactives will be used here as a substitute for all interactive exhibits, elements, components, and experiences.

What Is Interactive?

I hear . . . I forget.
I see . . . and I remember.
I do . . . and I understand.

Variations on this proverb have been used repeatedly in articles about interactivity in exhibitions, and with good reason. It defines the difference between remembering and understanding and it does so in terms of action taken by the learner. It has implications for any museum that hopes to help children gain understanding as a way to make meaning. In order for kids to learn by doing, we must create and define an active role for them within our exhibitions.

Every reader of this book shares at least one thing in common— we learn when we read. Most history museum exhibitions use written words to communicate ideas. When trying to reach children with these ideas our usual approach fails us. Children as old as ten are still learning to read rather than reading to learn. History museums cannot rely on kids either to have the skills to read and grasp the content of the text or to enjoy the experience of reading. So how can a history museum engage young people who either cannot read or do not enjoy reading? To reach this large and important audience, history exhibitions must engage them in meaningful activity. History messages need to be delivered without extensive label copy and interactive experiences must engage young children with ideas about what came before and why it matters.

The term interactive has many different meanings for museum professionals. Interactives are sometimes called hands-on experiences. These terms are often used interchangeably to describe exhibition activities such as pushing a button to illuminate a display, lifting doors or flaps to reveal information, or manipulating props from the museum's teaching collection or reproductions of collection items made for touching. Whether they are called interactives or hands-on activities, these exhibits invite visitors to do more than simply listen or read to obtain messages. They must act.

The narrowest definitions of an interactive describe exhibition experiences that offer visitors a way to provide input and, in return, perceive a response tailored to their specific action. Think of a game of computerized chess. The player moves a piece and the computer responds to the player's input, countering the move. The experience is shaped by the actions of the person in a real time, give-and-take relationship with the computer. The broadest definitions of the term interactive include anything a visitor does in the exhibition beyond looking or reading. Loosely defined, interactivity can be found in a conversation between visitors provoked by the exhibition content, when a child touches a replica of an object to feel its surface, or even when visitors are engaged in concentrated looking at objects.

In this chapter, an interactive will be defined somewhat narrowly as a discrete activity within an exhibition, unfacilitated by museum staff, that engages kids' minds, bodies, and/or emotions, invites them to do something, and responds to their actions, which furthers their understanding of exhibition content or messages. This definition will satisfy few museum professionals. For many it sets too high a standard. For others, it lumps the innovative, complex, multi-stage interactive experience with the more passive push button and its corresponding light-up panel.

Ultimately it is the spirit, not the definition, of interactivity that should prevail. Interactives are tools for engagement to be tested with visitors and measured for success. Whether in an art museum, science center, or history museum, an interactive must engage and enlighten visitors and invite them to become active participants in their own learning. If it does not, there is more work to be done.

Interactive Exhibitions or Exhibition Interactives

Interactive exhibitions are museum spaces designed with the goal of communicating messages through physical, cognitive, social, and/or emotional engagement. For example, an interactive exhibition about the history of the bicycle would approach the subject as a platform for interactivity, providing experiences with building, designing, buying, riding, and racing bicycles that communicate the messages of the exhibition. The concepts are experienced, not simply read or heard. *Sensing Chicago* at the Chicago History Museum and the redesign of the National Canal Museum in Easton, Pennsylvania, are two examples of interactive exhibitions in history museums. Both projects began with a commitment to provide an experience with history driven by interactivity. All subsequent decisions about content, collections, and design were measured against this primary goal.

Exhibition interactives, on the other hand, are elements within a traditional exhibition—a kiosk or device that engages people's minds, bodies, and/or emotions with a particular idea. Exhibition interactives can serve to punctuate a concept—a sort of experiential illustration—or they can provide further explanation of an idea or mechanism or process. They can create opportunities for group interaction and discussion or simply alter the pace and style of the exhibition experience. In the 2007 Chicago History Museum exhibition *Mapping Chicago: The Past and the Possible*, visitors were invited to explore the history of Chicago through three-dozen maps from the museum's collection. One area of the exhibition featured the history of a regional globe manufacturer. A globe activity in this portion of the gallery challenged kids to assemble the world by applying the printed vertical sections of the map, or gores, onto a blank sphere. The activity reinforced the relationship between maps and globes and invited kids to use their previous knowledge and their puzzle-solving skills to experience and understand the difficult and detailed work of the globe maker.

Unfortunately, exhibition interactives are often the products of a tortured birth from a shortsighted and ill-considered process. In many instances interactive solutions are pursued for all the wrong reasons. In my museum career I have witnessed the following scenarios play out as launching points for the development of exhibition interactives. On one project the exhibition content had been developed, the design was underway, and the collections were being prepared when a few project team members began searching for interactive opportunities so that there was "something for kids to do" in the gallery. Recognizing that kids would not be interested in the exhibition without opportunities to be active in the experience was insightful. Waiting to begin developing interactives until after most of the significant content and design decisions had been made was not.

In another case, the content developers could not locate appropriate objects or images to support a key exhibition message. They suggested that an interactive be developed to cover this important content. After considerable effort the subject matter failed to conform to an interactive experience and the initiative was abandoned. In yet another case, a label writer could not explain a complicated exhibition concept within the limits of available space. Project designers were asked to create an interactive to tackle the subject instead. After a flurry of activity they realized that a subject too complicated for text and graphics might be too complex to be addressed by an unfacilitated interactive experience. A flipbook full of information and images was developed instead, and was erroneously described as an interactive by members of the project team.

Successful interactives are usually hard to develop, difficult to design, and challenging to build—even when the content is well suited to an interactive experience. The unique and complex nature of interactives requires that they emerge early in the development process and that the entire project team commits to them. If the project team waits until after content questions are resolved and collections decisions are made before turning their attention to interactive development, not only will they have less time to work on the interactives, but also they forego opportunities to select content or choose collections that might support a greater level of interactivity in the exhibition. Tight schedules constrict development, prototyping, testing, and evaluation time, and contribute to the failure of interactive ideas to develop into successful working experiences within exhibitions. More importantly, within the project team, this approach reinforces the secondary status of interactives in our work. The reputation of the interactive element as an add-on or bonus feature (something unnecessary to the exhibition experience) contributes to the lack of attention paid to them and can undermine the efforts made to develop them.

In 2000, Experience Music Project (EMP) opened in Seattle, Washington, in a building designed by Frank Gehry, inspired by the energy of rock and roll and the colors of popular electric guitars such as Fender and Gibson. Everything about this museum was meant to be different. Even the name defied efforts to categorize it. In reality, EMP is an experiential history museum that explores the "do-it-yourself" creativity of rock and roll music through rare collections, audio and video experiences, and interactivity. It sets an example for the kind of experiences every history exhibition can provide.

Andrea Weatherhead, principal of WEATHERHEAD Experience Design Group, led the team that developed *Sound Lab*, an interactive gallery within EMP that provides visitors with an opportunity to experience what it is like to play in a rock band. Here, visitors actually play the classic 1960s rock and roll song *Louie Louie* on a real guitar either with other visitors or accompanied by the house band (a recording of the song performed by studio musicians). What experience could be a more meaningful and obvious in a rock and roll history exhibition than playing in a rock band? What could be a more daunting task for both visitor and museum staff?

I can't play any musical instrument, but I played *Louie Louie* at EMP. The "Guitar Interactive" in *Sound Lab* helped me do something I couldn't do when I walked in. And it helped me realize something about learning by doing. I never had any appreciation for the experience of playing in a band until I played EMP's guitar. More importantly, I couldn't really understand how it must feel to play with skill and con-

FIGURE 10.1. A boy plays a guitar in *Sound Lab*. Courtesy Experience Music Project/ Science Fiction Museum and Hall of Fame.

fidence and to make music with others. It helped me understand the ideas, the emotions, and the history that inspired that museum.

Weatherhead has said that the project was shaped by a commitment to excellence and to "the founder's vision." According to Weatherhead, "Paul Allen set extremely high goals, but not oppressive criteria." The project was defined by a combination of Allen's vision, the team's commitment to excellence and interactivity, and the creative environment in which they worked. The goal of "Guitar Interactive" was for visitors to play rock and roll on the guitar. Any solution to the interactive dilemmas the designers faced "that took you further from an experience playing the guitar was seen as an obstacle to the goal of playing rock and roll."[1]

The goal of the EMP team to connect the message of the experience with the action required to make the interactive work was beautifully articulated by Don Hughes, vice president of exhibitions at the Monterey Bay Aquarium. In remarks made during a session on exhibition design criticism at the American Association of Museums conference in 2009 Hughes said, "The movement of a good interactive moves the story forward. Visitors reach into a well and pull up a bucket full of water content, visitors turn the page of a diary to show the author's notes on the back, or sweep away sand to reveal a hidden flat fish. The visitor's action uniquely moves the story forward."[2] Playing a guitar in order to experience playing a guitar achieves Hughes' vision.

Inspiring Research

Unfortunately, the research into the effectiveness of interactive history exhibits designed for kids is extremely limited, and what exists largely comes from the evaluations of individual projects. This level of analysis often falls short when we try to establish baselines for interactives across museums. However, two important science museum research projects have identified some valuable criteria to consider when developing interactives for history museum exhibitions.

There are good reasons to look to science museums for important data about interactives as tools for engaging kids and communicating content. These organizations see interactivity as their primary experience driver and they have a long track record of creating experiential and interactive learning environments. Science museums typically weigh content and collections decisions against their ability to support a meaningful interactive experience for visitors, especially kids. Perhaps more important, science museum exhibitions reflect the way science is both taught and conducted. Hands-on chemistry, physics, and biology laboratory experiments are mimicked in science exhibitions that explore a wide range of subjects from the physics of light to the human capacity to remember to remarkable innovations such as interstellar navigation and genetic engineering. So what prevents history museums from embracing this approach and developing the sorts of experiential learning environments that we find in so many successful science museums? What keeps us from developing inquiry-driven experiences that invite kids to explore both the results of the work of historians and the work itself?

Like history museums, science museums often exhibit complex and intangible subject matter. A typical science museum exhibition might explore the weather or the hidden forces behind tornados. Is that challenge so different from presenting the history of complex and disputed events, such as the American Civil War or the development of the airplane? People cannot experience war in an exhibition about the Battle of Gettysburg. Likewise, an exhibition about tornados cannot give people an experience with a tornado. And yet a science museum would develop interactives to engage visitors in a learning experience about tornados. They would methodically explore the forces that cause tornados, including objects that speak to the force of storms. A science museum would trace the path a tornado took and analyze the destruction after the fact to understand its strength and weaknesses and imagine how we might experience and respond to tornados in the future. History museum professionals simply do not see history exhibitions in this way. We do not develop exhibitions that bring people into the process of doing history. Instead we share the results of the effort. In this way history exhibitions reflect only the way history is commonly taught, not how historians think, gather information, and interpret evidence. Nevertheless, there are lessons we can learn from science museums.

The Exploratorium's Active Prolonged Engagement (APE) study and the Philadelphia-Camden Informal Science Education Collaborative (PISEC) study provide important insights for history museums interested in developing interactive experiences for kids. It is important to note that both studies looked at family audiences rather than kids only. Family research always includes children as part of the study group and, since kids do not come to museums without adult caregivers, family-centered research is seen as a legitimate path to studying how kids behave in museums.

The PISEC study developed from a partnership between four Philadelphia-area science institutions. The project "aimed at increasing understanding of family learning in science museums and identifying the characteristics of successful family learning exhibits"[3] as a tool for developing interactive experiences and future studies that show how a successful interactive works in various contexts. The brilliant outcome of the work was the development of the seven attributes of family-friendly exhibits:

- **Multi-sided**—family can cluster around exhibit
- **Multi-user**—interaction allows for several sets of hands (or bodies)
- **Accessible**—comfortably used by children or adults
- **Multi-outcome**—observation and interaction are sufficiently complex to foster group discussion
- **Multi-modal**—appeals to different learning styles and levels of knowledge
- **Readable**—text is arranged in easily understood segments; and
- **Relevant**—provides cognitive links to visitors' existing knowledge and experience[4]

These attributes can be a tool for developing entire exhibitions or they can be used to develop specific family-friendly interactive experiences. At the Chicago History Museum, the exhibition team for *Sensing Chicago* found that these criteria could be successfully applied to history interactives. For example, the "Smell" exhibit, an interactive map, was developed and designed to employ all the attributes of family-friendly

FIGURE 10.2. Two kindergarteners share smell experiences in the Chicago History Museum's exhibition, *Sensing Chicago*. Courtesy John Russick.

exhibits. The concept for the experience was initially modeled on a competitive game show. Visitors tried to "name that smell" before other visitors could register their choice. However, the idea fell short when measured against the PISEC study's attributes. When the project team decided to make the activity multi-sided and increase the multi-user factor to include more than two visitors at a time, we followed a path that led us to create one of the most successful social experiences in the gallery. In the final version, groups of visitors gather around a tabletop map of Chicago smelling the odors of the city, past and present, discovering their sources, sharing stories and memories, and daring each other to "smell this." The experience is also one of the least complicated and least expensive of the exhibition's interactives.

A challenge for the "Sound" exhibit in *Sensing Chicago* was to design it to meet the PISEC study's multi-modal attribute. We wanted people with different cognitive and physical abilities to enjoy the activity on a variety of levels. The room includes sixteen colored discs on the floor. Each circle triggers a unique sound associated with one of three different scenes from Chicago's past. The goal of the activity is to identify the right set of five sounds for each scene. Older kids often search methodically for the appropriate sounds that link to the three historic scenes.

Younger children quickly jump from sound spot to sound spot trying to solve the puzzle as fast as they can. And very young visitors often jump up and down making one sound trigger until they are satisfied. All three groups are encouraged to participate, and the groundwork is laid for family or other social experiences in which kids of varying ages work collaboratively to meet a challenge.

The attributes of the PISEC study serve as tools for creating successful family-friendly interactives in both science museums and history museums. For history in particular we can use the PISEC study's framework to see how our understanding of the past is constructed and shared. Attributes such as "multi-sided," "multi-user," "accessible," and "readable" remind us of the collaborative nature of history and the obligation we have to share what we know consistently and equitably. "Multi-outcome" and "multi-modal" speak to the various interpretations of history and the value of multiple perspectives in historical interpretation. "Relevant" connects to our need to make history meaningful to the living.

A 2007 research project at the Exploratorium revealed that some of the museum's interactive exhibits were better than others at engaging visitors in active prolonged engagement, or APE. The APE study looked at the design of activities that held visitor interest and inspired experimentation. The study is valuable to any museum professional interested in interactivity. One of the study's most important messages is that even in a museum such as the Exploratorium, which is built around the idea of interactivity, new data and subsequent new thinking about how to develop, design, and produce interactive experiences continually influence the way the museum does business. In fact, this tireless effort to measure visitor experience goals against actual visitor experiences is an essential part of developing good interactives and effective exhibitions.

The APE study shows that the Exploratorium is trying to engage people with content in deeper and more meaningful ways. Joshua Gutwill, acting director of visitor research at the Exploratorium, suggests that the staff of the museum is not satisfied with creating experiences that simply allow people to play around on the way to getting "the right answer." Their goal is to put "visitors in the driver's seat, deciding for themselves what to try next, rather than following a set of instructions from the museum."[5] History can take a lesson. History exhibition project teams might suppress their desire to be authoritative and instead try simply to engage visitors with ideas. Perhaps then visitors would be drawn more fully into the historical process and be exposed to something more similar to historical thinking, something distinctly different from the brutal recollections of date and name memorization that color so many of our grade school social studies experiences.

Another valuable finding of the APE study was made during an investigation of the "Circuit Workbench" station, an activity design to engage visitors in an experience with electrical circuitry. Researchers were surprised to observe that even when the users were engaged for a prolonged period of time with the activity they "never turn to the exhibit graphic to answer their questions, but try either building a circuit or explaining it to themselves."[6] "Visitors continued to try to figure it out for themselves rather than read the label text for a definitive and immediate answer."[7] Here the challenge for history museums is clear. Can history exhibitions develop and design experiences that do not pose and then answer questions? Can they let kids noodle about, look through historical materials, and draw their own conclusions? Are they comfortable with kids thinking about history rather than thinking they know the answer? And are they able to make satisfying exhibitions that do not draw conclusions, but rather draw kids into the story? An experimental exhibition at The Field Museum in Chicago explored some of these questions.

In 1998, Richard Faron was directing exhibition development at The Field Museum when the initial work on *Sounds From the Vault*, an interactive exhibition featuring prized objects from the museum's collection, was conceived. Faron's hopes for the museum's collection can be summed up in a few lines. "The Field Museum is a collections-driven museum, but every object in our collection was at one time a tool or a household item. How do we get back to the coffee cup nature of these things?"[8] For most history museums, filled with manufactured goods that lack the mark of a human maker, Faron's dream seems like a strange desire. Most of us pine for the unique, the unfamiliar, or the exotic object to display. Faron hoped to strip away the aura so visitors might see the humanity in these objects and make a connection.

The concept for *Sounds From the Vault* emerged after a few encounters with a rarely seen but important collection of musical instruments that no living person had ever heard. In fact, not even the museum's curators knew how to play these instruments or what they sounded like. Faron recalls the day he walked through the collection with Bruce Oslin, a musician and eventual collaborator on the project:

> He wanted to grab every object and play it. It was the most natural reaction. It was instinctual. The instruments were designed by and for people and even though we didn't know how to play them, they invited us to take hold of them, cradle them, and use them. "Sounds" was born that day.[9]

FIGURE 10.3. Visitors compose their own music through a touchpad interface, which triggers prerecorded sounds made with these museum artifacts. Photograph by Diane Alexander White © 1999, The Field Museum.

The core idea of *Sounds From the Vault* was to inspire "conversation and play"[10] through objects. Visitors virtually play these instruments "driven by a customized computer network that makes the interactions [between visitor and object] immediate, elegant and seamless."[11] Since no living person knew how to play these instruments, it was reasoned that there was no right or wrong way to use them. Playing the instruments also provided the museum with a way to reduce the barriers between object and visitor to foster a relationship defined by visitors rather than the museum. The technology-driven interface between object and visitor required the museum to acquire recorded sounds from the instruments. Local folk musicians were brought in to experiment with the instruments and imagine how an expert might have made music with them.

In the exhibition, visitors were invited to "play" the historical instruments through drum-pad technology. Visitors used their hands to hit or stroke various pads, which would then play back different tones and rhythms recorded by the musicians during their earlier experiments. As the visitors spent time with each instrument's drum pad they could develop a relationship with the object and experiment with its musical values.

The museum could not offer visitors guidance for playing traditional tunes or mimicking techniques because they did not know any of that information. The interactive experience was remarkable if for no other reason than that visitors were doing just what the museum was doing—experimenting, listening, and wondering. Perhaps in untrained hands these objects expressed something even more closely connected to their original function.

Exhibition experiments such as *Sounds From the Vault* force us to consider what sort of experience we hope visitors will have in our history museums. Is it always about acquiring information? Is there room for the imagination, play, and experimentation? And is it possible that these could be the primary goal rather than an acceptable side affect?

The Challenge to Be Interactive

Interactives are commonplace in science museums, children's museums, and more recently natural history museums, aquaria, and zoos. But history and art museums struggle with interactivity as a primary visitor experience.

For the most part, art museums maintain that looking at original works of art is their primary visitor-experience objective. Most design elements and other tools of interpretation, such as interactives, are seen as intrusions into the relationship between artwork and visitor. In some ways, history museums are like art museums without the art. In an art museum without art, you might find artists' smocks, paintbrushes, easels, bowls and fruit from famous still life paintings, photographs taken at the sites of recognizable landscapes, and oral histories of aristocrats, milkmaids, and field hands who were captured in various important works. An art museum without art would use these materials to help visitors experience and imagine the artwork that isn't there. In this scenario, the art is akin to a historical event, place, or person, such as the Saint Valentine's Day Massacre, the deck of the *Titanic*, or President John F. Kennedy. Like the unseen art, visitors can't experience them as real people, places, and things. The museum, at best, can only approximate them with supporting materials and encourage visitors to use the context created by the exhibition to imagine the history for themselves.

But rather than see this reality as a limitation, perhaps it is a history museum's greatest asset, and provides the museum with a path to creating interactive experiences. After all, history is interactive. It is a work of and by people. It is a story that is always changing and never complete. History exists only in our minds and is shaped by our personal choices and experiences. Despite the fact that history stems from this dynamic intellectual process, waiting for people to define and redefine it, depending on new interpretations and new input to maintain its relevance, somehow history exhibitions fail to present history as something we do in the present rather than something that happened in the past.

It is often said that museums bring history to life. But what if we came to recognize that history is life, a living process ripe with real-life interactive opportunities? What are some of the visceral experiences that museums could provide that might give visitors some insight into the lives and events of the past? How difficult is it to throw a baseball ninety feet across home plate? What does the recoil of a World War I Enfield rifle feel like against your shoulder? How long does it take to grind a handful of grain with a stone? What did Chicago's Union Stock Yard smell like? What does it feel like to be in a real coal mine?

Some exhibitions remind us that history offers wonderful and engaging interactive opportunities. In 2006, the Museum of Science and Industry in Chicago renovated the exhibition of their World War II–era German submarine, the U-505. The museum constructed a new space to house the hulking vessel and the exhibition content is communicated through a wonderful marriage of object, story, and experiences. The gallery has a host of interactives. Key stories about the ways people operated the sub are communicated through these activities, both inside and outside the submarine. Visitors experience navigating the submarine, working its periscope, and using the ballast to raise and lower the ship. These experiences are not gratuitous. They drive the visitor experience. Kids go to these stations to learn about how this historical object worked, how people in the past lived and worked within it, and the significance of the ship and the people who captured it. Although this history exhibition was developed at a science museum, it demonstrates that historical content is at the core of many fascinating interactive experiences in other museums.

At the Churchill Museum and Cabinet War Rooms in London a high-tech interactive offers visitors an opportunity to sift through the seemingly endless documents related to former British Prime Minister Winston Churchill and World War II, and peek inside the world of the historian. Although the interactive is primarily for adults (it is largely a reading experience and the height of the tabletop demands a viewer be tall enough to stand and look down to view the documents), the digital display allows visitors to explore the past in whatever manner they prefer. Visitors can touch and open files, move digital copies of documents, and enlarge them for easy reading. Churchill's thoroughly documented and researched life is suddenly open for further inspection and interpretation. Visitors are presented with a chance to glimpse the historian's challenge, to find meaning within the materials; not merely to see them as evidence that support a pre-existing theory about Churchill's tenure as prime minister, but to imagine a new and unique interpretation of the man or his times constructed from their own reading of these original sources. At the very least, visitors gain some insight into the effort needed to understand a life they have not lived.

What might an equivalent experience for kids be like? Some might argue that certain challenging or complicated subjects are simply not appropriate for kids or, in some cases, for interactivity. For example, what would an exhibition about slavery, racism, or the holocaust for kids look like? How could an interactive exhibition about AIDS or people with disabilities respect these serious, complex, and emotional subjects? On the surface, the challenge of interpreting these topics in a meaningful way seems to defy an interactive solution. In fact, some intellectually or emotionally challenging subject matter may be simply inappropriate for very young children. Museums must measure what they hope to communicate to kids against a clear and thorough understanding of the cognitive and emotional development of this audience. For example, research indicates that very young children are ill prepared to encounter the horrors of slavery or the violence of the Holocaust. However, in 1993 the U.S. Holocaust Memorial Museum in Washington, DC, opened the exhibition *Remember the Children: Daniel's Story*. Although not driven by interactivity, the exhibition was developed and designed so that elementary and middle school children could learn about the holocaust through the fictional account of a young boy's encounter with Nazi terror.

Some exhibition teams have successfully interpreted challenging subject matter for families using interactives. The 2007 exhibition *RACE: Are We So Different?* at the Science Museum of Minnesota explored this complex and often controversial subject using a number of interactives. In one section, visitors listened to the sound of other people's voices and tried to identify the speaker from a collection of portraits. While playing this matching game, visitors were challenged to consider the associations they make between voice, appearance, and race.[12] The exhibition *Dialog in the Dark*, which first opened in Germany in the late 1980s, recreates familiar settings—a park, market, café, and cityscape. In darkness and accompanied by a visually impaired guide, kids and families try to navigate the different environments and perform "routine" challenges at each site. Through the guide's questions and coaching, visitors learn "to see" through their other senses. The ambitious goal of *Dialog in the Dark* is no less than to "facilitate social inclusion of marginalized people."[13]

Setting lofty goals for interactive experiences is challenging, but not foolhardy. *Dialog in the Dark* tackles a serious, emotional, and delicate subject—human disabilities—and helps kids and adults imagine and experience what it would be like to be blind in a physical, visceral, and respectful way. While not every aspect of every subject will lend itself to an interactive interpretation, the challenge for museums is to consider kids first—who they are, how they learn, what they need—and then develop experiences with history that will be meaningful for them.

Can History Be Interactive for Kids?

"It's too heavy!" A couple of three-year-olds yelled to me at Chicago's Field Museum one day as they tried to move a massive block of limestone in the *Inside Ancient Egypt* exhibition. "Come help us, Papa!" (OK, they were my kids). Together we tried to do the impossible, move a giant cube of limestone even a fraction of an inch with our bare hands. We had fun but we failed to move the stone. The task revealed something to all of us. My kids realized that there are some things their father cannot do (no doubt many more will be revealed in future years). I realized that my children could not tell by looking or even touching the block of stone that it was too heavy to move. I had assumed that its size alone—or the resonant slap of a hand against the solid, cold mass—would communicate that fact. But those feedback mechanisms were not yet in place. Lastly, we all realized that a lot of Egyptians worked really hard to make the pyramids.

It is worth noting that I worked at The Field Museum in 1988 when that giant piece of rock was first put on that immovable sled. I was not a curator then. I was a 24-year-old exhibition preparator, still wet behind the ears, trying to figure out what Michael Spock and Janet Kamien were doing there. The Field Museum's then-president, Willard L. "Sandy" Boyd, recruited these two seasoned museum professionals from the Boston Children's Museum to run The Field Museum's interpretive program and exhibition department, respectively. I wondered why Boyd would bring in folks from a children's museum for this job. What did they know about natural history?

I didn't know then just how much I didn't know about creating exhibitions, anticipating audience needs, or even what museums are for. But I do remember wondering why we were spending so much time and effort on this rock that was neither from Egypt nor an artifact. Surely we could include another mummy or sarcophagus here. Why lose this space to an unadorned block of Indiana limestone? Twenty years and two kids later, I finally figured it out.

Once we recognize that kids experience and make sense of the world in vastly different ways than adults do, we can begin the long, complex process of developing museum experiences that appeal to and engage them. First, we must remind ourselves of what we don't know, or don't remember, about being a kid. And we must rediscover what kids do and don't know to find that bright line that separates the everyday experience from the fantastic. By revisiting the now-unfamiliar territory of a child's imagination we might find opportunities to develop experiences with history that would never come to us otherwise. In fact, we cannot reasonably expect to be successful in our efforts to develop experiences for this audience unless we become versed in being and thinking like children again.

Remembering how to think like a kid comes from research, observation, and communication. Conducting literature reviews and creating developmental frameworks and audience profiles provide insight on children. Observing kids and noting their behaviors in museums, or wherever you find them, helps us anticipate their actions in future exhibitions. Communicating with kids and their adult companions gives us an opportunity to find out what they like and do not like about their museum experiences and what they are interested in doing so we can develop meaningful exhibitions for them that harness their creativity, energy, and enthusiasm.

Museums can find inspiration for interactives that will connect kids to historical content by looking at the natural tendencies of kids. Kids seek to master new skills and are inspired by a challenge. They are always ready to test themselves, to see how they measure up, cognitively and physically. And they are interested in solving riddles and working out puzzles. Human history is filled with stories of discovery, artistic achievement, invention, experimentation, and innovation. And historians are always looking for answers and solutions as they grapple with the mysteries of the past. A kid's natural tendencies to explore and experiment dovetail nicely with these core mechanisms of history.

In 2008, the National Air and Space Museum in Washington, DC, opened an exhibition about the history of flight called *America By Air*. In one interactive, kids are challenged to navigate an airplane to its destination using a reproduction of an airmail pilot's map and matching locations drawn on the map with photographs of the real physical landmarks along the flight path. Once visitors put the photographic locations in the same order they appear on the map, they can successfully make the mail delivery. The activity leverages kids' interest in challenges and puzzles and their skill in finding similarities and differences to create a meaningful experience with a historical industry, a museum collection item, and a human experience from the past.

At the Chicago History Museum, a simple interactive delivers an important lesson about early bridge design. In a city whose geography is defined by rivers and lakes and lagoons, bridges are central to its development. Early Chicago "swing" bridges were constructed on massive platforms that stood in the middle of the Chicago River, supporting the bridge as it stretched from one shore to the other. The platform also functioned as a giant turntable that swung the bridge out over the river to allow tall ships to pass on either side. To explain how these mechanical marvels worked and how they facilitated both street traffic and river traffic, the museum developed an interactive designed for kids. In one simple, swift motion children mimic the movement of both the historical bridge and the ships and witness how street traffic was disrupted and that riverboats were only able to pass through town periodically. A simple message is communicated entirely without words.

Facing the Challenges to History Interactives

What are the challenges that stand between you and incorporating interactives into your history exhibitions? Here are six messages you might have heard about interactives that can get in your way.

Interactives...

- are noisy;
- break;
- are expensive;
- raise expectations that everything in our museum will be interactive;
- inspire bad behavior in the kids who come to our museum; and
- are just fun and games.

Do any of these sound familiar? Like any serious obstacle to progress, these attitudes and opinions are rooted in someone's real-life experiences and cannot simply be brushed aside. Because each of them is grounded in someone's reality the institutional experiences that inspired them must be addressed and the prejudices and compartmental thinking that nurture and sustain them must be challenged. Embracing interactives is

FIGURE 10.4. A 6-year-old discovers how early bridge designs defined traffic patterns on both the city streets and the Chicago River in the Chicago History Museum's exhibition *Imagining Chicago*. Courtesy John Russick.

about more than developing, designing, and installing interactive experiences. It requires a change of attitude and a commitment on the part of the entire organization.

Interactives are noisy.

Interactives often require pushing, pressing, tugging, or jumping to make them go. These bumps and bangs can lead to other sounds, such as excited talking or even laughing. Sometimes a handful of interactives are the only elements in an entire museum designed for kids. So why are we surprised that kids get excited about the few exhibit elements designed for them? Museum staff must learn to hear the laughter and loud voices of children as active participation in history learning.

Interactives break.

Interactives require a commitment on the part of the museum to manage their use and maintain them in good working order. If your museum is not ready for the maintenance challenge, consider the possibility that one offline interactive supports the stereotype and may encourage colleagues to shun interactive opportunities. Don't wait until things are broken to put a maintenance plan in place. Museum staff must develop plans and set aside resources for addressing interactive maintenance. It is also important to remember that a broken interactive means that someone has been using it.

Interactives are expensive.

Interactives are original, unique products created by many hands. They cost money to develop, design, prototype, test, revise, test again, fabricate, and maintain, but the payoff for developing a successful interactive is the difference between providing an experience with history for kids and not. If kids are a priority for the museum, they need to be a budget priority too.

Interactives inspire expectations that everything in our museum will be interactive.

If a museum invites kids to come into the building it must be prepared to provide for them throughout the museum. If exhibitions are not designed with kids in mind, the children who visit probably won't enjoy themselves, and they won't want to come back.

Interactives inspire bad behavior in the kids who come to our museum.

Interactives inspire kids to do what comes naturally—run, jump, think, discover, wonder, and explore. Don't mistake that behavior for bad behavior.

Interactives are just fun and games.

Michael Spock, speaking of his exhibition work at The Field Museum, once said that "[i]t's completely possible to hang on to what's important. It [the museum experience] can be serious and meaningful and fun and attractive all at once."[14] We should not fear fun. When it comes to kids, fun and learning go hand in glove.

Conclusion

To find opportunities for interactivity history museums must reverse the exhibition development process and start thinking backward. They must begin by looking for interactive opportunities to explore history and challenge themselves to communicate every big idea in their exhibitions with an interactive.

History has endless opportunities to engage kids through interactivity. We just have to look for them. We have to commit ourselves to developing interactive history exhibitions rather than history exhibitions that may or may not have interactives in them. To reach kids with a new history exhibition, do not begin by asking what will kids learn. Ask instead what will kids do, and how can we make that activity meaningful.

NOTES

1. Andrea Weatherhead described the development of the interactives for Experience Music Project, personal communication, John Russick, June 20, 2008.
2. From remarks at the 2009 American Association of Museums conference in Philadelphia, PA, May 3, 2009. Hughes spoke as part of the "Reviving the Exhibition Critique" session, which was chaired by Kathleen McLean.
3. Minda Borun and Jennifer Dritsas, "Developing Family-friendly Exhibits," *Curator* 40, no. 3 (September 1997): 178.
4. ———. "Developing Family-friendly Exhibits," 180.
5. Joshua P. Gutwill described the Exploratorium's approach to creating interactive experiences, personal communication, John Russick, May 16, 2008.
6. Joshua P. Gutwill, "Part 1: Observing APE," in *Fostering Active Prolonged Engagement: The Art of Creating APE Exhibits*, ed. Thomas Humphrey and Joshua P. Gutwill (San Francisco, CA: Exploratorium, 2005), 12.
7. Gutwill, personal communication.
8. Rich Faron described his goals for interpreting The Field Museum's collections, personal communication, John Russick, June 10, 2008.
9. Faron, personal communication.
10. "Playing the Field with Richard Faron, a Field Museum Exhibit Developer," *In The Field: the Bulletin of the Field Museum of Natural History*, (January/February 2000): 11.
11. "Playing the Field with Richard Faron," 11.
12. This interactive was first used at the Ontario Science Centre in the exhibition *A Question of Truth*.
13. *Dialog in the Dark* project website, http://www.dialogue-in-the-dark.com/?page_id=11 (accessed February 16, 2009).
14. Mary Gillespie, "Dreams of Field," *Chicago Tribune*, September 10, 1989, 29.

CHAPTER 11

Is it Real? Kids and Collections

Mary Jane Taylor and Beth A. Twiss Houting

"Is it real, Mommy?" a 10-year-old child asks her parent in the National Archives Rotunda as the two gaze at the Declaration of Independence. She echoes the thoughts (and sometimes the words) of the adult visitors around her.[1] Kids, as well as adults, are often amazed when they see something older than they are, something that predates their existence and proves that people before may have had similar needs and wants in life. They can be emotionally moved by certain objects, whether rare, storied, beautiful, or unusual. For example, we stand in awe of those things that have played a role in a grand historic event; they are physical evidence that the moment occurred and a literal touchstone to important people of the past. By just looking at the object, we almost feel as if we know that person or have witnessed the event.[2]

Collections of historic artifacts, or objects, are central to a history museum's character and often to a visitor's experience, no matter their age. Children enjoy real objects and understand the idea of collections. Museums do not need to cultivate a special collection for children. Rather, they can borrow interpretation and exhibition techniques from various types of museums to assist families with children in exploring historical collections. These techniques help to make the collections personally relevant for each member of the family. They also can provide opportunities for the family to experience the museum as a group, something of special importance to parents today.

Museums as Places for Children and Adults

Today's parents are seeking new kinds of learning experiences with their children. Nearly 75% of elementary-school aged children have parents who are part of Generation X. As William Strauss, Neil Howe, and other futurists explain, each generation is shaped by the expectations of the older generations with whom they live and by the society in which they grow.[3] These researchers have observed that Gen X parents, born between 1961 and 1981, are more interested in spending leisure time with their children than were previous generations. Many visitor research studies have shown that one of the primary reasons parents, especially mothers, bring children to museums is for the family to learn together.[4] Gen X mothers and fathers have made career sacrifices to spend more hours at home, and these parents want to spend time enjoying the company of their children. Whereas a Baby Boomer parent visited a museum *for* their child, a Gen X parent now wants to visit a museum *with* their child. This nuance is important; museums must now serve the needs of both parents and children. Gen X parents come to the museum expecting that they and their children will have a good time and will each learn something new.[5]

In addition, as technology shapes play and children find enjoyment and learning in virtual worlds, the chance to connect to real things takes on a new importance for parents. In their books *The Experience Economy: Work is Theater and Every Business a Stage* and *Authenticity: What Consumers Really Want*, Joseph Pine and James Gilmore discuss the economic phenomenon of people willing to pay for real experiences.[6] Museums provide visitors with authentic and unique experiences. Museums can be places for socializing and relaxation where visitors can learn more about a subject, about those with whom they came, and about themselves. The experience may be as uncomplicated as time spent looking thoughtfully at one object or as complex as an immersion experience that transports visitors back in time using all of the senses.

Many families wishing to spend time together doing real things come to a museum to learn about history. One particular advantage for a family visiting a history exhibition is that the family structure largely defines a child's personal history. All parents, for example, have experienced the repeated cajoling of their school-aged children: "Tell me again about the day I was born!" Young children are fascinated by photographs and videos of themselves as babies and toddlers. As kids grow, they frequently beg also to be told about the naughty childhood behavior of a beloved grandparent or a favorite uncle. Clearly, children are interested in stories of their own history and the histories of those closest to them. So how then can museums harness a child's natural curiosity about their personal past and parlay it into a broader interest in the history of their community and their nation?

In *The Presence of the Past: Popular Uses of History in American Life*, Roy Rosenzweig and David Thelen explain that museum visitors often view objects through the lens of their own past.[7] Despite whatever interpretive framework the museum may have created in the exhibition, guests may be drawn to a particular artifact simply because it reminds them of a person or place of importance in their life. A colorful quilt may evoke memories of a grandparent's house; an ornate mechanical cash register may recollect childhood visits to a local candy store. Scott Paris and Melissa Mercer extend this view, observing that older family members convey strong personal associations with museum objects by telling stories to their younger companions. Such tales strengthen family bonds and impart family history, as parents and other relatives relate the experiences of individual family members and of places and stories of past generations. These shared narratives ground children in their family's past and help them to connect that personal history to a larger human story. Through this storytelling around museum objects, children absorb their family's values and views of nation, religion, and ethnic and cultural identity.[8]

Parents and Children Learning Together in Museums

For history museums the great challenge in connecting children to history through objects is to integrate the experiences of children and the adults who bring them to the museum. To build history exhibits for children and their parents, museums need to understand how families learn together. In their work at The Children's Museum of Indianapolis in 2005, the Institute for Learning Innovation educated the museum's staff about the collaborative learning model advocated by theorists such as Lev Vygotsky. The Institute elegantly expressed the sociocultural approach to family learning in terms of four characteristics.

1. Families need environments that are developmentally appropriate for all members of their group, from toddlers to grandparents. Activities need to accommodate the varying abilities and limitations of family members, and be well designed to maximize learning.

2. Families are seeking playful and social experiences. During a museum outing, parents expect to talk with their children, to see and try new things, and for the family to learn together while having fun.

3. Families want to relate their experiences at the museum to their existing knowledge. In building on their knowledge, families find their own meanings from the museum visit.

4. Family learning must involve different styles of learning. No matter what their age, people have innate preferences in how they like to learn.[9]

When visiting with their families, children usually experience museum galleries with substantial parental involvement. Often, it is the parent who makes the decision to visit. For children who cannot yet read, adults selectively read label text aloud, literally deciding what information about an object or topic of interest the child will be exposed to. Kevin Crowley and Melanie Jacobs explain that this adult mediation involves complex calculations. "Parents need to decide what is worth noting based on their own knowledge and interests, their understanding of the child's knowledge and interests and their current goals for the interaction."[10] Not all parents feel competent and comfortable undertaking this challenging interpretive role, but well-designed experiences in exhibitions can assist parents in this task.

Family learning is hardly a one-way street. Throughout every interaction with their families, children are also gauging what they want to talk about based upon their interests and the situation. Many museum professionals have marveled as preschool-age visitors "held forth" in a gallery, passionately sharing with their family incredibly detailed information on trains or rockets. In his work, Kevin Crowley has coined the term "island of expertise" to define the phenomenon where children develop a special interest and a relatively deep knowledge on a particular subject.[11] Parental involvement is generally crucial for these young learners, as adults choose books, videos, toys, and family outings that build upon the child's demonstrated interest.

Museum objects play a critical and meaningful role for families whose children develop an island of expertise. Visits to museum galleries allow children to apply what they have learned from books and movies to actual artifacts on display. Kids also reconcile their previous knowledge with the qualities of the objects themselves—the rockets may be taller than expected, an operating steam engine may be louder than imagined. Crowley has found that when very young children begin to develop an island of expertise, parents are collaborative learners. During museum visits in the early stages of a child's burgeoning interest in a topic, adults verbally label objects, describe their physical characteristics, and infer functions. These explanations aid the child in making connections and drawing conclusions and make the museum visit a compelling and memorable learning opportunity for parent and child.[12]

But as children gain mastery of their chosen subject, even the most doting and involved parent acts more as audience than interpreter.[13] Crowley implies that parents are somehow shirking their responsibility to teach in the museum by not extending their child's learning in these situations. However, family learning is not just about increasing the child's knowledge. Museums need to integrate techniques into exhibitions that allow children and their parents simultaneously to assume the roles of learner and teacher.

To support child and adult learning, museum staff members need to have some knowledge of educational psychology. Educational researchers have described various systems of learning styles to explain preferred ways to process, acquire, and use new information. Museum research on how adults and children respond to the decorative arts, a subset of historical artifacts, verifies that there are four learning styles that apply to object-based learning.[14] In a Winterthur study of visitor reactions to a Rococo-Revival side chair, museum educators asked people of all ages what they saw and thought about when they looked at the chair. The answers to these simple questions revealed that adults and children over age 7 naturally approached the object in one of four ways: description, classification, association, or evaluation. The study showed that these styles are not hierarchical and that a facilitator's skillful questioning can encourage visitors to use all of the four learning strategies to examine objects, not just their preferred strategy.

Many history museums have begun to use research on learning styles as a tool to develop exhibitions. In this process, museum staff members have taken care to ensure that interactive exhibition elements appeal to learners with different approaches to processing information and acquiring knowledge.[15] Moving forward, exhibition teams can begin to plan collection installations just as carefully so that artifacts are appealing for all learners, especially family groups.

Children and the Power of Objects

Children understand the concept of collecting. The impulse to collect is a trait of many children, if not most.[16] They begin in their preschool years hoarding similar items. Children seem to have at least three interests in collections that are not unlike those of the great collectors who created the backbones of many museums. First, children like to acquire and own things: "Do you see what I have? It's mine." For example, for the child with the most baseball cards, the collection confers status. Second, children as young as age 2 like to classify what they collect, arranging and rearranging objects as they explore their physical characteristics.[17] Third, a collection becomes a starting point for exploration and learning; for example, a child's love of coins can lead to a lifelong interest in archaeology or numismatics. To describe their collections, kids sponge up elaborate polysyllabic words far above their usual language level, as evidenced by the number of 4-year-olds who can correctly identify dinosaurs using long, complicated names.

Further, children share with all humans an innate attention to objects. Human brains are hardwired to perceive objects as a way of making sense of the world around them.[18] People continuously scan their environments for signs, often three-dimensional objects, to provide them with information.[19] When this visual data enters the brain, it is compared to a bank of other objects with similar characteristics until a match is found, or at least a match perceived to be very close to what is seen. To a child, the tip of a striped furry tail could signal a house cat, though it may belong to a never-before-encountered tiger hiding in its zoo cage.[20] Children, from birth, are building their visual memory banks based on objects they see. This framework of memory is an essential building block for later learning. In museum literature, educators typically argue that visual literacy skills account for the learned ability to recognize shapes and critically place them into context. However, it is the fundamental capacity of humans to create knowledge from objects that helps them live in the world from the earliest age. Brazilian educator Paulo Freire explained, "Reading the world always precedes reading the word, and reading the word implies continually reading the world."[21]

In addition to helping children build bigger memory banks as a scaffold on which to build later learning, viewing and discussing objects in museums helps children develop critical "prehistory" skills such as how to empathize with others, how to tell stories, and how to sequence events in time.[22] Object learning also fosters language development, as humans associate a set of sounds with a set of physical characteristics and later, in some societies, with symbols that lead to written language.[23] Experiences with real objects, then, should be part of how children experience museums with their families. As David Carr insists:

> What children see, feel, and understand in museums contributes to a continuously expanding cognitive record that becomes richer and more complex over the lifespan. Not only do strong images and engaging information become permanent parts of our repertoires of memory, these images and information help us to reinterpret what we have seen and known in the past.[24]

Carr makes a case for developing object-rich environments for children because exposure to collections increases the sophistication of their thought and communication. These encounters also develop children's ability to explore objects with their senses and their imaginations and begin to make judgments about what objects mean and why they are important.

Catherine M. Cameron and John B. Gatewood describe the experience some visitors have when viewing museum objects as "numinous," that is, similar to an experience one has when in the presence of the holy.[25] A relationship with an object enables visitors to relate to it personally on a deep level and inspire flights of the imagination, a sort of time travel. In fact, viewing real objects in museums can be the most satisfying part of a museum visit. In a study at the Minnesota History Center, visitors were asked to rate how helpful various activities had been to achieving the experience they desired that day in the museum. Notably, looking at objects on display always topped other activities, such as reading labels, watching videos, or hearing storytellers.[26] Even compared to touchable reproductions and discovery rooms, children more often rated viewing displays of historical objects as their favorite activity in the museum.[27] Richly contextual object displays also create lasting memories for kids. In their study of the museum experiences of 4- to 6-year-old children, Barbara Piscitelli and David Anderson found that long after museum visits, young children vividly recall certain object installations.[28]

Object-based History Exhibitions for Kids

Over the last half-century, museums have struggled—alongside other educational institutions—to understand how best to help children learn. New types of museums have modeled approaches that move far beyond the age-old tact of adult docents directing children's learning agendas. Drawing on the teachings of Piaget, Michael Spock's 1967 makeover of the Boston Children's Museum created a genuinely child-centered institution that fostered individual exploration and promoted experiential learning through play with touchable objects. The same impulses prompted the Winterthur Museum in 1960 and the National Museum of American History in the 1980s to create innovative hands-on rooms where children (and adults) would make personal discoveries through playing with objects.[29]

A few history museums have begun to see collections as a powerful tool for connecting kids and their families to history. Collections can stimulate a child's natural curiosity—What is that?—and their representation of truth and authenticity—Is that real? Exhibition teams are faced with three great challenges if they are to make history museum collections meaningful to kids:

1. to select objects that provide a foundation for a positive experience with history;

2. to interpret these objects so they communicate and illustrate key messages; and

3. to design exhibition spaces that foster conversations and exchanges between children, adults, and artifacts.

Through this three-part process, a museum's collection becomes a means for storytelling, making comparisons and identifying differences, and evoking empathy for and understanding of others. Creative displays, multimedia, and interactive experiences can allow children to have a more intimate interaction with the artifacts. A commitment to this thoughtful approach to object selection, interpretation, and design by museum staff will help surmount historical and psychological barriers that have for too long stifled efforts to create meaningful object-based history exhibitions for kids and their families.

Selecting Objects

There is no magic collection or object type that appeals to any given group. For example, museums cannot assume that a collection of historical toys will appeal to young children, that race cars will excite middle school boys, or that dolls will attract young girls. Rather, each individual child, teenager, adult, and senior, is attracted to those objects to which they can relate personally or culturally. Because a child's world is made up primarily of clothes, toys, games, school, and household furnishings, these types of objects often resonant with them. However, children can be just as attracted to a sophisticated piece of nineteenth-century agricultural machinery, a Renaissance painting, or a prehistoric arrowhead. It is a common misconception that none of these items is relevant to a child ages 4 to 12; in fact, children are as varied in their tastes and interests as adults.[30]

Therefore, museums do not need to collect especially for children, but must seek opportunities to develop meaningful exhibitions for kids using objects that kids can relate to. In 2001, The Children's Museum of Indianapolis acquired the contents of the bedroom of Ryan White, the Indiana boy who contracted HIV through a blood transfusion, was banished from his school and vilified in his hometown, and fought for the rights of HIV patients everywhere before he died of AIDS in 1990. According to Andrea Hughes, educator and curator for the museum's American collection, Ryan's mother, Jeanne White-Ginder, wanted the entire contents of Ryan's room to go to a museum because she saw the room as a whole and wanted its contents to be taken together. The museum accepted all of Ryan's things—furniture, posters, toys, clothes—and began to develop the exhibition *The Power of Children: Making a Difference* (opened 2007). The plan was to tell Ryan's story along with the stories of two other amazing children from history, Holocaust victim and diarist Anne Frank and American civil rights icon Ruby Bridges, to help children understand that kids have made important contributions in history. The museum recreated Ryan's room in hopes that visitors to the museum would be able to identify with him. Hughes explained,

> by including all of Ryan's things in the exhibition, we saw an opportunity to show our visitors that Ryan was just a normal kid, a normal kid who happened to have AIDS. The contents of his room became the tool for showing kids that he was like them so they could relate to Ryan and see that we are all capable of making the world a better place.[31]

Interpreting Collections

Again, to locate objects suitable for kids, museums do not need to rewrite collection policies or launch new collections initiatives; rather, they need to explore how to make the objects they collect relevant for their audiences, including children and families. Of paramount importance is how museums use their collections to meet audience needs and expectations.[32]

When interpreting objects in a history exhibition for kids, museums must consider issues of context carefully and avoid using language as the primary content-delivery mechanism. At the same time, they must choose the words they do use wisely. For example, in describing time-related concepts, museum staff must recognize that children under the age of 8 understand "old" to mean prior to today and "long ago" to mean perhaps prior to their life times. Between the ages of 9 to 11, children can begin to understand the difference between more precise amounts of time (such as one hundred versus three hundred years ago) and can associate time with specific events (such as the landing of the *Mayflower* and the American Revolution).[33]

As history museums have begun to offer object-based experiences especially for children they have sometimes used storytelling as an interpretive tool to link to collections in a family-friendly manner. At the Abby Aldrich Rockefeller Museum at Colonial Williamsburg, the *Down on the Farm* exhibition relates the travels of Prince, a carved wooden terrier from the big city. The story of Prince wandering the countryside from farm to farm in search of his country cousin is told in verse; kids follow the dog's adventures by reading book pages mounted at their eye level. The Museum's paintings and drawings of rural America illustrate the story, along with carved decoys, copper weathervanes, and whimsical wooden sculptures of pigs, cows, roosters, and other farm animals. Adjacent to the gallery is a hands-on area for families to create their own picture stories.

Designing for Collections

Design is the critical third step in the process of connecting kids to history through objects. Once again the challenge is to put audience first to ensure cognitive, emotional, and physical access to the materials. Family-friendly exhibitions must convey from the entrance that they are designed for adults and children because both children and their adult companions make instant judgments when standing at the title wall. While kids are deciding whether a museum space looks like fun or not, parents are assessing whether the gallery is a safe and welcoming place for their family. Artifacts installed in family-focused galleries must be protected from damage. But museums often fail to realize that enclosed cases and Plexiglas barriers do not indicate that families should stay away. Rather, such safeguards send an all-important signal to parents that a gallery is a secure and comfortable place for their family to learn and play.

Exhibitions for kids also must be built with the physical requirements of their visitors in mind. The seven characteristics of family-friendly exhibits developed by the Philadelphia-Camden Informal Science Education Collaborative are an excellent resource for museums (see Chapter 10, Making History Interactive).[34] Two of these characteristics are particularly critical to the installation of objects: displays should be multi-sided, so families can cluster around; and objects must be accessible—mounted so that the youngest visitors can see them. Often, display cases are pushed against a wall so that only the front of an artifact is fully visible. Moving cases out toward the middle of the gallery even a foot or two can allow a family group to gather around and see an artifact more easily in the round. Likewise, cases and object displays are often designed above the eye level of preschool-aged children, sending a not-so-subtle message to kids and forcing parents to lift their children repeatedly in order to have a family viewing experience.

Research from natural and social history museums suggests that children are most affected by and best remember physically large objects and exhibition spaces. This research also hints that kids prefer and

FIGURE 11.1. Protected behind Plexiglas barriers, authentic objects in period room vignettes provided historical context for the exhibition *KiDS! 200 Years of Childhood*. Courtesy Winterthur Museum.

best learn from displays that provide context.[35] For history museums, placing objects in life-like vignettes and showing furnishings in period room settings offers a way to create physically large and well-contextualized artifact displays. In Winterthur's 1999 exhibition *KiDS! 200 Years of Childhood*, the introductory section featured three object assemblages populated by child mannequins. Protected by Plexiglas barricades, these displays visually portrayed the different physical manifestations of childhood during three different historical time periods. Importantly, they also immediately conveyed that objects were an integral way to learn in the exhibition. With their painted architectural backdrops, the attractive vignettes grouped individual decorative arts objects into memorably large scenes of domestic life of the past. While modern kids could recognize significant differences between the displays and their own homes, the concept of domestic space was familiar.

The design team for *The Power of Children: Making a Difference* developed massive and complex period settings to inform the stories of Anne Frank, Ruby Bridges, and Ryan White and to help kids empathize with these courageous historical figures. Along with Ryan White's recreated bedroom are a 1,500-square-foot replica of the Franks' hiding place that includes Anne's writing desk and Ruby Bridge's recreated classroom, with one occupied and twenty-eight empty desks.[36]

Using Light, Sound, and Media to Highlight Objects

History museum collections contain many, many objects that can connect us to amazing people, places, and events in the past, but they often fail to excite the imagination at first glance. These collections are filled with materials from the machine age, objects whose true power usually needs to be released. An ordinary baseball bat alone fails to communicate that it hit the homerun that won the World Series; a well-tended and unblemished bible does not immediately appear to be a witness to several presidential inaugurations unless its story is revealed. Museums too often rely on labels to interpret these objects, but this approach does not take into account the fact that many kids have limited reading skills. There are ways to use media, sound, and lighting effects to draw kids into a deeper experience with objects.

The exhibition team that created *The Power of Children: Making a Difference* at The Children's Museum of Indianapolis used a tremendous amount of Ryan White's personal affects to create an authentic experience. However, one particular object, a reproduction of his angel nightlight, is used powerfully in a sound and light show as a metaphor for Ryan's life and death. During the show, the nightlight burns brightly as it and other artifacts throughout Ryan's recreated bedroom are spotlighted and visitors hear of his courageous battles. When the story concludes with Ryan's death, the nightlight is extinguished and the spotlight on it goes out. Through the nightlight, a common feature in children's bedrooms around the world, kids and their parents connect with Ryan and his mom.

At the Abraham Lincoln Presidential Library and Museum in Springfield, Illinois, the extravagant object theater experience "The Ghosts of the Library" sets a new standard for media-driven object interpretation. Here, visitors experience an extensive and entertaining program about the power of objects to fuel our imaginations, lead our research, and preserve our history. Designed for families, the show includes a live actor who interacts with historical figures that almost come to life. Likewise, the object theater "Rise of the Machines" at the New Mexico Museum of Natural History and Science features a host of objects, mostly out-of-date computer equipment, that talk to one another and explain their role in the personal computer revolution of the last quarter of the twentieth century. This funny, informative, and accessible sound and light experience helps give meaning to objects that alone have no character, no identity, and no fame.

The traveling exhibition *Benjamin Franklin: In Search of A Better World* staged by the Benjamin Franklin Tercentenary combined light and sound components with a variety of immersive and hands-on in-

FIGURE 11.2. A young visitor standing in the Cockpit of Parliament is accused by solicitor-general Lord Wedderburn of treason against the Crown, sharing Franklin's experience. Installation image from *Benjamin Franklin: In Search of a Better World* as seen at the Denver Museum of Nature & Science. Courtesy Page Talbott.

teractives to explore the robust activities of Franklin's life by reuniting many of his possessions. Rather than design the exhibition to showcase one historical object after another, the Tercentenary staff considered the needs and interests of its multifaceted audience, a significant portion of which consisted of families and school groups.

One of the most successful components of *Benjamin Franklin*, according to associate director and chief curator Page Talbott, was the video of a thunderhouse being blown up by lightning. It was placed next to the actual thunderhouse Franklin had used, causing visitors to exclaim about the reality of the object and their new understanding of its purpose. In another example, an audio track and set design provided context for a painting of a little-known historical figure, solicitor-general Lord Wedderburn, and helped visitors to empathize with Franklin as they stood as he had in the Cockpit of Parliament taking the verbal blows Franklin withstood as members of Parliament accused him of treason.

Immersive and interactive, the exhibition design placed the components that appealed to children and other tactile learners next to the artifacts. This side-by-side juxtaposition of objects and related interactives was essential to the exhibition's success: it insured that visitors could access the artifacts and the exhibition's main messages through moments of personal discovery.

Conclusion

Children are interested in history and objects whether or not they realize it on a conscious level. They are fascinated, after all, in their own past and that of their families. They understand that there was a yesterday, even if it was only a week ago rather than two hundred years ago. Children learn how to navigate in the world alone and with others through their interactions with objects in their daily lives.

A few history museums have begun skillfully to create object-based history exhibitions for families by blending the object installations of traditional history exhibits with the interpretive techniques of hands-on discovery from children's museums and the message-driven interactive exhibits of science museums. These history museums embrace the mission-related stories their collections can tell and simultaneously acknowledge that visitors will make their own meanings as they negotiate new experiences, merging prior knowledge with new. For visitors of all ages, objects in these exhibitions provide both cognitive and affective learning opportunities by calling up memories and then refashioning them to connect with historical content.

The key to making artifact-rich history exhibitions work well for children is to honor human learning characteristics and to select objects, interpret objects, and design for objects with kids in mind. If children and adults can see an exhibition's objects in context and can acquire pertinent and easily digestible information about them, artifacts can resonate with families. The skills for examining objects are innate in humans and, if presented in an age-appropriate manner, artifacts can make the abstract lessons of history powerfully tangible and real to kids and their families.

NOTES

1. Beth A. Twiss-Garrity, "Object Lesson: Relics, Reverence, and Relevance," *Common-Place* 2, no. 4 (July 2002), http://www.common-place.org/vol-02/no-04/lessons/.
2. Hilde S. Hein, *The Museum in Transition: A Philosophical Perspective* (Washington, DC: Smithsonian Institution Press, 2000), 87.
3. William Strauss and Neil Howe, *Generations: The History of America's Future, 1584–2069* (New York: William Morrow and Company, Inc., 1991).
4. Susie K. Wilkening, "Authenticity and Outdoor History Museums" (presentation at the annual meeting of the American Association of Museums, Denver, CO, April 28–May 1, 2008).
5. James Chung and Tara May, "X-Tended Family: Attracting the Post-boomer Audience," *Museum News* (November/December 2005).

6. B. Joseph Pine II and James H. Gilmore, *The Experience Economy: Work is Theater and Every Business a Stage* (Boston, MA: Harvard Business Press, 1999); James H. Gilmore and B. Joseph Pine II, *Authenticity: What Consumers Really Want* (Boston, MA: Harvard Business Press, 2007).

7. Roy Rosenzweig and David Thelen, *The Presence of the Past: Popular Uses of History in American Life* (New York: Columbia University Press, 1998), 16–7.

8. Scott G. Paris and Melissa J. Mercer, "Finding Self in Objects: Identity Exploration in Museums," in *Learning Conversations in Museums*, ed. Gaea Leinhardt, Kevin Crowley, and Karen Knutson (Mahwah, NJ: Lawrence Erlbaum Associates, Inc., Publishers, 2002), 401-24.

9. The Indianapolis Children's Museum, "Family Learning: An Extraordinary Opportunity" (pamphlet published by The Indianapolis Children's Museum, 2005).

10. Kevin Crowley and Melanie Jacobs, "Building Islands of Expertise in Everyday Family Activity," in *Learning Conversations in Museums*, 337.

11. Crowley and Jacobs, "Building Islands," 333.

12. Crowley and Jacobs, "Building Islands," 333–356.

13. Sasha D. Palmquist and Kevin Crowley, "From Teachers to Testers: Parents' Role in Child Expertise Development in Informal Settings," *Science Education* 91, no. 5 (2007), 712–32.

14. Pauline K. Eversmann et al., "Material Culture as Text: Review and Reform of the Literacy Model for Interpretation," in *American Material Culture: The Shape of the Field*, ed. Ann Smart Martin and John Ritchie Garrison (Winterthur, DE: Henry Francis du Pont Winterthur Museum, 1997), 135–67.

15. Anna Slafer, "Beyond the Button: The Art and Science of Interactive Development" (paper presented at the annual meeting of the American Association of Museums, Boston, MA, April 27–May 1, 2006).

16. Karen Rachel Jarmon, "The Meaning of Collecting in Children's Lives" (paper presented at the conference *Perceptions of a Past: Private Collections, Public Collections*, Winterthur, DE, October 6–8, 1994).

17. For a description of how children classify objects and its instrumentality to development of logical thinking, see Mary Ann Spencer Pulaski, *Understanding Piaget: An Introduction to Children's Cognitive Development* (New York: Harper & Row Publishers, 1980), 61–7.

18. Steven Pinker, *How The Mind Works* (New York: W. W. Norton and Company, Inc., 1997).

19. Paul Gabriel, "Visual Gateways to Memory: How the Brain Makes Visual Sense" (paper presented at the annual meeting of the American Association of Museums, Chicago, IL, May 13–17, 2007).

20. Stephen M. Kosslyn and Oliver Koenig, *Wet Mind: The New Cognitive Neuroscience* (New York: Free Press, 1992).

21. Paulo Freire and Donaldo Macedo, *Literacy: Reading the Word and the World* (London, UK: Routledge & Kegan Paul, 1987), xxvii, 25.

22. J. P. Dyson, "When Does Today Become Yesterday: History Exhibits for Young Audiences" (paper presented at the annual meeting of the American Association of Museums, Boston, MA, April 27–May 1, 2006).

23. Steven Pinker, *The Stuff of Thought: Language as a Window into Human Nature* (New York: Viking, 2007), 136–7.

24. David Carr, "Crafted Truths: Respecting Children in Museums," in *The Promise of Cultural Institutions* (Walnut Creek, CA: AltaMira Press, 2003), 131–2.

25. As referenced in Kiersten Latham, "The Poetry of the Museum: Numinous Experiences of the Museum Visitor" (paper presented at the annual meeting of the Visitor Studies Association, Grand Rapids, MI, July 25–29, 2006), 248.

26. Jane Marie Litwak and Andrea Cutting, "Evaluation of Interpretive Programming" (unpublished report, Minnesota History Center, April 1996).

27. Beth A. Twiss-Garrity, "Children as Museum Visitors," *Current Trends in Audience Research and Evaluation,* American Association of Museums (Committee on Audience Research and Evaluation) 13 (May 2000), 77.

28. Barbara Piscitelli and David Anderson, "Young Children's Perspectives of Museum Settings and Experiences," *Museum Management and Curatorship* 19, no. 3 (2001): 269–82.

29. Judith White, *Snakes, Snails, and History Tales: Approaches to Discovery Rooms at the Smithsonian Institution* (Washington, DC: Smithsonian Institution, 1992).

30. Twiss-Garrity, "Children as Museum Visitors," 77.

31. Andrea Hughes, educator/curator of American collections, The Children's Museum of Indianapolis, e-mail message to John Russick, January 26, 2009.

32. Stephen E. Weil, "From Being about Something to Being for Somebody," in *Making Museums Matter* (Washington, DC: Smithsonian Institution, 2002), 28–54.

33. Ronald Vukelich, "Time Language for Interpreting History Collections to Children," *Museum Studies Journal* (Fall 1984), 44–50.

34. Minda Borun et al., *Family Learning in Museums: The PISEC Perspective* (Washington, DC, Association of Science-Technology Centers, 1998).

35. Piscitelli and Anderson, "Young Children's Perspectives."

36. Early results of visitor studies show that families spend comparatively more time in the installation of Ryan's bedroom both before and during the object theater presentation than in other sections of the exhibition. The visitors also talk together in this area more often than in other parts of the exhibition. Tricia O'Connor, exhibit developer, The Children's Museum of Indianapolis, e-mail message to author, October 16, 2008.

CHAPTER 12

Write and Design
with the Family in Mind

Judy Rand

Not about Something, But For Someone

*The problem with history is that it's so remote, especially for kids.
What was it like back then? What did it sound like? Feel like? Labels
can sketch a story with details that engage the senses, giving just
enough context to invite people in.*

—Bonnie Wallace, writer[1]

Ever since the 1960s, when Michael Spock, Elaine Heumann Gurian,
and the Boston Children's Museum team pioneered hands-on learning
in a radical break with past museum practices, children's museums
have been creating exhibitions that are "not about something, but for
somebody."[2] This bold choice—to understand, focus on, and fully engage with the children who are visiting—creates an experience that's
different from the one we see in a traditional history museum, where
the curators or exhibit planning team "start with the collection" or "start
with the theme."

For those of us who have worked on theme- or mission- or object-
driven exhibitions, where the ideas that we want to share with visitors
are as important as the experience and the artifacts, this shift can be
unsettling. Deciding to design your exhibits "for somebody" will govern
the hundreds of decisions to come. Not the least of which will be the
struggle over the labels.

Proof that Less is More

One of the challenges for museums that want to connect with kids is
to break away from the notion that all content ideas are communicated
through words. As Chicago History Museum senior curator John Russick says, in history museums, "the most common solution for content
or message delivery is a label. There is no other part of our product that
we rely on to the same extent. Labels are like the Marines. 'When all
else fails, write a label.'"[3]

Most children's museums have few labels; those they do have are quite short. Most traditional history museums abound with labels, most of them quite long. Longer, that is, than the fifty-word limit that visitor research tells us will catch and hold a reader's attention. (Note: this paragraph is fifty words.)

The implications of writing shorter (and using fewer) labels might seem obvious. But if, as an exhibition curator, planner, or writer, you use words to organize your thoughts and convey your ideas, you may find that the way you've developed the exhibition can create mental roadblocks when it comes time to prepare the labels. Instead of starting the process assuming labels will carry messages, start instead where designer Andrew Anway does. Ask: "What if we did this kids' exhibition without ANY labels?" What if the experience had to communicate our ideas?

If the thought of stripping all the words off the walls gives you the shivers, read on.

Labels Are about More than Words

Label development should follow a process that begins with understanding your audience. Start with the families. Who are they? Why have they come? Next, develop a plan for communicating with them through labels. What do they need from us, from information to instructions? Only then comes the writing.

The writer's careful selection of words, chosen to engage visitors in a clear, concise, and captivating manner, anticipates graphic design. Graphic designers orchestrate the visual presence of the text—words, color, images, space, and shape—to express something more than the text alone. The presentation of the words is more than half the battle. Placement of labels is also critical to their success. And woven throughout this process is evaluation—testing labels with visitors to ensure that what we think the label is communicating is, in fact, what the user is understanding.

Designing exhibits to engage all ages means more than appealing to different learning styles. It means ending the habit of relying on text.

Consider the USS Constitution Museum. After tracking and timing family visitors in two exhibitions (*Old Ironsides in War and Peace* and the family exhibition *A Sailor's Life for Me?*), the team discovered that families spent "an average of seven minutes in *War and Peace*," a traditional history exhibition with "many long text panels totaling nearly 4,500 words, sensational objects, and a few interactives." On the other hand, "families spent nearly 22 minutes" in *A Sailor's Life For Me?*, with just 1,500 words of text. "...[J]ust as important," reports exhibits director

FIGURE 12.1. *A Sailor's Life for Me?*, Writer: Sarah Watkins. Graphic design: Jon Christensen. Photograph by Greg Cooper. Courtesy USS Constitution Museum.

Robert Kiihne, families "talked to each other significantly more" in the family exhibition.

As they developed *A Sailor's Life For Me?*, team members asked themselves, "Can we convey this idea *without* a paragraph of text?" Where they had to have a panel, they limited it to fifty words. For each panel they asked, "What is the main point we want to convey?" This enabled them to distill "a fifty-page draft document" into fifteen pages of labels. "We weren't dumbing down," says curator Sarah Watkins. "We were lightening up."[4]

The Chicago History Museum team embraced a new process to develop their children's gallery, *Sensing Chicago*. Instead of "defining the historical focus and then designing exhibitions" they identified a target audience and considered their needs, interests, and abilities. Drawing on the children's museum practice of creating audience profiles and developmental frameworks, the team decided that those abilities—the kids' own energy, inquisitiveness, imagination, and sense of fun and play—would guide the exhibition process. Extensive testing convinced the team to let the experience be the first step.[5]

It seems straightforward. If we write, design, and place labels so visitors can easily see them, read them, and use them, we increase the chances that more people will read those short, simple labels. But before we write labels, we have to know who we're writing for. That means thinking about the labels from the beginning, not sending them in at the end like Marines.

Getting Started: Understanding Kids and Families

Think of the family as a co-ordinated hunter-gatherer team actively foraging in the museum to satisfy their curiosity about topics and objects that interest them.

—Paulette McManus, museum researcher[6]

As we "lighten up" our labels and let the experience come first, what does this change mean for writers and designers who still must convey—in a short, simple, interesting way—whatever it is that the labels *say*? It means that as you reduce the number of labels and words, you want to make *sure* readers can read them; you want to make *sure* every word counts.

To start, it helps to get a picture of how family members interact in exhibitions. Who reads? When do they turn to labels? Paulette McManus, studying visitors at London's Museum of Natural History, tells us that "Families in exhibitions behave differently from other visitors."[7] They play. They have long conversations. And they're not likely to be seen reading labels, unless grown-ups are present. Even then, reading usually means glancing at text. McManus describes how families "forage, broadcast and comment":

The family . . . moves in a loose formation to explore the selected area. The children may physically lead in this exploratory behavior. As family members encounter interesting items they report back to the family group as they broadcast [facts] to each other. The parents are likely to identify or name new items encountered by the children and . . . to comment on, or interpret, the information broadcast by the children much more than the children are likely to comment on the information broadcast by their parents.[8]

This research finding—that family members share the exploration and information gathering—is just part of the picture of family behavior that teams can gain from visitor research. For example, visitor research dispels the myth that "Nobody reads the labels." To paraphrase Lincoln and Lynn Dierking: some of the people read some of the labels some of the time.

Do kids read labels in family exhibitions? Audience researcher Jeff Hayward says the rule is, "Adults read, children do."[9] Children set the pace for the visit; parents try to keep up, and read where they can. Families moving through a family exhibit full of moving parts—and moving kids—will find many things competing with flat little labels for their attention.

And adults interact with their children in different ways. "Some parents really like to play with their children; others prefer to stand back (or sit down) and watch their children learn independently," says senior exhibit developer Cathy Donnelly of The Children's Museum of Indianapolis.[10]

Reading behavior is hard to measure in museums. Tools like tracking and timing don't capture all the skimming-the-headlines and sharing-with-others that's going on. For a more detailed picture, Paulette McManus videotapes—and studies—hours of visitor conversations and behavior. One of her findings holds the key to writing labels for families: **parents read label text out loud to children.**

The bottom line is, people read to meet their needs: to name something; to answer a question; to find meaning; to find something to share. People who read labels share what they read with family members. As museum researcher Judy Diamond observes, parents use text and graphics to supplement their own knowledge and as direct teaching aids when they read labels out loud to their children.[11] Foraging family members like to find facts—and bring them back to each other. When they can find the labels with ease—when they can read and understand the labels with ease—when they find the labels answer their questions, offering information that's useful and interesting, readers will share what they read with others, reading out loud to their kids and companions. What they read—and share—sparks conversations. And conversation, says museum researcher Minda Borun, is at the heart of family learning.[12]

Planning Labels for Kids and Families

When you sit down to write, the function of a label is the most important thing. Ask,"What do I need this label to do for the visitors?"

—Eileen Campbell, writer[13]

Having a good grasp on the way families behave in exhibitions gives the project team the information they need to begin developing a label plan. As Chan Screven explains, labels have different functions.[14] From the big introductory panel to how-to instructions, you can use labels to invite; personalize; focus attention; describe; narrate; anticipate and answer questions; explain; persuade; instruct; and encourage conversations. But before writers start writing, they must take time to consider the purpose and intent of each label. Knowing what the label needs to do shapes decisions about language, design, and placement that are yet to come.

1.   A label can *invite* families into the exhibition and give the parent-reader a quick sketch of the story.

> ## Join Our Crew
>
> **Come in and join USS Constitution's War of 1812 crew.**
>
> All healthy, strong and brave souls are welcome to apply. We will soon set sail against the enemy for "free trade and sailors' rights."
>
> This is your chance to serve your country and see if a sailor's life is for you.

A Sailor's Life for Me?, USS Constitution Museum. *Writer:* Sarah Watkins.

2.   A label can *personalize* the experience, connecting the unfamiliar to the familiar.

> ## History Stinks
>
> **Use your nose to smell Chicago's past.**
>
> **What does Chicago smell like to you?**
>
> The Southeast side used to smell like the steel mills. In these factories, thousands of Chicagoans made steel for skyscrapers and bridges around the world.
>
> In fact, Chicago was once America's largest steel maker.

Sensing Chicago, Chicago History Museum. *Writer:* John Russick.

3. A label can *focus* the visitor's attention.

A Bit of Africa at Owa Market

Craftspeople in Africa create beautiful, useful objects by carving, weaving, beading, and tying knots.

Many of the things for sale at Owa Market were made by hand in West Africa.

Look carefully at the objects on the shelves.

Can you find carved faces?

Can you find something woven?

World Brooklyn, Brooklyn Children's Museum. *Writer:* Elizabeth Reich Rawson.

4. A label can *describe* the action so vividly that the reader can feel it physically.

Water = power

Take a garden hose. Turn it on just a trickle, and it makes a gentle stream. Turn it on twice as hard, and the stream becomes a bubbling river. Now, turn it on full blast, and the rush of water takes out just about anything in its path.

That's the power of water.

Mill City Museum. *Writer:* Kate Roberts.

5. A label can **narrate** a story about another place or time.

"It was an assembly line."

"When I'd give the kids a bath, I would take all four
of 'em and I'd put 'em all in according to age.

The twins would be way in the back, then Peggy,
and then Dick would be way up by the faucets.

I started with Dick, wash him up. She would be
at the door with the towels. Finally when I'd get
Dick, I'd take him, stand him up on the toilet.
She would wipe him down, put his diaper
and that on"—"his jammies back on"—
"then we went to Peggy."

"It was an assembly line. It really was."

—Dick and Angie Krismer

Open House: If These Walls Could Talk, Minnesota History Center. *Writer:* Benjamin Filene.

6. A label can **anticipate** and **answer** visitors' questions.

What does Gullah mean?

Nobody knows for sure what the word Gullah means.

Some people say it was originally Gola, shortened from
the name of the West African country Angola. In Georgia,
my Gullah people are called Geechee.

Tales from the Land of Gullah, Children's Museum of Houston. *Writer:* Christina Schmidt McKee.

7. A label can *explain* what's going on.

Lots of people worked on the canal

From boat captains to lock tenders to dock workers,
hundreds of people kept the canals running.
Men, women and children all worked together
to keep the boats moving.

National Canal Museum. *Writer:* Eugene Dillenburg.

8. A label can *persuade* the reader to see something in a new light,
    or try something new.

Baking Mexican treats in Sunset Park

If you've never been to a Mexican bakery—a *panaderia*—
you're in for a treat. The Lopez family opened their bakery
in Brooklyn in 1987. It's been a neighborhood favorite
ever since.

In fall, the store fills with the smell of fresh-baked holiday
breads for Day of the Dead.

World Brooklyn, Brooklyn Children's Museum. *Writer:* Elizabeth Reich Rawson.

9. A label can *instruct*, helping visitors play the game (and get the idea).

On the line in a meat packing plant

Instructions
Look at the clock. You have 60 seconds.

- Take an empty tray
- Fill each tray to the correct weight
- Pass trays to the canner on the other side of the table
- Find out how much money you made

Time + Work = Money

Minnesota History Center. *Writer:* Jim Roe.

10. A label can ***encourage conversations*** within families. Whether it's a label on a dinner plate at a long table . . .

> ### Sit down and load up a plate!
>
> This table represents 1 meal Mary Dodge Woodward would have cooked for the hungry field gang.

Mill City Museum. *Writer:* Kate Roberts.

Or a question a mom is sure to notice on a flapper panel . . .

> ### Who cleaned all those rooms?
>
> ### Robert W. Matthews house, St. Paul, 1900
>
> A family with a house this size would probably have employed two or three servants to cook and clean and care for the children.
>
> It was common for family teams—a mother and daughter, two sisters, or a brother and sister—to work as domestics in a single household.

Families, Minnesota History Center. *Writer:* Brian Horrigan.

Or a label any reader will read out loud . . .

> ### Look up.
>
> You're standing at the bottom of a grain bin.

Grainland, Minnesota History Center. *Writer:* Jim Roe.

Labels rooted in real-life experiences can—and do—start lively family conversations.

Who's Talking?

"Voice" is the personality of the exhibition, the written equivalent of the designers' "look and feel." Though an exhibition may include diverse voices, using verbatim quotations, we seek one unified voice to "host" the exhibition. With that in mind, when planning labels, you need to decide how close, or distant, your labels' tone of voice will be. Will you use third person (the impersonal "they"); first person (the forthright "I" or "we"); second person (the conversational "you")?

The USS Constitution Museum exhibits team tested labels written in third person against labels written in first person.

Third person:

> Every morning sailors holystoned (scrubbed) the deck. They took off their shoes, rolled up their pants and then got on their knees and scrubbed with water and sand. Sailors disliked this chore especially when it was cold.

First person:

> One of the things I dislike the most about being a sailor is holystoning (scrubbing) the decks each morning day after day. The worst is when it's cold. We take off our shoes, roll up our pants and get on our hands and knees, add salt water and sand, then **scrub. scrub. scrub**.

> *A Sailor's Life for Me?*, USS Constitution Museum. *Writer:* Sarah Watkins.

As researcher Minda Borun reports, "First person was preferred by 64% of visitors; third person by 36%. The reasons visitors preferred first person were: it is more personal, active, allowed the visitor to connect with the story, and would appeal more to kids."[15]

Though using second person ("you") may feel odd to some writers, it's the key to making labels sound conversational. When a label addresses "you," it can trigger the imagination, enabling whoever's reading—or hearing—the label to project themselves into the action. For example, in *World Brooklyn*, Elizabeth Reich Rawson rewrote some labels using "you" to help kids imagine themselves doing the mixing, the eating.

Second person:

> Fufu flour comes from yams or plantains. You mix it with water into a thick hot paste, then eat it with tomato sauces and stews.

> *World Brooklyn*, Brooklyn Children's Museum. *Writer:* Elizabeth Reich Rawson.

By defining the labels' voice and directing the conversation to the reader through the familiar "you," the team begins to think about the ways they'll relate to their readers.

Who's Listening?

Now it's time to see the label-reading experience from the visitors' point of view. If you were the visitor, wouldn't it be great to go through the museum with an insider? Someone at your elbow, someone friendly, who knows the inside story. Who can answer your questions. Point out interesting things you might miss. Someone who'd also know when to be quiet, waiting until you needed them. The labels are a stand-in for that "ideal companion."[16]

The ideal companion might be someone like Whoopi Goldberg; it might be someone everyone on the team knows ("Connor in Education! Funny and gung-ho."). What traits make this person an ideal companion? Is he or she lively, knowledgeable, friendly? Quiet, caring, sincere? Those traits will tell the writer what tone of voice to use.

The label writer takes on the persona of that ideal companion. Even in the early stages, the writer should walk through the developing exhibition plans, asking, at each element not "What do I want to say?" but rather "What do visitors really need here?"[17] Answer these questions and now, for the first time, you're ready to write.

Write for the Family; Talk to the Kids through the Parents

[In] the labels for World Brooklyn, *the third- to fifth-grade reading level is to ensure we reach parents and make it easy for them to read or relate the information to their children. You know the three- to six-year-olds are not reading the labels.*

—Elizabeth Reich Rawson, writer[18]

It's easy to see how history museums might try to please everyone by writing "some labels for grown-ups, some for kids." But label expert Beverly Serrell advises museums not to write two-level labels.

Don't write different labels at different levels. Writing for different vocabulary or developmental levels—labels for kids, labels for adults—makes labels twice as hard to write, more expensive to produce, and it creates visual clutter in the exhibit. Most visitors, given a choice, will choose to read labels that look easier, are shorter, and have larger print. Keep it simple: write one-level labels.[19]

If kids aren't likely to read, do you write "for parents"? And what does that mean? Do you "write for parents" who read for their own pleasure, while their kids are off "doing"? Many history museums do that, writing 125- and 250-word labels. But "writing for parents" to read out loud to kids and companions requires a different approach—fewer labels with fewer words.

There are two basic approaches to writing labels for parents with kids. The first is to compose short-and-sweet labels that parents scan quickly on their own, emerging an instant expert, ready to translate the meaning for their kids. Parents and teachers do this sort of thing all the time. But it's hard work. The "parents-will-translate" approach also makes adults the target for the experience, implying that the kids are novices whose status is secondary. The other approach is to write labels that parents read to, or with, their children. This establishes a very different experience for parent and child, as co-learners.

Forming New Habits: Writing to be Read Out Loud

To write labels that will sound natural—not forced—when parents read them out loud, you need to imagine how you would talk to the kids if you were there on the scene. Write the way you talk. Use short, simple sentences that sound clear when you hear them: the kind of writing that encourages parents to read out loud. You also need to identify the topics that hook kids. Parents will see them and want to share them.

It's harder than it sounds. It takes time, talent, and testing with visitors to write labels aimed-at-kids-for-parents-to-read in a tone that sounds genuine, not condescending or forced. As the writer, you need to stay within your persona as "the ideal companion," working on your "relationship" with visitors. Ask kids and parents to read your drafts out loud to you.

Asking Questions in Family-friendly Labels

Cathy Donnelly explains how understanding the particular audience for a specific exhibition can change the label writer's style:

> People are different. [Parents] come to the museum with all different kinds of experiences, expectations and parenting styles. When we interviewed . . . families for our *Global Perspectives* project, we asked them about labels with questions. We were assuming that asking questions [in the labels] would encourage parent-child discussion. This particular group emphatically told us, "No! I need information that I can quickly read and paraphrase for my child."

discover

The Day the Dead Get a Party

Don Paco Lopez Panaderia
displays a Day of the Dead
altar in the front window.

In Mexico, Central America, and South America, people set aside one day, November 2nd, to honor the lives and souls of those who have died. It's called Day of the Dead (*Dia de Los Muertos*). Instead of being sad, it's a joyous holiday.

Many families build an altar to honor loved ones who have passed away. Altars include a photo of the person, a few of their favorite foods, playful skeletons, bright flowers, and other offerings.

This altar celebrates Mexico's heroes. It was made for Brooklyn
Children's Museum by Cris Scorza (BCM), Jesenia Galvez,
Eric Galvez, Jessica Galvez, Andrea Lopez, and Karina Lopez.

BROOKLYN

FIGURE 12.2. *World Brooklyn.* Writer: Elizabeth Reich Rawson. Graphic design: Charita Patamikakom. Courtesy Brooklyn Children's Museum.

> Our model for encouraging discussion by limiting the information and suggesting questions frustrated these parents! . . . I do think that [knowing more about this] could help us write labels that appeal to a diverse audience.[20]

Taking advantage of visitor research, learning theories, and developmental frameworks, Brooklyn Children's Museum writer Elizabeth Reich Rawson uses interlocking sets of goals and guidelines that reveal her

**FAMILY INQUIRY: TO SUPPORT CONVERSATION AND
ENGAGEMENT WITHIN AND AMONGST FAMILIES.**

Consider how to use "productive questions" to foster interactivity and family learning.

- **Attention-focusing questions** fix [visitors'] attention on significant details. *Have you seen [X]? What have you noticed about [X]? What are they doing? How does it feel/smell/look/sound/taste?*

- **Measuring and counting questions** invite precise observations. *How many? How often? How long? How much?*

- **Comparison questions** help [visitors] analyze and classify. *How are these the same or different? How do they go together?*

- **Action questions** encourage [visitors to explore] the properties of unfamiliar materials [and] small events taking place, [or encourage visitors] to make predictions about phenomena. *What happens if? What would happen if? What if?*

- **Problem-posing questions** help [visitors] plan and implement solutions to problems. *Can you find a way to? Can you figure out how to?*

- **Reasoning questions** help visitors think about experiences and construct ideas that make sense to them. *Why do you think? What is the reason for? Can you invent a rule for?*

Point out things for readers to notice and observe. If there is a way to use senses, include them in the label: listen, touch, smell, and so on.[21]

museum's exhibit philosophy. For *World Brooklyn* labels, they not only set interpretive goals (such as "increase awareness of Brooklyn as home to people of many different cultures and countries"), but also focused on "how to make culture knowable" and "how to foster interactivity and family learning."[22]

When reaching out to children and families, traditional museums can learn a lot from children's museums—not just by visiting them, but by poring over the thinking that goes on behind the scenes. Rawson's brief on how to write "productive questions" for the *World Brooklyn* audience reveals this task to be harder than it sounds.

The Label Voice Has Personality and Perspective

Voice becomes an important resource for history museum staff learning to write labels for children and families. Some history exhibitions for kids create a character-guide to be the ideal companion. For example, in the traveling kids' history exhibition *Joshua's Journey: A Black Cowboy Rides the Chisholm Trail* from the Fort Worth Museum of Science and History, visitors read pages from 16-year-old Joshua Loper's diary.[23] The main character's perspective shapes the story. Perhaps this approach is a good model for other history museums. After all, history is about people who made choices, faced challenges, and interacted with other people. These character-guides provide perspectives on what it was like through their eyes and own experiences.

In *Remember the Children: Daniel's Story*, the children's exhibition at the U.S. Holocaust Memorial Museum, family visitors see the Holocaust through the eyes of a young German Jewish boy. Daniel is true to life, but didn't exist. There was no one real child's diary that told the whole story, so Daniel's words are based on the diary accounts of many children during the Holocaust.[24] Creating a composite character is not easy and takes time, research, and multiple reviews. The team and reviewers struggled over each sentence.[25]

Yet Daniel's voice—coming to visitors through overhead audio and labels—sounds real. "Have you ever been punished for something you didn't do?" he asks in the beginning. We follow his story through labels that look like pages from a diary.[26]

September 9, 1936

Dear Diary,

Because Father was once a soldier and got a medal for bravery, we haven't been forced to leave the ghetto. Some of my friends went to a place called a concentration camp. I'm not sure what that is. But people say it's worse than a prison.

Remember the Children: Daniel's Story, United States Holocaust Memorial Museum. Writers: Susan Morgenstein and Kathleen McLean.

In *Tales from the Land of Gullah*, created by the Children's Museum of Houston, a storyteller, Aunt Pearlie Sue, welcomes you.

Welcome to the Land of Gullah!

Travel back in time with me, Aunt Pearlie Sue,
to where I grew up in the 1940s—The Land of Gullah.

The smell of the ocean and the rhythms of my Gullah people filled the air.

Even today, when I close my eyes, I can still hear my mama singing songs, children pounding rice, fishermen rowing their boats, and my grandmother telling tales in her rocking chair.

Tales from the Land of Gullah, Children's Museum of Houston. *Writer:* Christina Schmidt McKee.

In *A Sailor's Life For Me?*, the USS Constitution Museum exhibits team prototyped thirteen full-scale photo cutouts: crew members and the families they left behind. The characters tell their own short-short stories in text bubbles by their heads. Though the USS Constitution Museum exhibits team also tested historical quotes, they found that the first-person texts prompted more family conversations.[27]

FIGURE 12.3. *A Sailor's Life for Me?*, Writer: Sarah Watkins. Graphic designer: Jon Christensen. Photograph: Greg Cooper. Courtesy USS Constitution Museum.

Historical first-person accounts, especially the words of adults, can be an obstacle for kids, even for parents reading to kids. Obscure or outdated language or references, and the need to establish the context in which the quote was written or spoken, can oblige the label writer to add a lengthy explanation just to make the words meaningful. History museums can use their experience with first-person voices drawn from the diaries, letters, journals, and oral histories in their collection to infuse labels with authenticity and accuracy. Family-friendly labels should use only those quotes that test well with visitors. A team's deep desire to use an original historical quote should not overwhelm the purpose of the label—to communicate simply and clearly with families.

However, quotes are not limited to the past, and contemporary voices can offer a youthful perspective. The Boston Children's Museum uses kids' perspectives in cultural exhibitions. For instance, in *Children of Hangzhou*, you "meet" four Chinese teens in the form of life-size photo cutouts who address you directly through labels:

> Ni hao!
>
> I'm Guo Qianyun (gwoh chien-yoon).
>
> I'm 16 and am studying Chinese opera at an arts school.
> I also love to shop, talk on the phone and play with my dog.
>
> Watch me practice and perform in the theater.

Children of Hangzhou, Boston Children's Museum. *Writer:* Gail Wang.

At The Children's Museum of Indianapolis, exhibit developer Tricia O'Connor uses authentic contemporary quotes to help tell Ryan White's story in *The Power of Children*:

> **"They don't want you back, Ryan.**
> **They're afraid you'll infect other kids."**
>
> —Jeanne White

The school said no

Now that he felt better, Ryan wanted to start 8th grade.

But school officials said he couldn't return.

There weren't any AIDS guidelines for school yet... and many parents were afraid.

They'd heard a lot of rumors.

"What they want to do isn't right. We can't let it happen to anyone else."

—Ryan White

Ryan fought back

He said he understood that parents were afraid, but "they should just listen to the facts."

"Dr. Kleiman and a lot of other experts had said you couldn't catch AIDS from being around someone who has it."

—Ryan White

The Power of Children: Making a Difference, The Children's Museum of Indianapolis. *Writer:* Tricia O'Connor.

Whether you invent a composite character, adapt one from history, or use first-person quotes, the goal is to create a label that's short enough for parents to skim quickly and read verbatim—in part or whole—to kids. The less searching, the less paraphrasing, the better.

FIGURE 12.4. *The Power of Children: Making a Difference.* Writer: Tricia O'Connor. Graphic designer: Heather Mills. © 2009 The Children's Museum of Indianapolis, Inc.

Designing and Placing Labels for Kids and Families

> *Despite some cynicism among interpretive professionals, visitors will read well-designed interpretive labels. However, how the labels are designed is critical.*
> —Stephen Bitgood, museum researcher[28]

The issues a graphic designer must consider when designing a label for kids and families include: size, shape, type size, typeface, white space, color, contrast, graphics, images, materials, texture, and the installation: lighting, scale, and placement.

Graphic designers use these tools to achieve unity and clarity, and pare away anything superfluous. The goal is a clean, uncluttered layout, with text and images that are highly visible and highly legible. Pictures or illustrations have to show the key idea. The few, carefully chosen words readers see on the label—short, to the point, simple, and clear—must telegraph the key idea for readers.

Visitor research can tell designers where to place labels to ensure they're visible to potential users. In "14 Helpful Research Findings," Beverly Serrell notes that "labels next to dimensional exhibits get read more than flat panels on the wall, with no objects nearby."[29] Stephen Bitgood's research advises that a label that "blends into the background may be ignored"; "lighting is . . . important in determining whether or not a label will be noticed" and "many labels are missed because of the traffic flow."[30]

FIGURE 12.5. *Dinosphere: Now You're in Their World!* Writer: Cathy Donnelly. Graphic designer: Chris Rozzi. © 2004 The Children's Museum of Indianapolis, Inc.

To make sure labels work for families, graphic designers can follow five key rules:

1.   Use a simple, legible typeface in large sizes.

2.   Use an initial capital letter; use lower case for the rest of the headline or sentence.

3.   Use lots of white space (wide margins around the text).

4.   Put one sentence on each line, or break the lines of text "according to sense."

5.   Place text next to what it refers to, using size, lighting, and color to make the relationship clear.

Look at the deceptively simple writing structure and design layout on the *Dinosphere* panels above: great examples of how a writer and graphic designer can organize and place information to drive a big idea home.

Family Labels Should Show More than They Tell

How do you design and write for people on the move, parents who have to skim as they go? How do you grab their attention, and hold it long enough for them to get the point? Writers and designers have learned to do this well in children's museums, aquariums, and zoos, places where it's easy to see how families "forage, hunt, and gather" on the move.

Writers at the Monterey Bay Aquarium have been writing for families for more than twenty-five years. Their approach is to lead with the main idea, up in the headline, so parents can get the message at a glance. They cut the paragraphs into short, easy-to-read segments. Since they want parents to read, the writers keep labels brief, writing not just to a word count but to line lengths and character counts. It takes careful editing to fit the limited space.[31]

Designers at the aquarium believe design should communicate quickly and clearly. Like the writers, they focus on audience needs: How big should the panel and type be? Big. Headlines? Bigger and bolder. How many characters can the eye read comfortably per line? Forty to fifty-five. How many lines tall should a paragraph be? No more than six. The Monterey Bay Aquarium kids' exhibition, *Splash Zone*, applies what exhibit developers, writers, and designers have learned from years of studying how families learn. Grown-ups can read headlines over the crowds, and decide whether to wait their turn or move on.

Location, Location, Location

> *You'll save time and avoid frustration if you consider label size, placement, and format from the very beginning of your exhibit development. Every sketch, every model, every case layout should account for object labels and text panels.*
>
> —Kate Roberts, writer[32]

Graphic and 3-D designers have to make countless design decisions, any one of which can make a carefully written label hard to find, hard to see, hard to read, hard to understand. Poor placement can undermine the best efforts of a label's writers and graphic designers. A label with instructions has to be in sight while you're doing the activity. If you have to face away from the label to work the interactive—and if your body blocks other people trying to read the label—people will rarely read that label and may become frustrated because the activity "isn't working right!"[33]

Beverly Serrell says labels for an interactive exhibit should go "where visitors' hands and eyes go when they use it."[34] In a family exhibit, that applies to placing any label: put it where people will see it as they engage with the exhibit. A gallery offers a range of surfaces for information, messages, directions, and instructions. But just like your words, they must be chosen carefully for access and readability.

When mounting photos for kids at the Minnesota History Center and Mill City Museum, exhibit designers make sure modern photos are in color and historical photos are in black and white, and that all photos are placed where children can see them, at kid height. Rather than putting the photos against a flat wall, the Mill City Museum created a semicircular space just right for a family, shaped so a parent can point to a picture, read out loud, and start a conversation with kids.

The team for the Minnesota History Center exhibition *Open House* created an introductory panel that recognizes both the value of clarity and brevity and the importance of placement.

OPEN HOUSE

IF THESE WALLS COULD TALK

What stories lie inside ONE ORDINARY HOUSE?

To find out, we picked a real, existing house and dug into its past. FIFTY FAMILIES lived at 470/472 Hopkins Street on St. Paul's East side across 118 YEARS.

Come EXPLORE their stories.

Open House: If These Walls Could Talk, Minnesota History Center. *Writer:* Benjamin Filene.

The *Open House* team knew that while some visitors may scan the forty-seven-word introductory panel, many won't stop. So they repeat the four key points—one by one, on doors leading inside the house—giving readers four more chances to catch the big idea.

1. ONE ORDINARY HOUSE
2. FIFTY FAMILIES
3. 118 YEARS
4. EXPLORE

At The Children's Museum of Indianapolis, writers tell a story with a case of artifacts . . . and just twenty-three words.

Look what we found digging for dinosaurs!

Last year, teachers and staff from The Children's Museum dug up these dinosaur fossils in South Dakota.

Dinosphere: Now You're in Their World, The Children's Museum of Indianapolis.
Writer: Cathy Donnelly.

It takes great discipline—and it takes time—to write labels that are this short.

In *Sensing Chicago*, the "Taste" exhibit uses the floor, ceiling, and spaces in between to offer instructions, information, and a compliment. The floor tells readers which sense to use: "Taste." The names of condiments circle a giant plate; on the plate sits a five-foot hot dog bun with the invitation: "You are the hot dog." Once a child is lying in the bun with soft "condiments" on top, a ceiling mirror reflects the delightful image with the compliment: "You look delicious."

Writing for the National Canal Museum, Eugene Dillenburg kept labels "short and to the point, as you need to with kids." He worked with designers to place labels where they'd be most useful for readers—on the large model, not on a hard-to-follow key or on a wall panel.

Locks use water to raise and lower boats.

Locks gently lifted boats up and down hills.

Lock Tenders' House

Entire families might work together tending a lock.

Coal Chutes

Coal chutes helped mine owners get coal
into the canal boats. Try it!

National Canal Museum. *Writer:* Eugene Dillenburg.

Creative history museum designers find ways to weave text right into the experience. In Minnesota History Center's *Open House*, words show up on a bed, a row of food cans, on dinner napkins and plates. In *A Sailor's Life For Me?*, questions and answers are screened on the tops and bottoms of tin plates in the mess area.

Top:

> ## Salt beef again?

Bottom:

> While at sea, we eat the same foods day after day, whether we like it or not.
>
> How'd you like to eat the same food every day?

A Sailor's Life for Me?, USS Constitution Museum, *Writer:* Sarah Watkins.

Exhibit designers who test full-scale mockups with actual text quickly learn the best places to put labels. Poor placement can undermine the best efforts of a label's writers and graphic designers. If busy parents can't find it and see it, they're not likely to read it, and your efforts go to waste.

Stronger Together

Label writers who work in or with history museums have unique advantages that other museums should covet. History museum exhibit developers and label writers:

- know a good human-interest story when they see one;
- are true storytellers who make the past come to life;
- through their storytelling, understand repetition, rhythm, and timing;
- have access to "the real thing"—authentic voices, and real-life, first-person stories;
- are fascinated with the way the past links to the present; and
- want to share their discoveries with visitors.

At the same time, children's museums have their own unique advantages. Their exhibit developers and label writers:

- know a lot about kids and families;
- know how to create authentic nonverbal experiences;
- write labels that are laudably short, simple, clear, and direct;
- are always learning and trying new things; and
- want to encourage visitors in the process of discovery.

What if your history museum team asked a nearby children's museum to co-create a history exhibition for kids? Or your children's museum invited a nearby history museum to do the same? Partnering could give both museums new energy, perspectives, and approaches.

A collaborative model for creating high-quality family exhibitions already exists on a national scale. Members of Science Museum Exhibit Collaborative (SMEC) and Youth Museum Exhibit Collaborative (YMEC) take turns creating high-quality traveling exhibitions. I can see a time when history museums and children's museums join forces as CHEC, the Children's History Exhibit Collaborative.

The labels will be amazing.

Courtesy Boston Children's Museum.

NOTES

1. Bonnie Wallace, e-mail message to the author, September 29, 2008.
2. Jeanette Steele, "New Children's Museum Will Let Youngsters Unleash Their Inner Picasso," *San Diego Union-Tribune*, April 27, 2008, http://www.signonsan diego.com/uniontrib/20080427/news_lz1n27museum.html (accessed September 15, 2009).
3. John Russick, personal communication to the author, October 1, 2008.
4. USS Constitution Museum Team, "Writing for a Family Audience," USS Constitution Museum Family Learning Forum online, http://www.familylearn ingforum.org/engaging-text/writing-for-families/writing-for-families.htm (accessed September 16, 2008).
5. D. Lynn McRainey and John Russick, "Learning from Kids: Connecting the Exhibition Process to the Audience," *Curator: The Museum Journal* 52, no. 2 (2009): 183–92.
6. Paulette McManus, "Families in Museums," in *Towards the Museum of the Future*, ed. Roger S. Miles and Lauro Zavala (New York: Routledge, 1994): 91.
7. McManus, "Families in Museums," 87.

8. ———. "Families in Museums," 91.
9. Jeff Hayward, e-mail message to the author, July 31, 2008.
10. Cathy Donnelly, e-mail message to the author, December 3, 2008.
11. McManus, "Families in Museums," 90.
12. Minda Borun, "Studying Learning Styles and Their Impact" (paper presented at the Visitor Studies Association Annual Conference, Grand Rapids, MI, July 2006).
13. Eileen Campbell, "Making Things Real" (paper presented at the American Association of Museums Annual Meeting, Portland, OR, May 2003).
14. Chan Screven, "Motivating Visitors to Read Labels," in *Text in the Exhibition Medium*, ed. Andrée Blais (Québec, Société des Musées Québécois: Musée de la Civilisation, 1995).
15. Minda Borun, "Why Listen to Your Visitor?" USS Constitution Museum Family Learning Forum online, www.familylearningforum.org/evaluation/power-of-evaluation/why-listen-visitor.htm (accessed September 16, 2008).
16. Judy Rand, "The Writing on the Wall" (paper presented at the American Association of Museums Annual Meeting, Chicago, IL, June 1989).
17. Judy Rand, "Rand and Associates Writing Guide" (training materials, Rand and Associates, 2002).
18. Elizabeth Reich Rawson, e-mail message to the author, July 23, 2008.
19. Beverly Serrell, *Exhibit Labels: An Interpretive Approach* (Walnut Creek, CA: AltaMira Press, 1996): 96. Italics in original.
20. Cathy Donnelly, e-mail message to the author, December 3, 2008.
21. *World Brooklyn* Preliminary Text Outline (Brooklyn Children's Museum, March 2006): 1, adapted from M. L. Martens, "Productive Questions: Tools for Supporting Constructivist Learning," *Science and Children* 36, no. 8 (1999): 26.
22. *World Brooklyn* Preliminary Text Outline, 26.
23. Fort Worth Museum of Science and History website, http://www.fwmuseum.org/jjourney.html (accessed September 18, 2008).
24. US Holocaust Museum website, http://www.ushmm.org/museum/exhibit/exhibit/ (accessed February 12, 2008).
25. Adrienne Kertzer, "A Multitude of Voices: The Production of Daniel's Story," in *My Mother's Voice: Children, Literature, and the Holocaust* (Peterborough, Canada: Broadview Press, 2002).
26. Suzanne Slesin, "Through a Child's Eyes, History and Tragedy," *New York Times*, June 3, 1993, http://www.nytimes.com/1993/06/03/garden/through-a-child-s-eyes-history-and-tragedy.html (accessed February 12, 2008).
27. USS Constitution Museum Team, "Audience Research Results: Labels with Historical Characters," USS Constitution Museum Family Learning Forum online, http://familylearningforum.org/engaging-text/questions-and-quotes/research-results-labels.htm (accessed September 16, 2008).
28. Garibay Group, "*Sensing Chicago* Evaluation," exhibit evaluation for the Chicago History Museum, August 2007, 42.

29. Serrell, *Exhibit Labels*, 235.

30. Stephen Bitgood and Donald Patterson, "Principles of Exhibit Design," *Visitor Behavior* 2, no. 1 (1987): 4.

31. Judy Rand, "Set the Mood, Show Me the Way, Tell Me a Story: The Invisible Work of Graphic Design" (paper presented at the American Association of Museums Annual Meeting, May 2004).

32. Kate Roberts, "Getting Visitors' Attention: Writing Exhibit Labels," *Minnesota History Interpreter* (Minnesota Historical Society) 24, no. 9 (September 1996): p. 4.

33. Stephen Bitgood, "The Role of Attention in Designing Effective Interpretive Labels," *Journal of Interpretation Research* 5, no. 2 (2000): 31.

34. Serrell, *Exhibit Labels*, 166.

CHAPTER 13

In a Language They'll Understand: Media and Museums

Gail Ringel

Introduction

A tower of monitors with a sweep of choreographed images depicts the history of music videos;[1] a living diorama shows Native Americans encamped on the plains;[2] the entire dramatic arc of the Civil War unfolds in just four minutes.[3] Why is it that so many memorable experiences in history museums are created by media installations? This chapter explores electronic media in many forms—from large screen theaters to interactive computers, ambient audio to object theater, audio, video, computers, and networks creating visitor directed experiences or fixed, unchanging parts of an exhibition setting.

Making It Work for Kids

This book is filled with detailed information about the building blocks for creating great history exhibitions for kids. Developmental frameworks and structured conversations with young visitors can provide invaluable direction in molding experiences that will resonate with and appeal to this audience. Curators and content developers may be weighing formal curriculum goals against the needs and interests of young learners. Incorporating play, thinking about multiple "ways in" to the material through the senses, imagination, and storytelling can all inform an exhibition plan or narrative. If the goal is to create a unique and memorable visitor experience, one that might transform young visitors by changing some fundamental understandings of the world around them, then it's helpful to look at the ways in which we typically communicate with all audiences and ask if some of these methods are particularly well suited to kids.

In this exploration it's important to keep content goals and authenticity at the core of the planning process. After all, history is not like many of the narratives that are part of a kid's experience. Feature films, adventure novels, and electronic games almost always depict other worlds and can be quite compelling, but they are not history—an important distinction that should not be lost on young museum visitors. Our work is not about simply providing a compelling experience for kids—if it was then we'd all just visit Disney World or a local arcade and be done with it. What's at stake is the ability to find compelling ways to present historical information and authentic experiences to young audiences to make the past more present and more relevant to their lives today. The task, at its core, is to bridge the huge divide between the world kids live in and recognize, and worlds that were different in fundamental ways and occupied these same places at another time.

Creating exhibitions that allow visitors to construct new understandings and empathize with the experiences of historical Others is difficult enough for adult audiences who bring prior knowledge based on education and life experience; to do the same for a child proves to be even more challenging. A case in point is a personal epiphany I had several years ago while working on the plan for a maritime museum in Mobile, Alabama. Although I grew up fairly close to an Atlantic seaport and had heard of various types of ships, skiffs, and freighters, my basic concept of travel involved moving over dry land; "shipping" goods in my view, paradoxically, depended primarily on trucks or train cars. When large lakes and rivers got in the way, the construction of bridges might be necessary. While I knew it was possible to move freight in large shipping containers on the oceans, the notion of a world *without* vast road systems for personal or commercial travel simply wasn't part of my historical perspective. Only while immersing myself in the nineteenth-century history of Alabama and its agricultural economy moving goods through Mobile, and then to the rest of the United States or Europe by sea, did I begin to understand an essentially different world. In a sense, adding new ideas about a different time is easy: back then, the shipping industry supported a large dockside community; in the past fortunes were made and lost trading cotton; long ago families took steamboats to arrive at their summer cottages. But changing our rootedness in the present? Removing features of the familiar landscape or changing fundamental ideas of how things work? That is a far more difficult task that involves rearranging ones' deepest and least questioned assumptions. *In the past, waterways were not barriers to travel. On the contrary, they provided the only viable highways of their time.* It's difficult for anyone to accomplish this fundamental shift during a museum visit. For young visitors, with a shallow life experience and little perspective on how societies evolve, it's truly daunting.

FIGURE 13.1. Visitors to *Five Friends from Japan* try on a kimono while "Sakiko's story" plays on a monitor nearby. Courtesy Boston Children's Museum.

What Is It about Media?

How do we know kids pay attention to and learn from media in museums? Evidence can be found at home as well as in a variety of informal learning settings. One has only to remember the tremendous popularity in the 1980s of "The Oregon Trail," a computer game developed by the Minnesota Educational Computing Consortium (MECC).[4] Young players were engaged in a range of challenges, from hunting for buffalo and squirrel to recovering from snake bites, while grappling with fundamental ideas about using limited resources to prepare for long journeys into the nineteenth-century American frontier.

Evidence that kids connect with media in museum settings is also available. Lynn Dierking and John Falk believe that children are particularly drawn to interactive computers[5] and an exhibition about Japanese culture created by Boston Children's Museum and the National Children's Museum that opened in 2004, *Five Friends from Japan*,[6] demonstrated the power of short video pieces to connect with young audiences. This exhibition presented the lives of five Japanese children to young visitors and their adult companions. Each of the Japanese children was portrayed in a four- to five-minute video piece within an immersive setting—part of their Japanese home. One boy's room had traditional tatami mat floors and was festooned with his baseball paraphernalia; a young girl's story was told beside the equipment and furnishings of her grandparents' tofu shop. A number of hands-on, interactive components were part of the experience—from trying on a traditional kimono in a bedroom to practicing Japanese writing skills at a touch screen computer—but most of the detailed information about the Japanese kids was conveyed through their video portraits. In each one, a child welcomes visitors into their home and talks about things most important to them: pets, sports, fun clothes, Harry Potter books, the way they help heat water for a traditional Japanese bath. These first-person narratives are edited in a snappy style reminiscent of children's television and punctuated with colorful graphics. Both form and substance target young viewers. The exhibition technology was entirely straightforward—push-button activated programs played on demand and reverted to a quiet "attract loop" at the end of the program.

A summative evaluation that canvassed young visitors and adults separately provided compelling data:

- 89% of children were able to identify one of the five exhibit subjects as someone with whom they'd like to be friends. They said such things as, "Ken is my favorite; I like baseball and Harry Potter too!" or "I liked Sakiko; she is a lot like me in some ways, but different too."

- 50% of children listed shared interests or personal qualities as the reason for their choice.

- 66% of children saw the Japanese children as being very different from each other. On the other hand, only 50% of adults described the Japanese children as very different from each other—it's possible that the personalities and interests of the exhibit subjects may have been more in tune with those of American children than adults, accounting for this discrepancy.

- Children were able to describe many similarities and differences between the United States and Japan. Such similarities and differences were typically factual observations based on the exhibition. Most personal characteristics ascribed to Japanese children were positive and nonstereotypical.[7]

Particularly telling are the statistics on the desire "to be friends with" one of the Japanese children—an emotive response to the exhibition. While not all forms of electronic media connect with visitors' emotions, carefully constructed stories with complementary music and effects can have deep affective impact. The high percentage of young visitors who saw the Japanese children as being very different from each other would have formed those opinions largely on the basis of the video portraits, the most detailed source of information about their personalities, activities, and preferences in the exhibition. The evaluation showed that children not only were drawn to the video installations, but also drew sophisticated conclusions based on viewing them. Of course, the experience of interactive gaming in which a child guides the narrative is dramatically different from the experience of passively watching a film or video. In order to make good choices about the various types of electronic media that might be used in a history exhibition we must begin by better understanding our audience.

What Is It about Kids?

Planning for young audiences in history exhibitions benefits from a focus on three characteristics of these visitors: they live in a media-rich world; they are capable of tremendous and sustained focus in museum environments; and their lives are fundamentally different from the lives of those responsible for planning exhibitions—even a difference of fifteen years can introduce significant changes in worldview as a result of our rapidly evolving social, economic, and technological environment. We may well have reached a moment at which the World Wide Web has fostered a global youth culture in which kids around the world have more in common with each other than do kids and adults in any one country.

What exactly does it mean to assert that youth live in a world fundamentally different from that of older people? While children over the age of about five can certainly imagine some features of "long ago" with the right kinds of prompts and stories, it is difficult, nevertheless, truly to bridge the gap between the present and the past. Consider any history involving communications. In the last ten years, cell phones have saturated the market and fundamentally transformed the way information travels. American households are increasingly foregoing the use of landlines, and many other households rarely use theirs. Children growing up today may assume that it's possible to reach anyone at any time. How, then, to explain to them why Americans fought the British in the Battle of New Orleans in the War of 1812 after the war was officially over? The Treaty of Ghent ending the war was signed on December 24, 1814, but without that knowledge, General Jackson continued to fight on for two weeks until the battle finally concluded. No phones?

Couldn't they have sent a copy of the treaty through e-mail? While kids might be interested in history, they lack the experience, the time depth that shows how enormously things can change from one decade to another. And the rate at which our world is changing continues to accelerate, exacerbating the problem.

Focus and Control

Another interesting attribute of young visitors in museums is their apparent ability to focus on one activity for considerable spans of time provided the activity has been thoughtfully planned to attract and hold them. I refer to this as the attention span paradox because it flies in the face of the conventional wisdom that young children typically have less patience and staying power than do their adult companions. At Boston Children's Museum it's possible to observe children playing with bubbles, puzzles, and blocks, at the controls of a Bobcat earth mover, floating boats, or creating in the *Art Studio* long after their parents have determined it's time to move on. Children seem more able than their parents to lose themselves in the task at hand. They probably are not thinking about the grocery shopping or what to make for dinner; they have no worries about what happened at work yesterday or some expensive car repair. They do not seem concerned about seeing the whole museum during their visit, or for that matter, about leaving at all. Maybe that is why so many of them are weeping when mom says it's time to go—they just did not see it coming. This phenomenon is so common that we refer to it as a measure of success—the number of kids crying when it's time to go home. This behavior could very well be a sign of the difference between how kids and adults experience their museum visit and think about its place in the larger sweep of a day's or week's activities.

How does this relate to media? Linear media experiences in museums, with a beginning, middle, and end, are often designed to appeal to both adults and kids, and the quality of the media installation will have them equally rapt or squirming. But put controls in the hands of visitors, make them authors of their own experience, and the differences between kids and adults are apparent. Many kids have an almost limitless appetite for fiddling with interactive media (e.g., Game Boy or PlayStation) or real-time strategy games for computers (e.g., the Sims, Age of Empires). For some kids, the attraction of multimedia installations may be simply pressing buttons to see what happens; there isn't a lot of processing or intentional activity going on. But for others, a computer terminal represents a world that opens up to one's touch, a rich environment for exploration and experimentation.

The "*Monitor* Center" at the Mariner's Museum in Newport News, Virginia, uses this medium to wonderful effect in a touch screen computer interactive through which visitors can "author their own experience" as they design a Civil War–era ironclad vessel.[8] The media experience is located deep within the overall exhibition; visitors have already passed through a space chronicling the history of naval architecture and armaments leading up to the American Civil War and are about to enter a reconstruction of some of the USS *Monitor's* interior. The goal of the computer exercise is to design the best possible ironclad—a boat that will be evaluated based on its buoyancy, handling, speed, armor, and firepower. To do this, each visitor chooses a design for the boat's hull, gun deck, type and amount of armor, propulsion, and armament. There's information available if you're looking for guidance and consultation, or you can simply forge ahead and build—which I suspect is the chosen approach of most visitors.

At the end of my first effort, the screen showed a group of dour naval judges in nineteenth-century attire giving me a thumbs down as my vessel was shown sinking. "You've shown that iron really cannot float!" was the verdict. My second attempt was more successful, although the group of naval architects and politicians commented, "Perhaps you should design coal barges instead of warships," and they christened my boat the VSS *Adequate*. The cartoon image of these judges was based in its historic period, but it was also amusing; their comments were certainly designed to make me laugh (they succeeded). But in addition to entertaining, they provided a memorable experience based on specific information and naval design criteria that the exhibit developers felt were important. The structure of the experience was such that it invited continued interaction. While my effort was only "adequate," the experience offered me the opportunity to delve deeper and aspire to building a more successful vessel. Experiencing the decisions and challenges involved in designing an ironclad could bring all visitors a more nuanced appreciation for the history of this one very famous ship, the USS *Monitor*, at the same time that it provided an engaging experience for a younger audience. The interaction focused on content, but it also provided feedback, rewards, and entertainment.

Interactive computer environments in exhibitions offer an opportunity that kids may have difficulty finding in other areas—the potential for control and mastery. John Falk and Lynn Dierking coined the term "free-choice learning" to describe what's happening in museums, but most choice is exercised simply by moving on and ignoring the parts of the exhibition that aren't interesting. Open-ended activities with "loose parts" and multiple potential endings, role play, and some virtual environments support genuine personal choices, as do many interactive media installations. For children, making choices that direct an activity can be powerful, if not mesmerizing. Where else do children find the opportunity to control their lives? The week is full of school schedules, mandatory curriculum, proper attire, weekend activities they may not have chosen, meals that someone else is planning. With the near disappearance of unstructured outdoor play for the majority of children in the United States, there's little opportunity to make choices that direct activity. This is age related—obviously older kids are making some choices about their clothing, appearance, and leisure activities. Museum experiences that include a choice of activities will be good places for kids to learn, and specific museum activities, such as interactive computer-based experiences or more experiential spaces that respond to the presence and decisions of kids, can be truly compelling.

If we put kids in control, are we sacrificing authenticity? Are choice and authenticity inevitably in tension with each other? Incorporating some degree of personal meaning making in a museum experience does not necessarily imply that visitors create their own historical narratives or rewrite history. One of the charms of electronic media is that its multi-channeling character can help in the effort to present a more nuanced recitation while engaging the active imaginations of learners. Media may actually enhance our ability to explore history from many perspectives—those of a privileged citizen or the working class, a person with deep family history in one location or a newcomer, male or female, Black or White; a rural resident or a citizen of small town or bustling metropolis.

A Media-rich World

In addition to having a distinct worldview, an impressive ability to focus, and the desire to make choices and demonstrate control, kids today live in a media-rich world. Ten years ago, this may have meant widespread exposure to cable television and personal computers on which they could e-mail, play games, and surf the Web—with the completion of an occasional homework assignment thrown in. Today, it is best represented by ubiquitous cell phones. While parents may give their kids phones to satisfy a nervous need to stay in touch continuously, kids are using phones for their own purposes. Text messaging, taking and sending photos, and anytime, anywhere connections make for strong social networks and enable kids to share the minutiae of everyday life.

"Disconnected," a 2008 documentary film produced by students at Carleton College in Northfield, Minnesota, followed the lives of three students after they voluntarily gave up all access to their computers.[9] After finding that professors would not accept handwritten assignments they struggled to produce documents on an electric typewriter. More significantly, they had trouble communicating with professors and doing research; they missed a range of campus activities without access to e-mail and resorted to a car stereo to listen to music; they spent more time outdoors and learned to play Ping-Pong. Two students dropped out of the experiment after three weeks; one lasted for five weeks and it was a struggle. They all reported feeling socially isolated and "out of the loop." It is almost impossible to appreciate the impact of technology until it's abruptly withdrawn from the fabric of our lives.

As technology continues to evolve we've seen the convergence of personal computers with phones so that the information, entertainment, and networking power of computing can now be taken virtually anywhere. Increasingly, cell phones look like mini touch screen computers with full Internet capability. So when a history exhibition for kids such as *Sensing Chicago* at the Chicago History Museum[10] gives kids an oversized computer touchscreen with which to create and e-mail a picture postcard, it's connecting to the media-rich world of its target audience. In this particular case the graphic design and catalogue of available images (apart from the personal photo created by visitors) reference an earlier time in the history of the city. It's as if a bridge is being built, one chosen image at a time, connecting Chicago's past to today's museum visitor.

Is media a good thing for kids? The Alliance for Childhood, an advocacy group focused on the healthy development of children, is a vocal critic of the television and computer saturation currently experienced by many children; they join a number of researchers who contend that screen time is harmful. Their studies show that communing with computers and television isolates children and can stunt emotional growth—and certainly some screen experiences, such as hours of daily, isolated television viewing, may have this result.[11] But what if electronic media are harnessed to create powerful shared experiences? What if they give rise to an emotional landscape that immerses young visitors in another time? When screens, big or small, are embedded within a well-designed exhibition experience they contribute to a rich and varied social experience that engages the intellect, senses, and particularly the emotions in ways that few other interpretive media can. While museum films and

FIGURE 13.2. Visitors to *Sensing Chicago* e-mail postcards of their own design. Courtesy Chicago History Museum.

video are a poor way to convey detailed information, they are one of the best ways to create memorable, immersion experiences for visitors that foster strong emotive connections.

Some media experiences, such as the "Sound" exhibit in *Sensing Chicago*, go beyond using screens to engage visitors. Connecting with a more playful spirit, this installation creates a lively interactive space that is roughly fifteen feet square and includes sixteen colored "hot spots" on the floor that are audio triggers. As one or more visitors hop around in the space, they conjure up an increasingly varied audio tour of Chicago's past connected to images of the Union Stock Yard, a jazz club, and the Great Chicago Fire.

A willingness to be playful or silly in public is not the only thing that separates young visitors from their parents. People born later than 1985 with ready access to a number of personal computing and communication devices have grown up in a multitasking and parallel-processing world. They are inputting while checking facts online, listening to streaming music or sports, connecting through online social networks or instant messaging, bouncing from blogs to YouTube to Wikipedia; they are awash in information and their days are defined by a creative remix of taking it in, processing, and repositioning by sharing with others. The implications for electronic media in museum experiences are twofold. First, with young visitors accustomed to complex, multiple, simultaneous streams of information, the design of media for museums might likewise need to be more complex in order to communicate to this audience, This is for you; this is consistent with the media world you live in. Second, the experience of living in a media-rich world may well increase one's capacity to take in multiple streams of information. While designing a video wall for the Birmingham Civil Rights Institute in 1991, I was questioned by a skeptical board member whether the multiple streams of images and information would be overwhelming or confusing for children. My answer was simple: if we put the board member and a group of young kids in a room together with the video wall, played it once, and measured who learned more or found it most compelling, my money would be on the kids.

Choosing the Right Medium

Planners will create media more attractive to kids if they choose content goals for their connection to young audiences, create a "gee whiz" spectacle, or introduce humor. But the endless variety of media installations can be overwhelming and it may be useful to think about the options with the help of a typology, a systematic way to describe the impact and appearance of installations. Every media installation has its own effect on the visitor experience and the dynamics of behavior within social groups at museums. To decide what type of media component might fit in the flow of an exhibition and when, it helps to think about the overall pacing of the visit. Consider the qualities *intrinsic* to that moment in the story or exhibition narrative. Does the story require some basic information to set the scene? Is there a dramatic moment in the narrative when pulling together many strands of content and emotion is needed? And think about the *extrinsic* factors too, such as how long people have to walk before they find a place to rest or how many things compete for their attention.

Great exhibitions, like great stories, are carefully constructed to provide an experience with highs and lows, moments when you pause to take it all in and times when your heart beats a little faster. A long narrative piece is going to slow people down but can have great emotional impact. An interactive catalog may engage somebody for quite some time—but not if another compelling exhibit component is right beside

CONTENT AND TONE

Messages: With authenticity as an essential requirement, the field still remains fairly open when determining the best possible content for kids in electronic media. The target age must inform these choices—a range of 4–12 years is very broad and too large to be truly meaningful. By narrowing that target for specific installations, or accepting that a large group experience will include kids of many ages, one can identify some common themes that should resonate with young audiences. For example, kids are generally part of families, so family issues may be familiar and encourage identification with the story. Questions of fairness resonate quite well with children over the age of about 7 or 8, so a civil rights program might focus on whether it's fair to deny people equal rights. Stories organized around questions of self and group identity may find a natural audience with "tweens" or teenagers.

Humor: While kids may relate to stories about childhood and may comprehend the meaning of nostalgia, a sense of the absurd or humor may be most likely to pull them into a story. The voice of most museum exhibitions is a voice of authority. Humor can change the tone of discourse between the museum and visitor and sends a message that communicating about history is a bit like other communication in the life of a child. Inspiration can be drawn from many sources—children's books, theater, the Internet, and, obviously, television. Not surprisingly, many of the same things that make adults laugh make kids laugh too—surprises, absurd developments, people saying or doing things that make them appear foolish. In younger audiences language skills may not be as well developed; slapstick and broad humor will be more effective. People falling down, spilling things, and failing dramatically at simple tasks (even for 6-year-olds) are funny. Doing something that flagrantly violates what is normally considered to be polite behavior is funny. Snubbing authority is funny.

The difficulty of humor is that everyone does not agree on what exactly is funny and, further, humor is deeply embedded in culture. But if one makes a careful study of Warner Brothers cartoons (Bugs Bunny, Road Runner) and the work of Matt Groening (The Simpsons) one can't go too far wrong. The issues of cultural sensitivity can often be creatively engaged by testing scripts, storyboards, and rough cuts with audiences representing diverse cultures and backgrounds.

Chart of Media Experience

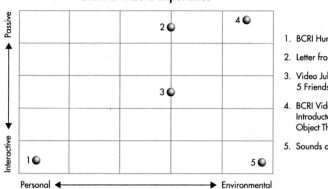

1. BCRI Human Rights

2. Letter from Birmingham Jail

3. Video Juke Box
   5 Friends from Japan

4. BCRI Video Wall
   Introductory Theater
   Object Theater; Home Place, MN

5. Sounds of Chicago

FIGURE 13.3. Chart of Media Experience.

it. Locating a dense electronic encyclopedia near the start of the visitor experience can be disastrous because visitors are anxious to dive in and move forward into the heart of the exhibition. Even if some visitors are engaged at that point, they'll form a bottleneck for other anxious guests trying to enter right behind them. The choice of a particular type of media installation should follow a consideration of likely visitor behavior based on both intrinsic and extrinsic factors. When would the audience benefit from an immersive experience or spectacle that floods the eyes, ears, and emotions? When are people ready for highly detailed information? At what point in a visit are families likely to stick together, and when might the kids have a chance to break away and explore on their own? The chart of media experience (Figure 13.3) is a simple tool that helps to conceptualize the different qualities of media installations and suggests how choices about different formats might be made.

The X-axis represents a range of experience from personal or intimate to more environmental or shared. The Y-axis indicates the level of interactivity from highly interactive at the bottom to fairly passive at the top. An important thing to remember is that the chart is merely descriptive—there's nothing good or bad about the media best described by any one spot. It simply provides a way of looking at the variety of experiences media can bring to an exhibition. That said, if it's true that young visitors tend to be more social and are particularly intrigued by exerting some control over their environment, then history exhibits seeking to engage younger visitors will do well to choose media installations that are higher in those attributes. A few examples drawn from one institution will illustrate the range of possibilities.

Using the Chart

The Birmingham Civil Rights Institute in Birmingham, Alabama, uses a variety of dramatic exhibit settings to tell the story of the Civil Rights Movement emphasizing local stories and their place in, and impact on, a larger national and international story.[12] The visitor experience begins with an introductory theater culminating in a dramatic reveal: an iconic photograph taken by Elliot Erwitt in 1950 shows a black man bent to drink from a water fountain labeled "Colored." The image dissolves as the screen rises to show a wall with similar "Colored" and "White" drinking fountains. Visitors exit around them to enter an exhibition gallery detailing the era of segregation in Birmingham.

Throughout the galleries there are a number of discreet media installations. In an exhibition on human rights is a touch screen interactive database of stories from all over the world. This example belongs at one end of the X-axis—the personal side. Visitors navigate through the database either by choosing to explore a category of human rights issues, such as women's rights, or by choosing stories from a particular geographic location. This media installation is personal because one visitor determines the path of the experience and the screen serves just one or two people at a time. At the other end of the spectrum are environmental experiences. A fragmented video wall made to look like a storefront selling televisions tells the story of demonstrations in Birmingham in 1963. The soundtrack featuring participants in those events looking back at their personal histories fills the space around the installation and groups of people naturally congregate to take it all in together. Another example of an environmental experience is the introductory theater, although this more traditional setting has a different experiential quality.

On the Y-axis of media experience, the range is from interactive to passive. In the gallery depicting life in segregated Birmingham is an interactive video jukebox that features performances by many groups on the "chitlin' circuit"—Black performers who traveled throughout the South to entertain Black audiences in segregated venues. The jukebox is quiet unless a visitor selects one of the performances. This very simple expression of visitor preference is sometimes known as "push a button, see a movie." Increasingly powerful computers and wireless connectivity make ever more personalized media interactions possible. One can imagine a handheld device, a personal information or interpretive system, offering more information, images, or video in response to specific inquiries. These systems may suggest connections to other areas of the exhibition or a wide range of supplementary information to enhance the museum experience. An artificial intelligence system can further tailor offerings to the visitor's preferences.

A more passive experience is the spot in the Birmingham Civil Rights Institute where visitors can stand by the bars of the jail cell that held Martin Luther King, Jr. in 1963. An audio installation features King reading the "Letter from Birmingham Jail." It takes a few moments to hear the entire program; when it stops people generally move on. This is a very simple, completely passive, yet powerful installation. The audio piece draws attention to the physical setting and really holds people; many visitors linger for several minutes and stand listening as they stare at the little cell.

On the chart of media experience, there are two axes so each media installation can be described on at least two continua; the "Letter from Birmingham Jail" is both passive and environmental. There is no interaction involved and the program is part of a setting that can be experienced by many people simultaneously. For virtually every spot on the chart one can describe or invent some kind, or several kinds, of media experience. If one plots the qualities of all media experiences within a given exhibition, it's safe to say that a history exhibition with a dispersed set of dots offers a rich and varied visitor experience.

Theater + Objects = Object Theater

News footage and photographs play an important role at the Birmingham Civil Rights Institute where artifacts are few and far between, but other museums and stories may have more extensive collections—and object theater may be a natural choice in those settings. Metaphorically speaking, the media installation gives those objects a voice, allows us to hear their stories. Whether iconic ceremonial pieces that mark special occasions or humble material culture of everyday life, objects have much to tell us about their context and significance. A theater that brings them to life both engages our cultural affinity for storytelling and communicates to young audiences that collections of historical objects hold great meaning. Even a collection of primitive computer processors, a group of objects not known for excessive charisma, was recently animated in an imaginative production at the New Mexico Museum of Natural History and Science.[13] A brief and engaging history of one "killer technology" after another is embodied in their physical form and attributes. A large screen with fast-paced montage of period video, photos, and documents set to pop music of the late-twentieth century animates a whimsical story in which the unimpressive "boxes" are made literally to speak for themselves.

At the Minnesota Historical Society an object theater, *Home Place Minnesota*, focuses primarily on stories about childhood.[14] For adults, it often elicits a longing for childhood and the special feeling of belonging that comes with a strong sense of place. For children, it explores childhood as a special time and trusts that they understand the complex emotional landscape that is nostalgia.

The intimate theater setting comes alive with first-person narrative, much of it told from a child's point of view. The production has the feeling more of live theater than of film. A series of stage sets—a Victorian home, a train platform, a 1950s living room—uses objects and images to evoke different periods and places in Minnesota's history. Daniel Spock, director of the Minnesota History Center Museum, attributes some of kids' fascination to the "gee-whiz" nature of object theater; the audience never knows what is going to happen next. With music and lighting effects, a turntable that whisks set pieces in and out of view, the audience is fascinated by both the physicality of the presentation and by the "empathetic engagement" engendered by program content.

People of different ages have storytelling and emotional connections in common; a media installation that capitalizes on these qualities is doing what media does best. Interestingly, research at Minnesota Historical Society shows that people who viewed *Home Place Minnesota* were more engaged in their visit to the museum overall than were those who did not. Spock speculates that by stimulating the *emotional* centers in the brain, visitors may well improve their ability to take in and retain more *intellectual* material as well during their visit.

And then, of course, there is magic. When there are no objects and very few images, electronic media may provide the only way to engage the imagination, particularly of young visitors. At the Ulysses S. Grant National Historic Site, in St. Louis, Missouri, the small farmhouse where young Grant met his wife, Julia Dent, was recently opened to the public. The house has been restored but the interior furnishings were lost in a fire long ago. The National Park Service, steward of the site, made a decision not to fill the premises with other period furnishings or reproductions; they saw this decision as a way to preserve the integrity of the historic site and built a separate interpretive center nearby. But this left a very empty looking house for visitors. Even with a knowledgeable guide, this visitor experience still challenged the imagination.

FIGURE 13.4. A combination of images, strong narrative, objects, and "gee whiz" effects makes object theater an effective storytelling medium. Courtesy Minnesota Historical Society, www.mnhs.org.

FIGURE 13.5. Media magically brings history to life at the Ulysses S. Grant National Historic Site. Photograph by Karen Elshout.

To populate the house and evoke a bit of its history, a media installation was added to the dining room. Just above the fireplace, a large mirror (actually a flat screen monitor) was installed that looks as if it belongs there. When visitors enter, the image of an empty room dissolves as if in a "magic mirror" and the reflection shows a fully furnished room with Grant and his in-laws seated at the table.[15] They are debating the merits of a hot issue of their day—the laws relating to slavery.

History, Kids, Media, and Meaning

Although the decision to use electronic media in exhibitions for children is an easy one, as Selma Thomas observes, it's not about the media but about understanding the interpretive purpose it serves. Thomas, a historian and longtime producer of media for exhibitions, describes media as modern Western culture's form of storytelling.[16] The ability to create compelling narratives that conjure up the past for today's visitors is critical to the success of exhibitions. Truly great installations combine carefully chosen content and a powerful arc of emotions to take visitors on a journey that will not soon be forgotten. Further, as the retelling of our history becomes more nuanced, as our construction of the past fragments to include more points of view, more narratives, more challenges to authority and power, we may find that electronic media are the best way to juxtapose ideas and alternative readings and allow visitors to provide input and shape exhibition content.

The virtual environment can be powerful and seductive. If kids entering history museums are familiar and comfortable with certain types of media, then exhibition teams can consider these when pondering how best to engage this audience. We have entered an age of self-constructed information and narratives. We live in a time when individuals have considerable power to gather their own facts and construct their own realities. Access to the Internet has provided an unprecedented ability to share these realities and posit alternatives to the institutional voice offered in museums of culture and history. How institutions choose to engage the public and use new media is likely to define the terms of a conversation about whose history and what narratives are worth telling. If the last quarter of the twentieth century was about opening up the academy to alternatives—about giving women, minorities, children, and people with different backgrounds a voice—then the first quarter of the twenty-first century may well be taken up with sorting out how this translates into the public experience of his-

tory. Exploring the area between personal meaning and social significance, providing an opportunity for individual choice to guide exploration while still offering access to professionally researched, documented,
and constructed history could be the next battleground in the struggle
for control of historical interpretation. For young audiences, this delicate
balance between personal choice and public narrative will be particularly
important. If we started out by asking who kids are, we may well end up
wondering what history is.

NOTES

1. "Video Killed the Radio Star," produced by the Rock and Roll Hall of Fame and Museum, Cleveland, OH, 1995.
2. "Ancient Voices: Stories of Colorado's Distant Past," Native American diorama produced by the Colorado History Museum, 2004.
3. "Civil War in Four Minutes," Abraham Lincoln Presidential Library and Museum, Springfield, IL, produced by BRC Imagination Arts in association with Illinois Historic Preservation Agency and the Capital Development Board, 2005.
4. "Oregon Trail," developed by John Hoffmann, Anthony Stone, and Pablo Jara Meza in 1971 and produced by MECC, 1974.
5. Lynn D. Dierking and John H. Falk, "Audience and Accessibility," in *The Virtual and the Real: Media in the Museum*, ed. Selma Thomas and Ann Mintz (Washington, DC: American Association of Museums, 1998), 64.
6. *Five Friends from Japan*, media and traveling exhibition produced by Boston Children's Museum and National Children's Museum, Gail Ringel, executive producer, 2004.
7. Jeff Hayward and Brian Werner, "Summative Evaluation of Five Friends from Japan," (unpublished report, Northampton, MA: People, Places and Design Research, 2004), 8.
8. "Design Your Own Ironclad," USS *Monitor* Center at the Mariner's Museum, Newport News, VA, produced by Two Rivers Studios, 2007.
9. Pamela Babcock, "Unplugged," *Carleton College Voice* (Northfield, MN), Spring 2008, p.18. Also see the web site about the documentary film http://disconnecteddocumentary.com/ (accessed August 25, 2009).
10. *Sensing Chicago*: "Sound" exhibit and "Postcard", Chicago History Museum, Chicago, Illinois, produced by Monadnock Media with Amaze Design and Chicago History Museum, 2006.
11. Coleen Cordes and Edward Miller, eds., *Fool's Gold: A Critical Look at Computers in Childhood* (College Park, MD: Alliance for Childhood, 2000), http://drup al6.allianceforchildhood.org/fools_gold (accessed August 25, 2009).
12. I discuss the following exhibits: "Introductory Theater," "Video Jukebox," "Birmingham: 1963," "Letter from Birmingham Jail," "Human Rights Database," Birmingham Civil Rights Institute, Birmingham, AL, produced by Dave Davis, Donna Lawrence Productions, and Jackie Shearer, Gail

Ringel, executive producer, 1992.

13. "Rise of the Machines," in *STARTUP: Albuquerque and the Personal Computer Revolution*, New Mexico Museum of Natural History and Science, Albuquerque, NM, produced by Weatherhead Experience Design Group, 2006.

14. *Home Place Minnesota*, Minnesota History Center, St. Paul, MN, Paul Martin, executive producer, 1993.

15. "Magic Mirror," Ulysses S. Grant National Historic Site, St. Louis, MO, produced by Hillman & Carr, 2007.

16. Selma Thomas and Ann Mintz, eds., *The Virtual and the Real: Media in the Museum* (Washington, DC: American Association of Museums, 1998).

Andrew Anway is the founder of Amaze Design, a firm specializing in the planning and design of museums and museum exhibits. He has thirty years experience in project planning, interpretive design, and management. He has led international teams in the development of national museums for the governments of Malaysia, Australia, Qatar, and the United States. Through collaborations with leading institutions including the Chicago History Museum and the National Children's Museum, Andrew continues to be inspired by the joyful capacity for learning that children bring to their museum experiences. Andrew holds a BA in history from Boston College.

Leslie Bedford is director of the Leadership in Museum Education Program at Bank Street College. A member of The Museum Group, she consults on exhibitions, programs, and staff development. She began her museum career as director of the Japan Program at the Boston Children's Museum before serving as deputy director for programs at the Brooklyn Historical Society. A graduate of Vassar College and Harvard University, she attended the Museum Management Institute in 1993. Leslie received her PhD in Museum Studies from Union Institute and University in 2008; her dissertation, "Working in the Subjunctive Mood," explores exhibitions as art form and imaginative experience.

Jon-Paul C. Dyson is vice president for exhibit research and development and director, National Center for the History of Electronic Games at Strong National Museum of Play. He also is editor of the *American Journal of Play*, a peer-reviewed, interdisciplinary journal devoted to the study of play. In his ten years at Strong he has led the development of numerous play-based and history-based exhibitions, including *Reading Adventureland, Berenstain Bears: Down a Sunny Dirt Road*, and *DanceLab*. He holds a BA from Oberlin College and a PhD in American intellectual and cultural history from the State University of New York at Buffalo.

Benjamin Filene is associate professor and director of public history at the University of North Carolina Greensboro. Prior to UNCG, Benjamin was senior exhibit developer at the Minnesota Historical Society. He served as lead developer on the exhibition *Open House: If These Walls Could Talk*, winner of a WOW Award for innovation and an Award of Merit from the American Association for State and Local History. Benjamin received his PhD in American Studies from Yale, and published *Romancing the Folk: Public Memory and American Roots Music*. He serves as contributing editor for the *Journal of American History*'s exhibition review section.

Robert Kiihne is director of exhibits at the USS Constitution Museum. He began his museum career as a high school summer interpreter and college art installer. He has held many titles over the last nineteen years at the USS Constitution Museum—all created for him. Robert is very interested in how to engage all visitors on a shoestring budget and believes that prototyping is a moral imperative. In 2004 he became the project manager for The Family Learning Project, which tracked or interviewed over 2500 families through prototype exhibits designed to engage families. Robert also believes in the importance of ice cream.

Neal Mayer has been designing three-dimensional environments for storytelling ever since his third grade teacher told him he could build a diorama instead of writing a book report. He began his professional museum experience twenty-five years ago as a founding staff member of the New York Hall of Science and has since continued to devote his professional life to museum design and education. In 1998 he and three partners founded Wondercabinet Interpretive Design, an exhibit planning and design firm specializing in environments for learning. Neal received a bachelor of industrial design from Pratt Institute.

D. Lynn McRainey is the Elizabeth F. Cheney director of education at the Chicago History Museum. Lynn has led interdepartmental initiatives to redefine adult and school programs; chaired an institutional visioning committee; and served as project director for the children's exhibition *Sensing Chicago*. She has over twenty years experience in museum education at art, history, and children's museums. Lynn received a Fellowship in Museum Practice from the Smithsonian Institution and participated in the Getty Leadership Institute program Museum Leaders: The Next Generation. She has an MA in art history and a BA in American studies from the University of Virginia.

Judy Rand is a leader in the field of interpretive exhibit planning, cited for excellence in exhibit writing. Museums use her "Visitors' Bill of Rights" to help them think about visitors' needs. In her years at the Monterey Bay Aquarium, Judy established the Exhibit Research and Development Department. A member of The Museum Group, Judy is an independent exhibit developer who works with museums nationwide, including the Monterey Bay Aquarium, National Constitution Center, and The Children's Museum of Indianapolis. She's helped create more than eighty exhibitions on topics ranging from bats to belfries, microbes to dinosaurs, and Jimi Hendrix to Jewish chicken farmers.

Anne Grimes Rand is executive vice president of the USS Constitution Museum, a free museum on Boston's Freedom Trail welcoming 300,000 visitors annually. Anne is responsible for the visitor experience, working to create engaging exhibits and programs where families can have fun and learn as they explore history together. She has twenty years of museum experience, twelve as curator of the USS Constitution Museum. She earned her BA at Dartmouth College and MA at Brown University, and participated in the Seminar for Historic Administration. When not thinking about maritime history exhibits, Anne prefers to be on the water under sail.

Elizabeth Reich Rawson is an independent consultant and an adjunct professor for Bank Street College and Johns Hopkins University. As senior exhibition developer and project manager for Brooklyn Children's Museum from 1997 to 2010, she led teams for award-winning projects such as *World Brooklyn* and *Pattern Wizardry*. Her work has been recognized by the American Association of Museums, the Association of Children's Museums, the National Endowment for the Humanities, and the American Association of State and Local History. Liza received an MA in history museum studies from Cooperstown Graduate Programs and a BA in historic preservation from Goucher College.

Gail Ringel is vice president for exhibits and production at Boston Children's Museum. An interpretive planner and media producer for twenty-five years, Gail leads the development of exhibitions for children and families that balance the arts, sciences, and humanities. Recent projects include *Five Friends from Japan*, winner of a 2003 American Association of Museums Muse award; *Accessibility*, 2005 recipient of Association of Children's Museums Universal Design for Learning award; and the complete renovation of exhibitions at Boston Children's Museum in 2007. Gail is a graduate of Cornell University and consults on museum projects for cultural, history, and natural history museums.

John Russick is senior curator at the Chicago History Museum. John has over two decades of experience in a variety of museums, including The Field Museum and the National Museum of American History. He was lead curator for *Sensing Chicago*, a history exhibition for children, which received an honorable mention in the Nineteenth Annual Excellence in Exhibition Competition, 2007. His most recent publication, *Historic Photos of Chicago Crime: The Capone Era* features images from the Chicago History Museum's permanent collection. He holds degrees in history and historic preservation from Northern Illinois University and the University of Texas at Austin, respectively.

Sharon Shaffer is the executive director for the Smithsonian Early Enrichment Center, a model program in museum-based education for young children. Sharon is the founding director for the program and oversees the lab school for young children while also providing leadership for educational outreach. She designs seminars in object-based learning and arts-centered curriculum, consulting with schools and museums nationally and internationally. Sharon has a PhD in social foundations of education, has served as president for the Early Childhood Art Educators Division of the National Art Education Association, and teaches as an adjunct professor at the University of Virginia.

Daniel Spock has a twenty-six-year career in the museum field, which began as a planetarium guide. Over the course of his career he has worked as an exhibit designer and exhibit developer, including thirteen years at the Boston Children's Museum. He then moved into the realm of administration and program leadership at the Minnesota Historical Society. Dan is an ardent proponent of visitor-centered, experiential interpretive approaches that value visitors as active learners. He has consulted and lectured at a variety of museum and learning institutions. Dan has a BA in art from Antioch College.

Mary Jane Taylor is a museum educator with sixteen years of experience in program and exhibition interpretation, interactive and audio tour production, and visitor research. Throughout her career, she has worked extensively with school and family audiences. As curator of education for interpretation at Winterthur Museum & Country Estate, she won the 2004 American Association of Museums Excellence in Exhibition Writing award for her interactive history exhibition for families, *Kid Stuff: Growing Up at Winterthur*. Mary Jane has degrees from the Winterthur Program in Early American Culture at the University of Delaware, James Cook University of North Queensland, and Wittenberg University.

Beth A. Twiss Houting, director of education for the Chester County Historical Society in Pennsylvania, has worked in and consulted for a variety of art and history museums over the last thirty years, including Winterthur and the National Constitution Center. Her areas of interest are in hands-on object learning, exhibition interactivity, and visitor research. Beth has an MA in the Winterthur Program in Early American Culture as well as a certificate in museum studies from the University of Delaware.

The following references are selected sources cited by chapter authors and offer readers a sample of the available research.

Ackerman, Diane. *A Natural History of the Senses.* New York: Vintage Books, 1990.

Alexander, Edward P. *Museums in Motion: An Introduction to the History and Functions of Museums.* Walnut Creek, CA: AltaMira Press, 1996.

Alleman, Janet, and Jere Brophy. "History is Alive: Teaching Young Children about Changes Over Time." *The Social Studies* 94, no. 3 (May–June 2003): 107–10.

American Association for the Advancement of Science. *Benchmarks for Science Literacy: Project 2061.* New York: Oxford University Press, 1993.

American Association of Museums Standing Professional Committee on Education. *Excellence in Practice: Museum Education Principles and Standards.* Washington, DC: American Association of Museums, 2002, revised 2005.

Ames, Kenneth L., Barbara Franco, and L. Thomas Frye, eds. *Ideas and Images: Developing Interpretive History Exhibits.* Nashville, TN: American Association for State and Local History, 1992.

Barton, Keith C. "Oh, That's a Tricky Piece!: Children, Mediated Action, and the Tools of Historical Time." *Elementary School Journal* 103, no. 2 (2002): 161–85.

Bedford, Leslie. "Storytelling: The Real Work of Museums." *Curator: The Museum Journal* 44 (2001): 27–34.

Bergen, Doris, and Doris Fromberg, eds. *Play from Birth to Twelve Years: Contexts, Perspectives, and Meanings.* New York: Routledge, 2006.

Berk, Laura E. *Awakening Children's Minds: How Parents and Teachers Can Make a Difference.* Oxford: Oxford University Press, 2001.

——. *Child Development*, 7th ed. Boston, MA: Allyn and Bacon, 2000.

——. *Infants and Children: Prenatal Through Middle Childhood*, 6th ed. Boston, MA: Allyn and Bacon, 2002.

——. "Vygotsky's Theory: The Importance of Make-believe Play." *Young Children* 50, no. 1 (1994): 30–9.

Berk, Laura, and Adam Winsler. *Scaffolding Children's Learning: Vygotsky and Early Childhood Education.* Washington, DC: National Association for the Education of Young Children, 1995.

Bitgood, Stephen. "The Role of Attention in Designing Effective Interpretive Labels." *Journal of Interpretation Research* 5, no. 2 (2000): 31–45.

Bitgood, Stephen, and Donald Patterson. "Principles of Exhibit Design." *Visitor Behavior* 2, no. 1 (1987): 4–6.

Borun, Minda. "Why Listen to Your Visitor?" USS Constitution Museum, Family Learning Forum Online, http://www.familylearningforum.org/evaluation/power-of-evaluation/why-listen-visitor.htm.

Borun, Minda, Jennifer Dritsas, Julie I. Johnson, Nancy E. Peter, Kathleen F. Wagner, Kathleen Fadigan, Arlene Jangaard, Estelle Stroup, and Angela Wenger. *Family Learning in Museums: The PISEC Perspective.* Washington, DC: Association of Science-Technology Centers, 1998.

Borun, Minda, and Jennifer Dritsas. "Developing Family-Friendly Exhibits." *Curator: The Museum Journal* 40, no. 3 (September 1997): 178–196.

Bradley Commission on History in Schools. *Building a History Curriculum: Guidelines for Teaching History in Schools.* Westlake, OH: National Council for History Education, Inc., 2005, http://www.nche.net/docs/NCHE_BAHC.pdf.

Bruner, Jerome. *Actual Minds, Possible Worlds.* Cambridge, MA: Harvard University Press, 1986.

Cadwell, Louise Boyd. *Bringing Reggio Emilia Home: An Innovative Approach to Early Childhood Education.* New York: Teachers College Press, 1997.

Caillois, Roger. *Man, Play, and Games.* London: Thames and Hudson, 1962.

Carr, David. "Crafted Truths: Respecting Children in Museums." In *The Promise of Cultural Institutions.* Walnut Creek, CA: AltaMira Press, 2003.

Charlesworth, Rosalind, and Dilek Buchholz. *Understanding Child Development.* Albany, NY: Delmar, 2003.

Chase, Henry. "Past Due and On Time!" *American Visions* (June-July 1994), http://findarticles.com/p/articles/mi_m1546/is_/ai_15495026?tag = artBody;col1

Chudacoff, Howard. *Children at Play: An American History.* New York: New York University Press, 2007.

Chung, James, and Tara May. "X-Tended Family: Attracting the Post-boomer Audience." *Museum News* (November/December 2005): 55–62.

Classen, Constance. "Museum Manners: The Sensory Life of the Early Museum." *Journal of Social History* 40, no. 4 (Summer 2007): 895–914.

Cole, Michael, and Shiela R. Cole. *The Development of Children.* 4th ed. New York: Worth Publishers, 2001.

Connell, Bettye Rose, Mike Jones, Ron Mace, Jim Mueller, Abir Mullick, Elaine Ostroff, Jon Sanford, Ed Steinfeld, Molly Story, and Gregg Vanderheiden. *Principles of Universal Design,* Version 2.0. Raleigh, NC: The Center for Universal Design at North Carolina State University, April 1, 1997. http://www.design.ncsu.edu/cud/about_ud/udprinciples.htm.

Cooney, William, Charles Cross, and Barry Trunk. *From Plato to Piaget: The Greatest Educational Theorists from across the Centuries and around the World.* Lanham, MD: University Press of America, 1993.

Cordes, Colleen, and Edward Miller, eds. *Fool's Gold: A Critical Look at Computers in Childhood.* College Park, MD: Alliance for Childhood, 2000, http://drupal6.allianceforchildhood.org/fools_gold.

Cotton, Kathleen. *Developing Empathy in Children and Youth.* Northwest Regional Educational Library, 2001.

Crowley, Kevin, and Melanie Jacobs. "Building Islands of Expertise in Everyday Family Activity." In *Learning Conversations in Museums,* edited by Gaea Leinhardt, Kevin Crowley and Karen Knutson. Mahwah, NJ: Lawrence Erlbaum Associates, Inc., Publishers, 2002.

Culp, George H., and Herbert N. Nickles. *An Apple for the Teacher: Fundamentals for Instructional Computing*. Monterey, CA: Brooks/Cole Publishing Co., 1983.

Davis, Elaine. *How Students Understand the Past: From Theory to Practice*. Walnut Creek, CA: AltaMira Press, 2005.

de Sanctis Ricciardone, Paola. "Collecting as a Form of Play." In *Play: An Interdisciplinary Synthesis, Play & Culture Studies Volume 6*, edited by F. F. McMahon, Donald E. Lytle, and Brian Sutton-Smith. Lanham, MD: University Press of America, 2005.

DeWitt, Jennifer, and Martin Storksdieck. "A Short Review of School Field Trips: Key Findings from the Past and Implications for the Future." *Visitor Studies* 11, no. 2 (2008): 181–97.

Dewey, John. "The Pattern of Inquiry." In *Logic: The Theory of Inquiry*. New York: H. Holt and Co., 1938.

Diamond, Judy. "The Behavior of Family Groups in Science Museums." *Curator: The Museum Journal* 29, no. 2 (1986): 139–54.

Dierking, Lynn D. et al. "Laughing and Learning Together: Family Learning Research Becomes Practice at the USS Constitution Museum." *History News* (Summer 2006): 12–5.

Dixon-Krauss, Lisbeth. *Vygotsky in the Classroom*. White Plains, NY: Longman Publishers, 1996.

Dodd, Jocelyn. "Interactivity and Social Inclusion." Paper presented at the Interactive Learning in Museums of Art Conference, Victoria and Albert Museum, May 17–18, 2002, http://www.vam.ac.uk/res_cons/research/conferences/learning/index.html.

Doherty, Martin J. *Theory of Mind: How Children Understand Others' Thoughts and Feelings*. New York: Psychology Press, 2009.

Durbin, Gail, ed. *Developing Museum Exhibitions for Lifelong Learning*. London: The Stationery Office, 1996.

Egan, Kieran. "Accumulating History." In *The Philosophy of History Teaching*. Middletown, CT: Wesleyan University Press, 1983: 66–80.

——. *The Educated Mind: How Cognitive Tools Shape Our Understanding*. Chicago, IL: The University of Chicago Press, 1997.

——. *Teaching and Learning Outside the Box: Inspiring Imagination Across the Curriculum*. New York: Teachers College Press, 2007.

——. *Teaching as Story Telling: An Alternative Approach to Teaching and Curriculum in the Elementary School*. Chicago, IL: The University of Chicago Press, 1986.

Egan, Kieran, and Gillian Judson. "Of Whales and Wonder." *Educational Leadership* 65 (2008): 20–5.

Eversmann, Pauline K., et al. "Material Culture as Text: Review and Reform of the Literacy Model for Interpretation." In *American Material Culture: The Shape of the Field*, edited by Ann Smart Martin and John Ritchie Garrison. Winterthur, DE: Henry Francis du Pont Winterthur Museum, 1997.

Falk, John H. "Visitors: Who Does, Who Doesn't, and Why." *Museum News* (March/April 1998): 38–43.

Falk, John H., and Lynn D. Dierking. *Learning from Museums: Visitor Experiences and the Making of Meaning*. Walnut Creek, CA: AltaMira Press, 2000.

——. *The Museum Experience*. 1992. Reprint Washington, DC: Whalesback Books, 1998.

Festinger, Leon. "A Theory of Social Comparison Processes." *Human Relations* 7, no. 2 (1954).

Fivush, Robyn, and Jean M. Mandler. "Developmental Changes in the Understanding of Temporal Sequence." *Child Development* 56 (1985): 1437–46.

Forman, George E., and David S. Kuschner. *The Child's Construction of Knowledge: Piaget for Teaching Children.* Washington, DC: National Association for the Education of Young Children, 1983.

Freire, Paulo, and Donaldo Macedo. *Literacy: Reading the Word and the World.* London: Routledge & Kegan Paul, 1987.

Gaidos, Susan. "Thanks for the Future Memories." *Science News*, June 21, 2008.

Gardner, Howard. *Frames of Mind: The Theory of Multiple Intelligences.* New York: Basic Books, 1983.

Gilmore, James H., and B. Joseph Pine II. *Authenticity: What Consumers Really Want.* Boston: Harvard Business Press, 2007.

Greene, Maxine. *Releasing the Imagination: Essays on Education, the Arts, and Social Change.* San Francisco: Jossey-Bass, 1995.

Gutwill, Joshua P. "Part 1: Observing APE." In *Fostering Active Prolonged Engagement: The Art of Creating APE Exhibits,* edited by Thomas Humphrey and Joshua P. Gutwill. San Francisco: Exploratorium, 2005.

Harris, Paul L. *The Work of the Imagination.* Malden, MA: Blackwell Publishing, 2000.

Hein, George E. *Learning in the Museum.* New York: Routledge, 1998.

Hein, George E., and Mary Alexander. *Museums: Places of Learning.* Washington, DC: American Association of Museums Education Committee, 1998.

Heine, Hilda S. *The Exploratorium: Museum as Laboratory.* Washington, DC: Smithsonian Institution Press, 1990.

———. *The Museum in Transition: A Philosophical Perspective.* Washington, DC: Smithsonian Institution Press, 2000.

Hendrick, Joanne, ed. *First Steps Toward Teaching the Reggio Way.* Upper Saddle River, NJ: Prentice Hall, 1997.

———. *Next Steps Toward Teaching the Reggio Way: Accepting the Challenge to Change.* Upper Saddle River, NJ: Pearson, 2004.

Hirzy, Ellen Cochrane, ed. *Excellence and Equity: Education and the Public Dimension of Museums.* Washington, DC: American Association of Museums, 1992.

———. "Mastering Civic Engagement: A Report from the American Association of Museums." In *Mastering Civic Engagement: A Challenge to Museums.* Washington, DC: American Association of Museums, 2002.

Hoffer, Peter Charles. *Sensory Worlds in Early America.* Baltimore, MD: Johns Hopkins University Press, 2003.

Hooper-Greenhill, E. *Museum and Gallery Education.* London: Leicester University Press, 2000.

Husbands, Chris. *What Is History Teaching?: Language, Ideas and Meaning in Learning about the Past.* Buckingham, PA: Open University Press, 1996.

Huizinga, Johan. *Homo Ludens: A Study of the Play Element in Culture.* Boston, MA: Beacon Press, 1970. First published 1950 by Roy Publishers.

Hutchison, David. *A Natural History of Place in Education.* New York: Teachers College Press, 2004.

Johnson, Paul E. *A Shopkeeper's Millennium: Society and Revivals in Rochester, New York, 1815–1837.* New York: Hill and Wang, 1978.

Kammen, Michael. *Mystic Chords of Memory: The Transformation of Tradition in American Culture.* New York: Knopf, 1991.

Kertzer, Adrienne. "A Multitude of Voices: The Production of Daniel's Story." In *My Mother's Voice: Children, Literature, and the Holocaust*. Peterborough, Canada: Broadview Press, 2002.

Kosslyn, Stephen M., and Oliver Koenig. *Wet Mind: The New Cognitive Neuroscience*. New York: Free Press, 1992.

Leon, Warren, and Margaret Piatt. "Living-History Museums." In *History Museums in the United States: A Critical Assessment*, edited by Warren Leon and Roy Rosenzweig. Urbana, IL: University of Illinois Press, 1989.

Lockridge, Kenneth A. *A New England Town: The First 100 Years, Dedham, Massachusetts, 1636-1736*. New York: W. W. Norton and Company, Inc., 1970.

Martens, Mary Lee. "Productive Questions: Tools for Supporting Constructivist Learning." *Science and Children* 36, no. 8 (1999): 24-7, 53.

McCracken, Grant. "CULTURE and Culture at the Royal Ontario Museum, Part 2." *Curator* 46 (October 2003): 421-32.

McLoyd, V. "The Effects of the Structure of Play Objects on the Pretend Play of Low Income Preschool Children." *Child Development* 54 (1983).

McManus, Paulette. "Families in Museums." In *Towards the Museum of the Future*, edited by Roger S. Miles and Lauro Zavala. New York: Routledge, 1994.

McNeill, William H., Michael Kammen, and Gordon A. Craig. "Why Study History? Three Historians Respond." In *Historical Literacy: The Case for History in American Education*, edited by Paul Gagnon and The Bradley Commission on History in Schools. New York: Macmillan Publishing Company, 1989.

Miles, Roger S., et al. *The Design of Educational Exhibits*. London: Unwin Hyman Ltd., 1982.

Millard, Anne. *A Street Through Time: A 12,000-Year Walk Through History*. New York: DK Publishing, Inc., 1998.

Mintz, Steven. *Huck's Raft: A History of American Childhood*. Cambridge, MA: Harvard University Press, 2004.

Mitchell, Robert W. "Pretense in Animals: The Continuing Relevance of Children's Pretense." In *Play and Development: Evolutionary, Sociocultural, and Functional Perspectives*, edited by Artin Goncu and Suzanne Gaskins. Mahwah, NJ: Lawrence Erlbaum Associates, Inc., Publishers, 2007.

Museums for a New Century: A Report of the Commission on Museums for a New Century. Washington, DC: American Association of Museums, 1984.

National Council for the Social Studies. *Expectations of Excellence: Curriculum Standards for Social Studies*. Silver Spring, MD: National Council for Social Studies, 1994 (published online 1996), http://www.socialstudies.org/standards/curriculum.

National Park Service. "Teaching With Historic Places." *History Education News* 1 (May 2008), www.nps.gov/history/nr/twhp.

Nelson, Katherine, and Robyn Fivush. "The Emergence of Autobiographical Memory: A Social Cultural Developmental Theory." *Psychological Review* 111, no. 2 (2004): 486-511.

Paley, Vivian Gussin. *The Boy Who Would Be a Helicopter*. Cambridge, MA: Harvard University Press, 1991.

Palmquist, Sasha D., and Kevin Crowley. "From Teachers to Testers: Parents' Role in Child Expertise Development in Informal Settings." *Science Education* 91, no. 5 (2007): 783-804.

Paris, Scott G., ed. *Perspectives on Object-Centered Learning in Museums*. Mahwah, NJ: Lawrence Erlbaum Associates, Inc., Publishers, 2002.

Paris, Scott G., and Melissa J. Mercer. "Finding Self in Objects: Identity Exploration in Museums." In *Learning Conversations in Museums*, edited by Gaea Leinhardt, Kevin Crowley, and Karen Knutson. Mahwah, NJ: Lawrence Erlbaum Associates, Inc., Publishers, 2002: 401–24.

Pellegrini, Anthony D., and Peter K. Smith. "Physical Activity Play: The Nature and Function of a Neglected Aspect of Play." *Child Development* 69, no. 3, (1998): 577–98.

Piaget, Jean, and Bärbel Inhelder. *The Psychology of the Child*. Paris: Presses Universitaires de France, 1969.

Pine, B. Joseph, and James H. Gilmore. *The Experience Economy: Work is Theater and Every Business a Stage*. Boston: Harvard Business Press, 1999.

Pinker, Steven. *How The Mind Works*. New York: W. W. Norton and Company, Inc., 1997.

———. *The Stuff of Thought: Language as a Window into Human Nature*. New York: Viking, 2007.

Piscitelli, Barbara, and David Anderson. "Young Children's Perspectives of Museum Settings and Experiences." *Museum Management and Curatorship* 19, no. 3 (2001): 269–82.

Poster, John B. "The Birth of the Past: Children's Perception of Historical Time." *History Teacher* 6, no. 4 (August 1973): 587–98.

Povinelli, Daniel J., Anita M. Landry, Laura A. Theall, Britten R. Clark, and Conni M. Castille. "Development of Young Children's Understanding that the Recent Past is Causally Bound to the Present." *Developmental Psychology* 35, no. 6 (1999): 1426–39.

Power, Thomas. *Play and Exploration in Children and Animals*. Mahwah, NJ: Lawrence Erlbaum Associates, Inc., Publishers, 2000.

Rand, Judy. "The 227-Mile Museum, or A Visitors' Bill of Rights." *Curator: The Museum Journal* 44, no. 1 (2001): 7–14.

Ravitch, Diane. "History's Struggles to Survive in the Schools." *Organization of American Historians Magazine of History* (April 2007): 28–32.

———. *National Standards in American Education: A Citizen's Guide*. Washington, DC: The Brookings Institution, 1997 (1995).

Reed, Elaine Wrisley. "Helping Your Child Learn History." Edited by Jacquelyn Zimmerman. U.S. Department of Education, May 1993. KidSource Online, http://www.kidsource.com/kidsource/content/history.html.

Reese, Elaine. "Social Factors in the Development of Autobiographical Memory: The State of the Art." *Social Development* 11, no. 1 (2002): 125–42.

Riney-Kehrberg, Pamela. *Childhood on the Farm: Work, Play, and Coming of Age in the Midwest*. Lawrence, KS: University Press of Kansas, 2005.

Rosenzweig, Roy. *Eight Hours for What We Will: Workers and Leisure in an Industrial City*. New York: Cambridge University Press, 1983.

Rosenzweig, Roy, and David Thelen. *The Presence of the Past: Popular Uses of History in American Life*. New York: Columbia University Press, 1998.

Schacter, Daniel L. *Searching for Memory: The Brain, the Mind and the Past*. New York: Basic Books, 1996.

Schug, Mark, and Robert Beery. *Teaching Social Studies in the Elementary School: Issues and Practices*. Glenview, IL: Scott, Foresman and Co., 1987.

Screven, Chan. "Motivating Visitors to Read Labels." In *Text in the Exhibition Medium*, edited by Andrée Blais. Société des Musées Québécois: Musée de la Civilisation, 1995.

Serrell, Beverly. *Exhibit Labels: An Interpretive Approach*. Walnut Creek, CA: AltaMira Press, 1996.

Shaffer, Sharon E. "Collections in the Classroom." *Smithsonian in Your Classroom* (Spring 2008): 2–4.

Singer, Dorothy G., and Jerome L. Singer. *The House of Make-Believe: Children's Play and the Developing Imagination*. Boston, MA: Harvard University Press, 1990.

Slesin, Suzanne. "Through a Child's Eyes, History and Tragedy." *New York Times*, June 3, 1993.

Smith, Mark M. "Producing Sense, Consuming Sense, Making Sense: Perils and Prospects for Sensory History." *Journal of Social History* 40, no. 4 (Summer 2007): 841–58.

———. "Still Coming to 'Our' Senses: An Introduction." *The Journal of American History* 95, no. 2 (September 2008): 378–80.

Smith, Mark M., ed. "The Senses in American History: A Round Table." *The Journal of American History* 95, no. 2 (2008): 378–451.

Sobel, David. *Mapmaking with Children: Sense of Place Education for the Elementary Years*. Portsmouth, NH: Heinemann, 1998.

Spencer Pulaski, Mary Ann. *Understanding Piaget: An Introduction to Children's Cognitive Development*. New York: Harper & Row Publishers, 1980.

Spock, Daniel. "A Practical Guide to Personal Connectivity." *History News* (Autumn 2008): 11–17.

Spock, Michael, ed. *A Study Guide to Philadelphia Stories: A Collection of Pivotal Museum Memories*. Washington, DC: American Association of Museums, 2000.

———. "Tales of Alonetime and Owntime in Museums". *Journal of Museum Education* 25 (2000): 15–9.

Stearns, Peter, Peter Seixas, and Samuel Wineburg, eds. *Knowing, Teaching, and Learning History: National and International Perspectives*. New York: New York University Press, 2000.

Strauss, William and Neil Howe. *Generations: The History of America's Future, 1584–2069*. New York: William Morrow and Company, Inc., 1991.

Sutton-Smith, Brian. *The Ambiguity of Play*. Cambridge, MA: Harvard University Press, 1997.

Thernstrom, Stephan A. *Poverty and Progress: Social Mobility in a Nineteenth Century City*. Cambridge, MA: Harvard University Press, 1964.

Thomas, Selma, and Ann Mintz, eds. *The Virtual and the Real: Media in the Museum*. Washington, DC: American Association of Museums, 1998.

Tilden, Freeman. *Interpreting Our Heritage*. Chapel Hill, NC: University of North Carolina Press, 1957.

Twiss-Garrity, Beth A. "Children as Museum Visitors." *Current Trends in Audience Research and Evaluation* (American Association of Museums Committee on Audience Research and Evaluation) 13, (May 2000): 71–81.

Tyack, David B., and Larry Cuban. *Tinkering toward Utopia: A Century of Public School Reform*. Cambridge, MA: Harvard University Press, 1995.

Urban, Wayne J., and Jennings L. Wagoner. *American Education: A History*. 3rd ed. New York: McGraw-Hill Company, Inc., 2004.

Vukelich, Ronald. "Time Language for Interpreting History Collections to Children." *Museum Studies Journal* (Fall 1984): 44–50.

Vukelich, Ronald, and Stephen J. Thornton. "Children's Understanding of Historical Time: Implications for Instruction." *Childhood Education* 67, no. 1 (1990): 22–5.

Vygotsky, Lev S. *Thought and Language.* Edited by Alex Kozulin, translated by Eugenia Hanfmann and Gertrude Vakar. Cambridge, MA: MIT Press, 1986. First published in Russia, 1934. Translated to English and published in the USA, 1962.

Weil, Stephen E. "From Being about Something to Being *for* Somebody: The Ongoing Transformation of the American Museum." In *Making Museums Matter.* Washington, DC: Smithsonian Institution Press, 2002: 28–54.

White, Judith. *Snakes, Snails, and History Tales: Approaches to Discovery Rooms at the Smithsonian Institution.* Washington, DC: Smithsonian Institution Press, 1992.

Willow, Diane. "Exhibitions as a Context for Engaging Young Children and Families with the Ideas that Technology Can Reveal." *Exhibitionist* 27 (Spring 2008): 78–86.

Wood, Chip. *Yardsticks: Children in the Classroom Ages 4–14: A Resource for Parents and Teachers.* Greenfield, MA: Northeast Foundation for Children, 1997.

Wurman, Richard Saul. *Information Anxiety 2* Indianapolis: QUE Publishing, 2000.

Note: Italicized page numbers indicate photographs, figures, and boxes.